BRITAIN I

1858–1947

Anthem Perspectives in History

Titles in the **Anthem Perspectives in History** series combine a thematic overview with analyses of key areas, topics or personalities in history. The series is targeted at high-achieving pupils taking A-Level, International Baccalaureate and Advanced Placement examinations, first year undergraduates, and an intellectually curious audience.

Series Editors

Helen Pike – Director of Studies at the Royal Grammar School, Guildford, UK
Suzanne Mackenzie – Teacher of History at St Paul's School, London, UK

Other Titles in the Series

Disraeli and the Art of Victorian Politics
Ian St John

Gladstone and the Logic of Victorian Politics
Ian St John

King John: An Underrated King
Graham E. Seel

BRITAIN IN INDIA, 1858–1947

Lionel Knight

ANTHEM PRESS
LONDON · NEW YORK · DELHI

Anthem Press
An imprint of Wimbledon Publishing Company
www.anthempress.com

This edition first published in UK and USA 2012
by ANTHEM PRESS
75-76 Blackfriars Road, London SE1 8HA, UK
or PO Box 9779, London SW19 7ZG, UK
and
244 Madison Ave. #116, New York, NY 10016, USA

British Library Cataloguing-in-Publication Data
A catalogue record for this book is available from the British Library.

Library of Congress Cataloging-in-Publication Data
Knight, Lionel.
Britain in India, 1858–1947 / Lionel Knight.
p. cm. – (Anthem perspectives in history)
Includes bibliographical references and index.
ISBN 978-0-85728-517-1 (pbk. : alk. paper) – ISBN 0-85728-517-3
(pbk. : alk. paper)
1. India–History–British occupation, 1765–1947. I. Title.
DS475.K65 2012
954.03'5–dc23
2012026715

ISBN-13: 978 0 85728 517 1 (Pbk)
ISBN-10: 0 85728 517 3 (Pbk)

This title is also available as an eBook.

CONTENTS

Conclusion 167

ACKNOWLEDGEMENTS

I thank warmly the principal and fellows of St Hugh's College, Oxford for a Schoolteacher Fellowship which enabled me to read in this field. Professor Roy Bridges and my editor, Helen Pike, were enormously helpful. Many thanks are also due to Ronojoy and Monojoy Bose, Melanie and Alastair Bridges, Janet Darby, Gary Griffin, Jonathan Keates, Michael Knight, Jing Liu, Andrew McBroom, Roger McKearney, Richard Macmillan, Michael Magarian, Hari Shah, the late Subrata Shome, Mary Short, Ronojit Sircar, David Ward and, above all, my wife.

PREFACE

British India is now a distant memory and, works of family piety and nostalgia apart, attention has naturally moved to Indian history. As a consequence, it is not easy to find a modern reliable account of the ninety years of Crown rule. This short book, written in the light of the historiographical revolution of the past generation, aims to meet this want.

Map of India

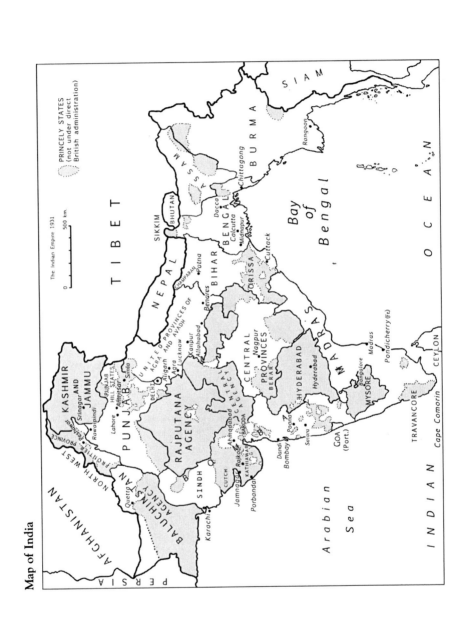

INTRODUCTION

1. The British Indian Empire

Britain's Indian empire comprised the territories of contemporary India, Pakistan, Bangladesh and Burma. The Straits Settlements of Penang, Malacca and Singapore were transferred in 1867 from British India to the Colonial Office which also controlled Ceylon/Sri Lanka. This immense tapering territory was about one thousand nine hundred miles both east to west and north to south, roughly the same size as Europe without Russia. Within this region there was great geographical diversity. In the north were the Himalayas, the world's highest mountain range, from which flowed three of the earth's great rivers, the Indus, Ganges and Brahmaputra. In peninsular India there was the high, dry tableland of the Deccan. In the west there were the 100,000 square miles of the Thar Desert. In the east at Cherrapunji a record 805 inches of rain was recorded in 1861.

This was an empire, not a unitary state with a single system of taxation and administration. New British provinces had been and would be added to the three presidency governments of Bengal, based in the capital city of Calcutta, and Madras and Bombay. What was called the Indian army was in fact the armies of these presidencies, with the commander-in-chief of the Bengal army exercising authority over the armies of Madras and Bombay. Elsewhere, the most important province was the Punjab, whose British officials thought of themselves as the most dynamic and innovative.

Scattered throughout the subcontinent were a large number of states under their Indian rulers. A semi-official work in the 1890s put the number by then at 688. Many were small and most were insignificant and grouped into agencies under British supervision. However, a dozen or so were large and important, uneasy survivors of the age of conquest and annexation. Hyderabad, ruled by the Nizam, had an area of 72,000 square miles and was the most heavily populated of these states, comprising nearly ten million people. Kashmir was almost the size of modern Britain but with a population of only 1.5 million. The government of Mysore, a state about the size of Belgium, was among the most sophisticated. The states had lost their external sovereignty, but retained varying degrees of domestic independence. They comprised two-fifths of India, but only one-fifth of the population.

The first census was published in 1872, giving a daunting total population of 241 million.[1] Of these, 186 million were in British India, 54 million in the states, and three-quarters of a million in the Portuguese and French enclaves. There were also 121,000 Europeans, of whom 60,000–70,000 were from British Army regiments, and 64,000 were Eurasians (mixed race). An official summarized the main divisions in the Indian population as 41 million Muslims, 16 million high-caste Hindus (Brahmans and Rajputs) 111 million 'mixed-population Hindus' and 17.5 million aborigines; with other small minorities, Sikhs, Christians, Jains, Parsis and Jews. Though there were scores of minor languages, the major ones numbered about fifteen. Censuses were to become important instruments of government policy. They not only extracted information from the population, but also classified people in increasingly refined ways and forced them to choose identities. By 1901 a paper slip had been created for each person and manually sorted into pigeonholes for each different statistical tabulation needed. By then Indians were 80 per cent of all subjects of the British Empire. Much was made of their complex variety, which could be held to justify foreign rule as an external arbiter.

2. An Empire of Opinion: The Legacy of the English East India Company

How had this foreign rule come about? To the powerful states which had governed parts, and occasionally most, of the subcontinent, there arose in the eighteenth century an unlikely successor. The Company's turbulent history dated from its Charter of 1600 which gave it monopoly rights over eastern trade. Dutch strength in the East Indies had encouraged more focus on India where the decline of the Mughal Empire opened opportunities for deals with local powers. This period of instability coincided with Britain's world-wide struggle with France which reached its climax during the Seven Years War (1756–63). By its end, the Company, assisted by British naval and military forces, had become the dominant power on the subcontinent. After the defeat of Tipu Sultan of Mysore in 1799 and the Marathas in 1818, this dominance was total although opinions differed about its depth. Sir Charles Metcalfe (Acting Governor-General, 1835) thought that 'our hold is precarious…[now that] our subjects have had leisure to enquire why they have been subdued…

they might understand that it [British power] does not rest in actual strength but on impression'.[2] By contrast, Lord William Bentinck (Governor-General, 1828–35) considered that, apart from anxieties about the vast mercenary army, 'our power is irresistible… It is universally declared to be so and I hope it may become actively instrumental in promoting the welfare and improvement of this great society.'[3]

The Company's untrammelled management of its own affairs was threatened by reports of oppression and corruption which reached London. A trading company, backed by an industrial revolution at home, now had the revenue of large tracts of the country in its hands, 'a kind of gift from heaven' as the Elder Pitt described it.[4] In the chaotic transition to foreign rule, officials heartlessly pressed on with raised taxes. It was reckoned that a third of Bengal's population died in the famine of 1770. In addition, the sheer scale of the Company's operations and the backwash of big money into British politics alarmed ministers.

With Pitt's India Act of 1784 a system of double government was established. A Board of Control – in effect, a cabinet committee – was set up to 'superintend, direct and controul' the Company's operations. Henceforth, the governor-general in Calcutta, whose authority over the other presidency governments of Bombay and Madras was enhanced, was to be a royal appointment, drawn from the ranks of senior figures in British public life. Subject to the vagaries of distance, war and peace were now to be decided in London. The Company had scores of MPs to speak for it, but among evangelical Christians and free traders there was a growing body of critics. When the charter came up for renewal in 1813, the Company lost its right to trade in India, though not in China. Now, the age of rule replaced the age of trade and of loot – the Indian word was coming into English usage.

The Company had been religiously neutral in a positive way. Its practice of making donations to temples and mosques and its refusal to allow Christian missionaries in its territories had enraged evangelical MPs. They now overturned the ban. There were already Christians in India. The Syrian Church dates from the earliest centuries of Christianity. Roman Catholics had spread out beyond Portuguese Goa and French Pondicherry. There were also chaplains for the European troops. Near Calcutta, in the Danish enclave of Serampore, William Carey had set up a pioneering biblical translation and printing press for Bengali and many other Indian languages. But after 1813, Protestant missions, initially from Britain and from Basel, began to send representatives and open schools in many parts of India. In the changing atmosphere, some leading officials made no secret of their religious zeal, and there were even officers in the Bengal army who engaged in off-duty bazaar preaching.

With a small number of foreigners controlling such a large population, the rule of the Company was sometimes called an empire of opinion. It was also an empire of knowledge. Vast enterprises were set afoot to gather information about the geology and resources of the country, about the people, their languages and religious customs. The Great Trigonometrical Survey had been set up as early as 1800 and pushed forward under George Everest to create the first reliable *Atlas of India*. Many other projects were inherited by the Crown after 1858 and were published or lay behind policy assumptions in the second half of the century. Multi-volume works on the tribes and castes of different provinces were being prepared. In the 1870s, W. W. Hunter was to begin work on the great *Imperial Gazeteer*, which, supplemented by local gazetteers, summarized masses of information of different kinds, and began to standardize the English spelling of Indian names. All this knowledge constituted not merely passive power. It was active power in that it defined the country using categories familiar and useful to the government, and steadily invited and required people to define themselves in the same ways.

The Company had decided in 1835 to discard Persian as its official language and promote English influenced by current pressures brilliantly summarized by the historian Thomas Macaulay, then law member of the Governor-General's Council, in his *Minute on Education*.[5] His argument was for progress. Through English, educated Indians would come into contact with the intellectual life of the West, and this knowledge would progressively transform Indian society. Macaulay stressed the secular character of the project. 'We abstain, and I trust will always abstain, from giving any public encouragement to those who are engaged in the work of converting natives to Christianity.' He further argued that the Company should abandon financial support for publishing in the classical languages of Sanskrit and Arabic because texts in those languages stayed in the warehouses whereas English books flew off the shelves, and everywhere (in Calcutta) students sought English lessons. The Company, he believed, should look at the market and acknowledge the choices already being made. He observed that 'it is unusual to find, even in the literary circles of the Continent, any foreigner who can express himself in English with so much facility and correctness as we find in many Hindoos'.[6]

He assumed that most people would continue to operate in the vernacular languages. But he also argued that the Company should try 'to form a class who may be interpreters between us and the millions whom we govern – a class of persons, Indian in blood and colour, but English in taste, in opinions, in morals, and in intellect.' Macaulay has been accused of racial arrogance in his confident assertion 'that a single shelf of a good European library was worth the whole native literature of India and Arabia'.[7] But here, and in a later essay on Bacon, he also rubbished the first thousand years of English literature and all the vernacular literatures of Europe before the seventeenth century. He was above all a champion of modernity who believed that in the East as well as the West the superior prestige of classical learning should be overturned. The Calcutta men who called themselves Young Bengal were already finding this a heady message. With western ideas and technology, they dreamed that the strength of India could be restored. Though small in number, their expectations would expand with their horizons. Macaulay's *Minute on Education* had also stressed the utility of English. In the years to come, would opportunities for employment in the government and the law be sufficient to meet these expectations?

Among the civil servants, as the Company called its officials, there was a strong sense of mission to modernize India and liberate its society from stagnation and superstition. This outlook was encouraged in a seminal work by a senior official at the London headquarters, James Mill's *History of British India* (1820). Among the proud examples of enlightened reform, there were the abolition of *sati*/widow burning in 1829, the campaign against *thagi*/thugs in the next decade and the suppression of the *meriah* human sacrifices among the Kond tribal people of Orissa. These cases illustrate the difficulties and ambiguities of intervention in cultures for which both understanding and empathy may be lacking. Indian groups had been pressing for the criminalization of *sati* but the government, nervous of conservative sentiment, dragged its feet for ten years during which time thousands of women died. In *thagi*, had Colonel Sleeman uncovered a sinister secret society which strangled and robbed travellers in the name of the goddess Kali, or could the activities of these groups be more accurately explained by the effects of the recent demobilization of tens of thousands of soldiers? Among the Konds, human sacrifices had been few and infrequent. Yet, by the time that the Meriah Agency was wound up in 1861, thousands had perished in the campaign and many of the *meriah* children had died in government boarding schools or fled back to the villages from which they had been liberated.

The civil servants, educated at Haileybury College where Malthus had taught, had been introduced to contemporary economic ideas and utilitarian thinking about government. If the greatest happiness of the greatest number was their touchstone, the peasant was obviously to be the prime beneficiary of British rule. This fitted with older British assumptions that in India the state was the ultimate owner of the land, and with the economist David Ricardo's opinion that 'the interest of the landlord is always opposed to every other class in the community.'[8] If the government were to cut out the landlords and deal directly with peasant and village community, a social revolution would follow. In 1856 this policy was attempted in the newly annexed state of Oudh/Avadh. The economic depression of the second quarter of the century was not a promising time to attempt bold measures. The growing military character of Company rule with its internal campaigns against states and social groups was destabilizing parts of the country. Nor was the enthusiastic embrace of western modernity by a few Bengalis reproduced in the wider country where there was conservative alarm at the growing changes.

3. 1857

On 10 May 1857 at the Company's base at Meerut, the *sepoys* shot their officers and marched the thirty-six miles to Delhi. There they acclaimed the last of the Mughal imperial line, the elderly poet Bahadur Shah, designated by the Company as King of Delhi. What the British called the Indian Mutiny had begun. The revolt of the Bengal army led to the collapse of British power across north India and the death or flight of Company officials and their families. Central India, especially the recently annexed Nagpur, a state larger than the Punjab, trembled in the balance. Uneasy peace prevailed in peninsular India, the maritime cities and the Punjab. Fortunately for the British, communications were still slow and this impeded the coordination and articulation of resistance.

The Company's response was swift and savage. They were able to draw on troops still in the Crimea and a military expedition on its way to China was diverted. In the recently annexed Punjab, the commissioner John Lawrence, was able to raise forces and bring them down to the siege of Delhi. Coming up the Ganges valley, British troops exacted vengeance with indiscriminate savagery. The new governor-general, Lord Canning (1856–62), horrified by attitudes that reminded him of enraged American slaveholders, tried to draw the slaughter to a close. Europeans in Calcutta referred to him derisively as 'Clemency Canning'.

The shock in Britain was immense, but the idea of a uniformly savage response can no longer stand. Christopher Herbert has reminded us of other voices and shown how the horrific and superficially triumphalist accounts of the Mutiny can be read in diverse ways.[9] Disraeli wondered whether 'instead of bowing before the name of Jesus, we were preparing to revive the worship of Moloch'. He asked the House of Commons whether it was a mutiny or a national rebellion. Many MPs protested at the destruction of the 26th Regiment of Native Infantry. Five hundred mutineers who had laid down their muskets and fled from their base at Lahore had been pursued and killed to a man on the orders of the commissioner Robert Montgomery, grandfather of the famous field-marshal. Nevertheless, the prevailing mood in Britain was undoubtedly one of retributive vengeance in the grimmest puritan tradition which greeted news of the slaughter of mutineers, and of Indians, with enthusiasm.

In trying to explain the rebellion, British contemporaries recognized the perceived religious threat to both Hindus and Muslims typified by the new ammunition cartridges greased with pig or cow fat. Some acknowledged that opposition to foreign rule had been deep and wide, crossing social and religious boundaries. When the commissioner for Mysore, Mark Cubbon, was later asked by the government why he had not submitted the names of those helpful in 1857, it might be thought it was because Mysore was hundreds of miles from the affected area. In fact, he said that a useful informer of possible trouble told him that his wife would poison him if his name were publicized. Cubbon added that, if known, those who had helped the British would be shunned from generation to generation.[10]

J. W. Kaye, the historian-official at the India Office in London, blamed the expansionist policy of Lord Dalhousie (Governor-General, 1848–56) for the uprising. Some dispossessed princes did join the revolt, others feared for their future. The Rani of Jhansi is now a nationalist icon. Among modern historians, Eric Stokes drew attention to the Company's destabilizing of rural society.[11] The Bengal army recruited heavily from Brahman farmers in Avadh. The ruthless annexation of the state in 1856 and the uncertainty created by the promise of radical land reform added innumerable recruits to the rebellion. From Delhi, a Company official, Syed Ahmed Khan, wrote in his *Causes of the Indian Revolt* (1858) that it was neither a mutiny nor a conspiracy, but a breakdown of trust between society and government.

The events of 1857 and the theme of united resistance to foreign rule has been the starting point for the nationalist tradition in modern Indian historiography. It has been represented as the last great protest of old India and/or the forerunner of modern nationalism. V. D. Savarkar's *The First Indian War of Independence, 1857* (1909) was an early influential exposition of the latter position.[12] More generally, the nationalist tradition has focused on the exclusion of Indians from leadership positions in their own country, economic exploitation, and the discrimination and arrogance which came with the extreme inequality of power.

The main current of British historical writing during the period of British rule in India questioned the basic assumption of the nationalists that India in all its variety was a politically meaningful concept. The Liberal Imperialist tradition celebrated the achievement of the *Pax Britannica* after the wars which convulsed much of the fragmented subcontinent in the eighteenth century. Britain's role in the nineteenth century was to modernize government and infrastructure under the rule of law, and draw India into the stimulating environment of the global economy.

For Karl Marx, this exposure to the free market was a disaster which had 'broken down the entire framework of Indian society'.[13] In the 1860s,

India, which had once been a textile exporting country, now took more than a quarter of all Lancashire cotton goods, which were themselves a third of Britain's total exports. Those historians who have seen economic exploitation at the heart of the relationship have focused on the destructive and dislocating effects of this shift on the country's weavers; on the high costs of the British establishments in India and in London; on the remittance of wealth to Britain; and on the government's financial reliance on the land revenue paid by the poor cultivators. Marxist interpretations of Indian history have remained important, while the idea of a 'drain' of wealth became central to most nationalist writing.

4. A Magna Carta for India

The prime minister, Lord Palmerston, anticipating the measures that might be taken by an incoming Tory government, abolished the Company and replaced it with direct control by the Government of India Act, 1858. The Queen's Proclamation, drafted by Lord Derby, followed in the same year.[14] It reassured the remaining princes of their security; it promised that there would be no racial discrimination in public appointments; and, at a time when the British state was still tied to the Church of England, it proclaimed secular governance for India. This offered a Liberal Imperialist vision for the future where civil servants, chosen for their ability and integrity, would oversee modernization based on the rule of law. The proclamation, however, raised questions which only time could answer.

How close would the new relationship with London be? The mid-nineteenth century saw a revolution in communications. The steamship bound the empire together closer than the vagaries of wind power had done. After 1869 the Suez Canal promised the transit of mails between London and Calcutta in weeks rather than months. Above all, the telegraph had the potential to reduce drastically the scope for independent action by the man on the spot. By 1866, 14,000 miles of line existed within India, and by 1870 the patchy, mostly overground line from London had been replaced by a submarine cable to Bombay. The immediacy of the effects should not be exaggerated; despite the recommendation of a Parliamentary Select Committee, it was not until 1888 that all government mail was transported using the Suez Canal route. London would now exercise greater control over foreign policy because, if these changes brought India nearer to Britain, they also brought the European powers closer to British imperial interests.

Would India become a live issue in British politics? What, in an age of transition would the character of these politics be? For British politics, the 1860s were a watershed. The mid-Victorian boom and the repeal of the

Paper Duties in 1861 were creating an informed public of newspaper readers. Many of them were enfranchised in the Second Reform Act of 1867. The personalities of Gladstone and Disraeli and the sharpening of party conflict helped project interest in British politics to the cities of India. The Reform Act was less a settlement than part of a process, and the emergence of mass politics in a world of information introduced an unpredictable element to the relationship between Calcutta and London. How would unaccountable bureaucratic rule sit with the beginnings of the modern cabinet in Britain? Would this more focused executive assert itself in India?

Above all, what would happen when western-educated Indians appealed to the proclamation in support of their rights? Could such claims be reconciled with the imperatives of liberal imperialism? Three trends were soon apparent that would keep alive the promises of this Magna Carta for India.

First, were the consequences of Macaulay's 1835 *Minute* and the 1853 *Education Despatch* of Sir Charles Wood (later Secretary of State, 1859–66). The latter authorized a scheme of state support for primary education in the vernaculars and the establishment of three English language universities. G. O. Trevelyan thought 'the class of scholars and the character of the instruction given [in these government schools] place them far above the level of Government schools in England.'[15] Financial stringency crippled their development but Calcutta, Madras and Bombay universities opened in 1857, setting a pattern of top-heavy education in the country. Between 1864 and 1868 some 5,000 students enrolled in the constituent colleges. The establishment of the High Court in 1861 opened a new career as a pleader, making law the most popular course for students. The employment of English-educated graduates was about to become a political issue.

Second, the Indian press was introducing these graduates in the maritime cities to a world of informed public debate. Bengal had seen 100 papers between 1818 and 1855, but circulation had been low and their lives short as ownership and editors changed to stave off financial failure. Elsewhere, the only Indian papers not under missionary control had been in Bombay and in the North-Western Provinces, mainly around Agra. But by the mid-century costs were falling and the urban population was growing. As the manuscript press disappeared, some of its lively independence was inherited by its successors. The English papers could be assertive, too, especially on behalf of planters. The hysterical fear and hatred they expressed during 1857 must have opened some Indian eyes.

The arrival of Robert Knight in 1861 in the editorial chair of the *Bombay Times* quickened the pace of change. He went on to merge several papers into the *Times of India*, before moving to Calcutta to found the *Statesman*, papers with famous lives ahead of them. In the eyes of Anglo-Indians (Britons resident in India) he committed the cardinal sin of working for Indian employers, in this case newspaper proprietors. For the government, he was a thorn in their flesh. His critical line was that all subjects of the empire had the same entitlements: freedom of speech and of the press; due process of law and open honest government. He also facilitated debate about the Indian economy by putting statistical information in his papers, and later founding the *Indian Economist*. At a time when other papers' coverage was local or provincial, his papers encouraged an all-India outlook.

For an authoritarian government, handling a free press was a tricky matter, especially when official advertising and the offer of small subsidies were no longer sufficient to secure general compliance. As early as 1830, Bentinck had complained that 'in all encounters with the editors at Calcutta, the government have been beat.'[16] Canning had felt obliged to introduce curbs during the Mutiny. His successor, Lord Lawrence (1863–69) toyed with the idea of an official newspaper on the lines of Napoleon III's *Le Moniteur*, but neither he nor his successors had the stomach for serious censorship. The solution pursued by Lord Mayo (Viceroy, 1869–72) involved encouraging W. W. Hunter to write anonymous articles in support of government policy, but this made it difficult to stop freelance anonymous writing by other officials or army officers and hence widened public debate.

Third, civil society began to blossom in the mid-century as clubs of all kinds appeared in the cities; among them were political associations. The British Indian Association had been formed in 1851. Despite its name it mainly defended the interests of landowners in Bengal, a self-interested position which soon provoked other groups into life. The following year a Bombay Association had been formed, with a substantial annual subscription of 25 rupees. Its first concern had been to petition Parliament about the Company's charter which was coming up for renewal in 1853. Indians or their agents had been lobbying in London for a century. However, more organized, standing groups were now forming. Dadabhai Naoroji helped to found the London Indian Society in 1865, to be overtaken the next year by the East India Association with many retired civilians critical of current policy. These pressure groups were bringing attention to all-India questions; and a few associated Indians were to take back their political experience in the coming years.

The Queen's Proclamation gave these individuals and small groups a frame of reference but only the future would tell how Indian government would be reconciled with the proclamation and whether its promises would be upheld by government in Britain. In the wider world, progressive trends seemed to be on the rise. The Union had triumphed in America and slavery had been abolished. There were signs of widening political participation in the British Empire. After the 1865 rebellion in Jamaica the Colonial Office ended the rule of the planters. 1867 saw the creation of the Dominion of Canada. But it was soon clear that not all trends were one way. In the USA, France, Germany and also Britain the extended franchise called forth strong conservative forces. For Britain a new world was dawning and, while still a superpower, she faced the uncertainties of mass politics at home and great power rivalries abroad as the European power balance broke down after the 1870–71 Franco-Prussian War.

Chapter 1

CROWN RULE TO 1880

1. Coercion or Collaboration?

Although the 1860s saw a drive to put a modern infrastructure into place, the opportunity for political initiatives was not taken. The viceroy John Lawrence, apparently baffled by the new bureaucratic world and nostalgic for patriarchal rule in the Punjab, appeared, 'like a senior foreman waiting for orders' in the words of the historian Sarvepalli Gopal.[1] Caution was the watchword. After 1857, the government was careful to pay attention to those notables and groups who spoke two languages, metaphorically and sometimes literally – the supporters or 'collaborators' who could transmit and interpret alien rule.

The question of how to explain the rule of a small minority of foreigners has exercised historians. For some, simple force is sufficient. The British could bring to bear at particular points coordinated military and financial resources. Purnaiya, Tipu Sultan's minister and *diwan* of Mysore, had said that it was not what he could see of British power that he feared, but what he could not see. 1857 revealed that the British were prepared to unleash colossal violence to maintain their position. The possibility of repetition hung like a menacing cloud on the horizon. It was not only a possibility; at Mala Kota in 1871 there was fighting involving the Kukas, a reforming Sikh sect who had been responsible for attacks on cattle slaughterhouses. After a trial, 49 men were blown from guns and 16 hanged; though Mayo disowned the action and dismissed the officer responsible.

However, the positive response of many Indians to aspects of British rule and the scale of their involvement has encouraged other approaches. Ronald Robinson's *Sketch for a Theory of Collaboration* (1972) argues that imperial domination was 'only practicable insofar as alien power is translated into terms of indigenous political economy... the financial sinew, the military and administrative muscle of imperialism was drawn through the mediation of indigenous elites from the invaded countries themselves'.[2] The ambiguous connotations of the term 'collaborator' have proved controversial. Does the word not conceal the extreme inequality of the relationship? It defines populations in terms of their association with or antipathy to British rule. Yet relationships between rulers and ruled may not always have been as asymmetrical as they seem. Without the knowledge and authority which collaborators provided, British power would have been magnificently helpless, as R. F. Frykenberg showed in his influential study *Guntur district, 1788–1848*. In return, the position of notables could be strengthened by British recognition and patronage and by access to the new legal procedures established by a government which knew little and enquired less of what passed at local level.

Governance after 1858

The Crown inherited the Company's methods, men and paperwork. The legal foundations of British India, the Code of Civil Procedure (1859), the Penal Code (1860) and the Code of Criminal Procedure (1861) were the outcome of several decades of preparatory work. The main changes introduced by the Government of India Act (1858) were a secretary of state responsible to Parliament and advised by a Council of India of 15 with experience of Indian government. In Calcutta, the governor-general, now given the title of viceroy, ran the Supreme Government through an Executive Council of five, and later six, members, all senior officials. After 1861 there were Legislative Councils in Calcutta, Madras and Bombay, and their nominated non-official members included Indians. They could only advise on the legislation that they ratified but their proceedings were public. Overall, the trend was towards greater concentration of authority. An Act of 1870 allowed the governor-general to overrule the Executive Council, and Lord Salisbury (Secretary of State, 1866–68, 1874–78) showed that a strong minister could ignore his council.

Below the viceroy were 900 men of the Indian Civil Service (ICS).[3] These civilians were fresh graduates chosen, after the abolition of patronage in 1853, by competitive examination. Salaries were probably higher than in any other bureaucracy in the world. Most retired after 25 years service to enjoy a pension of a thousand pounds a year whatever their final rank. High, too, were the expectations of integrity and initiative. Most were assigned to the 235 districts of British India where they were responsible for the land revenue, criminal justice and just about everything else. Some moved into judicial work, others into the Political Service which dealt with the states.

Carrying out their orders were 13,000 other civil servants earning 75 rupees a month, about half of whom were Eurasian or European. Below them were ten times as many Indians in the most lowly paid jobs. At the very top, a tenth of the 900 were in the central secretariats working an empire of paper. As Lord Curzon (Viceroy, 1899–1905) wrote, 'Round and round, like the diurnal revolution of the earth, went the file, stately, solemn, sure and slow.'[4]

What made the life of senior ICS men even more detached was the annual move to the hills. When Lord Lawrence was offered the viceroyalty, he had recently retired to London. Pleading age and health, and a dislike of Calcutta, he made his acceptance dependent on permission to spend the hot weather in Simla. A government train took the officials, the clerks, the files and the families 1,200 miles to this small town at 7,000 feet in the Himalayan foothills. Here, surrounded by the headquarters staff of the Supreme Government, the only viceroy who was ever fluent in an Indian language worked as far away from the people of India as could be imagined. As a personal concession became the rule, every provincial government began to follow suit, except for that of Assam, whose capital, Shillong, was already in the hills. Bombay moved twice each year, to Mahabaleshwar, then on to Poona. The Madras government was later spending more time at Ootacamund in the Nilgiri hills than it did in Madras.

By the time of Lord Lytton's arrival (Viceroy, 1876–80), Indian entry to the ICS had become a pressing question. The promise of the Queen's Proclamation was unambiguous, as it declared:

> [I]t is our further will that, so far as may be, our subjects, of whatever race or creed, be freely and impartially admitted to offices in our services, the duties of which they may be qualified, by their education, ability and integrity, duly to discharge.[5]

However, the promise had been given before there were any university graduates. When the first Indian, Satyendranath Tagore, passed the examination in 1863, the Civil Service commissioners nervously responded by changing the marking scheme to impede future Indian candidates. Despite this and the cost of coming to London, four Indians managed to pass in 1869, surviving claims that they had falsified their ages. One of these, Surendranath Banerjea, was dismissed from his post a couple of years later for a misdemeanour that many thought would have received only internal censure had he been British. In 1875 as numbers of applicants were picking up, Salisbury reduced the examination age from 21 to 19, an even bigger obstacle for Indian candidates.

It is likely, however, that Salisbury's decision was made in reference to British candidates to the ICS. Competitive examinations had replaced patronage in the Home Civil Service only in 1870, and a debate still raged in England and in India about their value. The proponents had a particular version of the meritocratic argument. They wanted educated young men of the upper classes and thought that examinations would, as Gladstone put it, show their 'immense superiority'.[6] ICS experience, however, was giving grounds for second thoughts. In *The Competition Wallah* (1864), G. O. Trevelyan caricatured the new men: 'The natives say that another caste of Englishmen has come out.' Instead of the old official 'secure with a favourite hogspear in hand and a double-barrelled Purdey slung across his shoulders', the new type could 'be seen walking with his arm round his wife's waist in the bazaar'.[7] Lawrence thought the competition *wallahs* 'know books better than men' but, citing a spectacular innings in a recent cricket match, conceded that there were, nevertheless, some active men among them.[8] In other words, examinations were letting in the wrong sort, especially in the eyes of aristocratic politicians. Sir Charles Wood thought that increasing the marks for Latin and Greek would keep at bay 'wild Irishmen…[and] middle class examination students'.[9]

If there were doubts about the British intake, the attitude to potential Indian recruitment was clear-cut. Bengali *bhadralok* (see Glossary) might, as uncovenanted officials, run government offices from the Punjab to South-east Asia. Nevertheless, British references to the *Babus* – a polite form of address in Bengali – were generally contemptuous. Lytton was sure they had no value as collaborators, describing them as 'the Baboos, whom we have educated to write semi-seditious articles in the Native Press, and who really represent nothing but the social anomaly of their own position'.[10] Yet some of them, despite the obstacles, were capable of passing the examination. A tiny trickle, slowed by official manipulation, would not satisfy Indians. But large-scale entry was unthinkable. The ICS was the core institution of British control. Its very existence was considered evidence of British superiority. Lord Mayo had earlier told his foreign secretary, 'Teach your subordinates that we are all British gentlemen engaged in the magnificent work of governing an inferior race.'[11]

How could this exclusiveness be reconciled with the Queen's Proclamation? On resolving the problem 'lies practically the fate of the empire', thought Fitzjames Stephen (Law Member, 1869–72). Lytton's solution was radical. He wrote in a secret note, 'We all know that these claims and expectations never can, or will be fulfilled. We have to choose between prohibiting them or cheating them…'[12] His answer was two services, one British and competitive, the other fairly generously provided for nominated Indians. But Lord Cranbrook

(Secretary of State, 1878–80) doubted whether the necessary legislation for a partial return to patronage not to mention rescinding the Queen's Proclamation would pass the House of Commons. Thus was born Lytton's compromise, the Statutory Civil Service of 1879. A few Indians would continue to take the London examination, while others from upper-class families would be appointed to positions on the recommendation of the provincial governments. These governments dragged their feet, and there was little demand from upper-class young men for arduous work in the bureaucracy. The service only lasted eight years, during which 57 appointments were made.

Angry disappointment was voiced in a furious press campaign, a major cause of the censorship introduced by the 1878 Vernacular Press Act. The Indian Association took up the cudgels on behalf of the western-educated. One of its founders, Surendranath Banerjea, went on a successful speaking tour of north India. For the first time western-educated groups were drawn together in an all-India response to a political question.

The Army[13]

The *Pax Britannica* was not as peaceful as it might seem. Internal security required the army's support of the civil authorities to repress many mute protests whose voices have been recovered in the last generation by the Subaltern School of historians. Three developments, in particular, triggered these outbreaks.

First, official interest in 'waste lands' and 'reserved forests' most affected the tribal peoples. The ban on shifting cultivation after 1867 and the 1878 Forest Act provoked numerous outbreaks, of which the rebellion in Chodavaram in the Godavari Agency from 1879–80, was especially violent. Second, British conceptions of property strengthened landlord rights at the expense of those who relied on customary entitlements. Third, rising rents, land revenue, taxes on salt and the excise triggered many protests. The Deccan Riots of 1875 targeted moneylenders in the context of rising revenue demands and the collapse of the cotton boom as the US economy recovered from the Civil War. Though local, these protests sometimes presented a significant challenge to British rule. In the aftermath of the Deccan famine in 1876–77, a Brahman clerk, Phadke, gathered a band of high and low caste youths to disrupt communications and restore some kind of Hindu *raj*.

There was a police force, about a third armed, numbering some 158,000 in 1879 at the time of the Eden Commission. It was similar to the rural Irish constabulary, but poorly paid and of low calibre. The army, therefore, remained vital for the stability of the Raj. As late as 1899–1901, it was called out 69 times to help the civil authorities.

The most basic support of British rule was the army. After 1858 its main purpose was internal security. First, it had to be made secure itself. Artillery was now exclusively in British hands. The number of *sepoys* was reduced from 238,000 to 140,000 and the ratio to European troops set at two to one. The Peel Commission of 1858 received much advice on how to 'divide and rule'. Mixing castes and nationalities throughout regiments was recommended to avoid the dangerous *esprit de corps* so recently in evidence in the Bengal army. Despite the promise of appointment on merit in the public services, there were now to be no Indian officers. 'So far as the [Indian] army is concerned, the Queen's Proclamation…is a dead letter.' General Chesney explained, 'The studious exclusion of Indians from all but the humblest places in the army is so conspicuous that only one inference can be placed on it – that we are afraid to trust them.'[14] Behind the *sepoys* were the British troops, their lesser numbers compensated by the strategic character of much of the new railway system, which was staffed by Europeans and Eurasians. They were barracked in 'the great cantonments – the lairs where British power lies silent and almost unseen, but ready to rush forth at a moment along every spider-thread of the network of railways which is now enveloping India'.[15]

The Indian army was also vital for the projection of British power across the Indian Ocean, and for Britain's standing as a great power. With over 200,000 troops in India as well as approximately 90,000 in the United Kingdom it was, at least before 1870–71, on a par with France and Russia. After its first duty in support of British rule, the Indian army campaigned to push out the frontiers in Baluchistan, 1876–79, Afghanistan, 1878–80 and Upper Burma, 1885. Then, as the second centre of the British Empire, it provided the manpower for numerous overseas expeditions. Under the Company, *sepoys* had been sent abroad as early as the Java Wars after 1810. If Aden and the Persian war of 1856 were part of the protection of the route to India, Britain's imperial interests seemed paramount elsewhere: the China Wars of 1839, 1856, 1860; Malaya in 1875; Egypt in 1882; the Sudan in 1896–98; the East African actions of the 1890s. The year 1867 had seen a strong but unavailing financial protest to London by Lawrence against Indian military participation in the invasion of Abyssinia.

The attraction of the Indian army was cost. Keeping European soldiers in India was vastly expensive. A Royal Commission of 1863 had noticed that in an average year, out of the 60,000–70,000 soldiers, 4,800 would die and 5,800 would be hospitalized; in the Madras army a quarter were treated for venereal diseases. Florence Nightingale showed that battle casualties were only a third of those caused by sickness. The figures for the *sepoys* were incomparably lower, and the costs of the Indian army were born by the Indian taxpayer.

In Salisbury's brutal words, India was 'an English barracks in the Oriental Seas from which we may draw any number of troops without paying for them'.[16]

After 1880 attention switched to the fighting efficiency of the army. The Eden Commission recommended a move from general mixture to 'class company' regiments. These socially homogeneous regiments would be increasingly recruited from the 'martial races'. Sir Frederick Roberts (Commander-in-Chief, 1885–93), who was the driving force behind these changes, began to focus the army on the north-west frontier. He believed the threat now was from Russia and that an army recruited and organized with internal security as its prime objective would not be equal to the challenge. 'Martial races' meant communities supposedly with the physical and psychological toughness the army now required, and they did not include Madrasis or Bengalis. The Madras army was run down, and the three armies were finally merged into one in 1893–5. This meant a turn to Sikhs and Gurkhas who had been so helpful in 1857. By 1904, the percentage of soldiers who came from the Punjab, the frontier and Nepal was at 57 and growing. A third of the army was Muslim, a fifth Sikh. Towns were shunned; rural communities with lower than average literacy were preferred as recruiting grounds. By 1912, some began to reconsider the prudence of this narrow recruiting policy. The Nicholson Committee recommended a broader approach for the sake of safety, but without effect.

With the favoured 'martial races', the idea of collaboration re-enters the equation, suggesting that coercion and collaboration are not mutually exclusive. Selective recruitment creates mutual dependence; it would not be easy for the government to move away from favoured districts. The doubling of the Sikh community from two million in the 1881 census to four million in 1931 (increasing their percentage of the Punjab population from 8 per cent to 13 per cent) has been explained by the army's preference for Sikhs with uncut hair who did not smoke, thus encouraging non-observants to reclaim their Sikh identity. The Punjab was the principal recipient of British irrigation investment. Between 1860 and 1910 ten million acres were brought under cultivation. The 1887 Chenab Canal Colony was founded for cultivators of 'proven loyalty', again in a recruitment area. Taking 40 per cent or more of the budget, the army has been seen as an incubus on the country, but in a garrison state, as India has been called, military spending could have a multiplier effect on parts of the economy and society.[17]

Landlords and Peasants

With British rule set on a more conservative and limited trajectory, landlords appeared to be the main beneficiaries of the post-Mutiny settlement. They and the government had a shared interest in social stability. The 'aristocratic restoration' focused on Avadh where the confiscation of the lands of the *taluqdars*, the 72 feudal barons who controlled two-thirds of the country, had been at the heart of the Mutiny. In return for their submission, Canning allowed them to recover control of their villages and secure a lower land revenue settlement. The tilt towards the landlords was only possible where a numerous class existed. In 1793 the *zamindars* of Bengal had been given a permanent settlement, a promise that their land revenue would be fixed in perpetuity. Instead of the land-investing, improving landlords as intended, they had become a *rentier* class. This disappointment had inhibited the spread of the policy. Much of the country, the south and west especially, was a land of peasant cultivators, individually assessed and paying their revenue through the village, the *ryotwari* settlement, as it was called in Madras.

The government, then, could not rely exclusively on landlords as intermediaries, but needed also to devote attention to the cultivators. Lawrence's council was split over where to put the emphasis. His foreign secretary, Sir Henry Durand, pressed the 'aristocratic restoration', arguing that in practice peasant support was of little value. But the viceroy still held to the ideal of a 'country cultivated by a fat, contented yeomanry, each riding his own horse, sitting under his own fig tree, and enjoying his rude family comforts'.[18] He even pushed through an Oudh Rent Act, 1868, providing protection for some cultivators against rent rises by the *taluqdars*. His Punjab Rent Act of the same year provided ampler security against landlords.

New ideas of property, British courts and the growing monetization of agriculture were threatening to destabilize a rural order which the British, despite a commitment to free trade, felt the need to shore up. After the Deccan Riots, 1875, the government became concerned at the scale of peasant indebtedness. It responded with the Deccan Agriculturists' Relief Act (1879), which tried to impede the sale of agricultural land to non-agriculturists. It was a political policy. The government wanted economic growth but baulked at the social consequences. As an official commented, 'the money-lender can never take the place of the large ancestral landlord or the substantial yeoman whom he dispossesses...'[19] Trying to be all things to all men involved some delicate balancing acts. With some growth in the economy between 1871 and 1893 the conflicts of interest and principle in these policies were, for the moment, sustainable.[20]

Muslims

The British feared the Muslims. They assumed that there was deep resentment at the loss of political dominance in the subcontinent which had left them under the rule of unbelievers. Despite mixed evidence, many, especially in Britain, believed Muslims to have been prime movers in the 1857 rebellion. Defeat had not brought passivity. The 1860s saw heavy fighting on the north-west frontier between British forces and fundamentalist Wahhabis. Near Delhi a new school for *ulema* (law doctors) was founded in 1867 at Deoband. Here boys studied a traditional curriculum with no English or modern science, and the printing press spread the message of uncorrupted scriptural Islam.

This background helps to explain the impact of W. W. Hunter's *The Indian Musalmans: Are They Bound in Conscience to Rebel against the Queen?* (1871). The author explained that support for Wahhabism was widespread in northern India. But all news was not bad. Hunter drew attention to recent *fatwas* which had declared that it was legitimate for Muslims to obey the laws of British India and that there was no obligation for *jihad*. He concluded that poverty was the real issue. If the government made special educational provision, Muslims would be able to compete for public employment and become a contented population.

Over the years the book became a key text in arguments about British policy and Muslim separatism. Some nationalist historians have seen here clear evidence of 'divide and rule', whereby the government now sought Muslim support by offering preferential help for education and jobs. However, the assumption that Hunter was commissioned to write a book as a policy recommendation is not substantiated. Mayo encouraged him to pull some of his journalism together in book form, as other officials were doing. The 1871 Education Resolution on special educational provision for Muslims was unconnected with Hunter. Shortly after, Chief Justice Norman of the Calcutta High Court was assassinated by a Muslim, as was Mayo himself in February 1872. Both events strengthened the case for constructive conciliation, and heightened European anxiety which made the book especially topical.

Although the author insisted that he was mostly talking about Bengal, he has been accused of treating Muslims as an undifferentiated mass, or at least of encouraging an official tendency to do so. India's Muslims were part of a worldwide community linked by belief, practices and the *hajj*. Yet in daily reality they were highly fragmented. Among the Sunni majority there were scattered Shia communities. Saiyyids claimed descent from the Prophet, Shaikhs an Arabian ancestry. Nearly half of all Muslims were rural Bengali descendants of converts. Comprising a sixth of the population of India, Muslims were unevenly distributed. Apart from Bengal, the other large Muslim presence was in the Punjab where they constituted a small majority. In Bombay Presidency they were about 18 per cent, though in its western region of Sindh there was a big majority. In the south, various communities amounted to about six per cent. In the princely state of Hyderabad, the Nizam headed the last important Muslim government in the country. Insofar as their spokesmen were responding to the challenges of secular modernity brought by British rule, the outcomes were equally varied. As well as the traditionalists, there was the 'protestant' textual Islam of Deoband and the 'modernism' of Syed Ahmed Khan. In 1879 the activist Jamal al-Din al-Afghani returned to India preaching pan-Islamism under the rule of the Ottoman Khalifa.

Despite the stereotypes fuelled by generalizing from Hunter, not all Muslims rejected western education. Even in Bengal, Abdul Latif's *Muhammadan Literary and Scientific Society of Calcutta* (1863) sought to promote it in ways consonant with religious belief. Amir Ali's *National Mahommedan Association* (1878) was less conservative and, taking the Hunter argument that Muslim decline followed from British rule, pressed the government for assistance.

Strikingly different was the position of Muslims in the North-Western Provinces and Avadh (NWP). In 1871–72 though Muslims were 13.5 per cent and 9.9 per cent of the population respectively, they constituted 17.8 per cent and 25.3 per cent of the school population. It was true that their presence in higher education was smaller, but English had made less headway here and the continuing use of Urdu in government favoured the urban Muslim population. Into the 1880s they still held 45 per cent of all uncovenanted executive and judicial posts in these provinces.[21]

It was from this province that the British government found its most useful ally in Syed Ahmed Khan, a former sub-judge in the Company's service from a family of Delhi courtiers. The shock of the Mutiny had convinced him that bridges must be built and made him ready to respond to the tentative overtures of the Mayo government. A visit to London in 1869 reinforced his belief that Britain was here to stay for the foreseeable future. Before 1857, his biographer recalled that 'his piety was terrifying'.[22] Now he re-thought a theology that would not just reconcile modernity with Islam but would positively welcome it as revelation through reason: 'Reason in man is itself a form of divine inspiration.'[23] His interpretation was anathema to traditionalists or to the Deoband *ulema*. Nevertheless, his earnest call to rally the Muslim community had a strong appeal. Believing education was the key to the future, in 1875 Syed Ahmed founded with official and princely support a college at Aligarh that would train an elite with a foot in both Muslim and western camps. Respectable families could send their sons to study English and prepare for public office without fear for their souls. Discreet government help for Aligarh was not the hand-out for a backward community suggested by the Hunter model. As Francis Robinson has argued, 'Aligarh College... [was] founded to preserve a strong position, not to improve a weak one.'[24]

Can we see here the beginnings of a 'divide and rule' policy? Anil Seal has summarized the main types of explanation for division between Muslims and Hindus. Following Hunter, Muslims have been thought of as a backward community who turned to a receptive British government for special treatment. A simpler version holds that the alien British rulers, so few in numbers, threw their weight behind first one group then the other. A third view holds that there were two nations essentially separate since the Muslim invasions long before the British arrived. All these approaches treat the Muslims as a relatively homogeneous bloc. However, at this stage the variety and fluidity of the situation defy firm conclusions that have been suggested by hindsight.

Rather than 'divide and rule' we may consider the 'balance and rule' approach of Canning. In a letter rejecting Palmerston's request in 1857 to demolish the Friday Mosque in Delhi 'without regard to antiquarian veneration or artistic predilection', he said:[25]

> If we destroy or desecrate Mussalman Mosques or Brahmin temples we do exactly what is wanting to band the two antagonistic races against ourselves...as we must rule 150 million of people by a handful (more or less small) of Englishmen, let us do it in the manner best calculated to leave them divided (as in religion and national feeling they already are) and to inspire them with the greatest possible awe of our power and with the least possible suspicion of our motives... But I beg you not to ask for anything to be done against the religion of either race.

Princes

From London, the Queen's Proclamation announced the end of the age of annexation. In India, Canning expressed his relief that the states, which covered two-fifths of the subcontinent, had not joined the great rebellion, but had been 'breakwaters in the storm, which otherwise would have swept over us in one great wave... the safety of our rule is increased, not diminished, by the maintenance of Native Chiefs well affected to us'.[26] Gratitude took symbolic form in the 1861 creation of the Order of the Star of India awarded to important princes who had been helpful in 1857. The next year *sanads* were sent out, promising to recognize adoptions. Failure to produce direct heirs had been as common as among the Tudor monarchs of England, and Canning's predecessor, Dalhousie, using the so-called 'Doctrine of Lapse', had created widespread alarm with ruthless annexations.

Official opinion was divided whether the states could become a useful support for British rule or were at best a passive advantage and at worst a nuisance. The 'forward' school of frontier policy wanted to be equally active across these internal borders and bring the princes under indirect control as a decentralized aristocracy. Lawrence's school of 'masterly inactivity' stood for vigilant non-interference both across the north-west frontier and in the states so long as local rulers observed treaties and the obligations of good government.

The Queen's Proclamation had declared that all treaties and agreements would be respected. By the mid-1860s they had become available in C. U. Aitchison's multi-volume publication.[27] However, Lawrence's legal approach to the states could not provide clear-cut policy guidance. Only 40 actually had treaties with the Company. Also, princes whose status was uncertain had not been among the 160 who received adoption *sanads*.

In this context, the proclamation's promise that 'We desire no extension of our present territorial possessions' did not, to the official mind, preclude extension absolutely.[28] The age of annexation might be over, but individual annexations in special cases could still occur. Mysore was a case in point. The elderly Maharaja had not received an adoption *sanad* and so could be considered as a prince to whom the official promises did not apply. Since his suspension in 1831 on a dubious technicality, the state had been in the hands of a British commission. Bureaucrats and Whig politicians alike baulked at the idea of a restoration to 'native rule'. There was a coffee planters' lobby and Mysore was strategically placed across peninsular India. The real determinant, however, seems to have been the desire to keep what they thought of as being already British. To return a state which had been under British administration for a whole generation seemed at odds with the trajectory of British rule in India. If Indians could be trusted to run a British-style administration in Mysore, then why not elsewhere? It was recognized that in the light of royal promises, taking Mysore would be a delicate matter. Sir Charles Wood warned Lawrence against annexing troublesome Bhutan: 'we must keep our good character – it may be needed for Mysore'.[29] However, the suspended Maharaja showed that two can play a legalistic game as he ordered his agents to bring various appeals before Parliament.

The arrival of the Tories in 1867 saw the beginnings of a shift from legal to political conceptions of state relations. Determined to prevent appeals to London, Lord Cranborne (later Salisbury) took matters into his own hands and provisionally recognized the previously ignored adoption of the old Maharaja. There was to be no annexation. Speaking in the House of Commons, Cranborne even queried the superiority of British administration 'in the estimation of the natives'. Lawrence wanted to answer this scepticism though he conceded there were inherent difficulties: the foreignness of British rule and the 'forgetful ingratitude of the people'. He sent a circular to the regional authorities asking for an opinion. Prompted by his covering letter, almost all replied without reference to 'the estimation of the natives', but expressed their own confidence that the people were happier and more prosperous under British rule.[30]

The Baroda poisoning case of 1875 illustrates the continuing lack of clarity in state relations. Baroda was a state of 7,000 square miles and two million people then suffering from the collapse of the cotton boom during the US Civil War. The residency of the state was the plum appointment in the hands of the Bombay government which was also responsible for the small states of western India. The Calcutta Foreign Department was trying to centralize control of all Political appointments and had recently taken Aden and the Gulf from Bombay. Mutual suspicion between the two governments was to complicate the case, especially when Bombay appointed as resident colonel Phayre who had been suspended for acrimonious relations in his last position in Khelat. The new Gaekwar of Baroda, Mulhar Rao, was another difficult man who had once been accused of trying to poison his predecessor.

Trouble arose immediately. Phayre objected to the Gaekwar's choice of wife, to being addressed with the informal '*tum*', and above all to Dadabhai Naoroji – 'a mischievous political agitator' – as *diwan*. However, the viceroy informed London that 'a very high opinion is entertained in many quarters of his [Naoroji's] character and abilities'. After a commission of enquiry had reported, both Calcutta and Bombay were losing patience, and Lord Northbrook (Viceroy, 1872–76) finally ordered Phayre's removal for flouting his instructions. At this point a telegram arrived: 'bold attempt to poison me this day has been providentially frustrated'. This raised the stakes and a tribunal ordered by Northbook offered no way forward. The three Indian members acquitted the Gaekwar. The three British, reversing the burden of proof, 'were unable to find any sufficient reason which would justify our declaring the Gaekwar not guilty'. On what grounds could the viceroy legitimately base any action? He told Salisbury that to annex Baroda 'would shake our power in India'.[31] After consulting the cabinet, Salisbury instructed Northbrook to depose the Gaekwar on grounds of unsuitability, not as a result of a trial where the evidence was dubious and the legal basis of the proceedings questionable.

The lack of clear guidelines for government action over Baroda probably focused Salisbury's mind in the case of Alwar, when he returned to office in the new Conservative government. The Alwar Despatch, 1875, marks the turning-point to a political policy. The ruler had died without producing an heir or having adopted one, so Canning's legal promise through *sanads* did not apply. The decision from London to support a suitable candidate was 'a policy, not a pledge... It aims at the perpetuation of Native rule, which is something wider than the perpetuation of the houses of Native rulers, and it is based on grounds of general policy, not an exclusive regard for their individual claims.'[32] Salisbury wanted a re-grant of the state which would bind it close to the overall aims of British government. Misunderstandings with Calcutta frustrated the new approach which was later unveiled with the restoration of the Maharaja Chamrajendra Wadeyar at the Rendition of Mysore in 1881. Mysore was to be the Model State. Here the Instrument of Transfer spelled out the form of government, including a nominated Representative Assembly and numerous British entitlements including the right to intervene in the case of any unilateral changes by the Mysore government.

The title of Empress of India, assumed 1 January 1877, came from England and from the Queen herself. Associating her name with the Indian government followed naturally from the establishment of Crown government in 1858. But the occasion of the Royal Titles Act, 1876, which authorized a new title, was a surprise. 'What does the Queen mean?' Salisbury asked Disraeli.[33] The viceroy, Lytton, was concerned that Indians would 'think it impossible that...the Queen should have adopted this title without any political purpose whatsoever'.[34] Nevertheless, it suited his purpose admirably. Like other viceroys, except Lawrence, he was an aristocrat, disliked middle class politics at home and in India, and greatly overestimated the aristocratic possibilities in India: 'if we have with us the Princes, we shall have with us the people'.[35]

However, with a major famine developing in the south, government spending, of half a million pounds sterling, was confined to staging an Imperial Assemblage. All the princes were invited to a theatrical gathering at the old Mughal capital of Delhi. A new title, Counsellor to the Empress, was conferred on eight rulers, and in 1878 new orders of chivalry for men and women were founded. There were occasionally female rulers, notably in Bhopal. The ceremonial, the pageantry and the establishment of ranked distance marked a permanent shift in how British rule was presented. In the 1860s, Lawrence's officials had not liked his walking to church; such informality was now inconceivable. This was 'ornamentalism', hierarchy made visible. Salisbury hoped the new title would help to legitimate British rule and 'to hide from our own people, and perhaps the growing literary class in India, the nakedness of the sword on which we really rely... and also lay the foundations of some feeling on the part of the coloured races towards the Crown other than the recollection of defeat and the sensation of subjection'.[36]

Lytton's Romantic literary background may have encouraged the idea of drawing the princes together in a 'feudal' aristocracy. There was also a hard-headed desire to oversee princely armies – in total, 320,000 troops and 5,226 guns – and reduce costs: £800,000 was paid by the states to the government, who spent half this sum on agencies and twice as much on pensions for deposed rulers. But what could be offered to them? Hyderabad's desire to recover the cotton land of Berar, taken under British control during a crisis in 1853, was certainly not on the agenda. Nor was addressing the numerous territorial grievances of other states; to discuss them would open a can of worms.[37]

'Feudal' implied a subordination that the minor states might accept; proud Hyderabad was a different matter. Salisbury foresaw that 'it is possible, however, that they may see this [their implied subjection] as clearly as we do'.[38] One advantage, however, which many princes exploited was the direct link to Windsor Castle. All external relations were supposed to go through the Calcutta Foreign Department, but the Queen made it clear that she was willing to receive letters from her feudatories.

Otherwise, the princes had nowhere to turn. Where, in the rest of the British Empire, the trend was now towards indirect rule, these princes were being drawn more closely into a system of support for British rule in the subcontinent. The turning-point was not the Mutiny but Salisbury's shift from the legal to the political in the Alwar and Mysore cases which laid the real foundations of paramountcy. It fell on fertile ground in Calcutta where, Sir Henry Maine, Lawrence's law member, had been developing his theory of divisible sovereignty. The English tradition of unified sovereignty, whereby a state was either sovereign or not, was now redundant – at least as a tool for dealing with the princes. How sovereignty was divided between a state and the British government was in each case a matter of fact, to be decided by the officials of the Political Department who would record individual decisions and treat them as applicable to all other states. 'Paramountcy rests on conquest, agreement and usage';[39] especially usage.

2. The Second Afghan War

Events in the late 1860s began to challenge the policy of masterly inactivity on the north-west frontier. After a civil war Sher Ali had emerged as Amir of Afghanistan and asked for British support. Stability suited Britain, but Lord Mayo was not inclined to give guarantees of support that might draw Britain across the border if the succession struggle were resumed, an arms-length approach continued by Lord Northbrook. Meanwhile, the khanates of Central Asia were falling to the advancing Russians. In 1867 the province of Turkestan was established and the Russian governor began to correspond with his neighbour the Amir. All of this raised fears that through the direct or indirect control of Afghanistan, the Russians might reach the border of British India. Given problems of distance and terrain an invasion might seem unlikely, but there was also the concern that a Russian thrust would provoke an internal rebellion.

After the Conservative election victory in 1874, forward ideas were in the ascendant. As the Balkan crisis deepened, London took charge of policy; there was now more at stake than the successful transformation of Afghanistan into an outer princely state. Disraeli chose the bold and theatrical Lord Lytton as viceroy and told him that 'The critical state of affairs in Central Asia demands a statesman, and I believe that if you will accept this high post you will have an opportunity, not only of serving your country, but of obtaining an enduring fame.'[40] Lord Salisbury thought the Russians were impregnable in Europe and could only be attacked in Asia. In 1876 Lytton arrived in Calcutta with the hope of 'bequeathing to India the supremacy of Central Asia'.[41]

First came plans to establish a 'scientific' frontier, by bringing the border tribes under control. Quetta was occupied for the Baluchi sector and, for the Pathan north, the Maharaja of Kashmir was approached to accept a British envoy in Gilgit. Then, if the Russian threat to the eastern Mediterranean were to become severe, a thrust by the Indian army towards Tashkent was envisaged which Lytton thought could 'easily sweep the whole Russian Powers out of Central Asia'.[42] These troops would have to pass through Afghanistan, 'a State far too weak and barbarous to remain isolated and wholly uninfluenced between two great military empires such as England and Russia'.[43] It would have to come under indirect British control.

Lytton told the Amir that he was an earthenware pipkin between two iron pots. Yet the viceroy's belief that Sher Ali could be intimidated into an agreement proved mistaken. A lengthy visit in the spring of 1878 by the Russian general Stolietov probably encouraged him to temporize, and raised British fears to a high level. Lytton prepared a mission to bring decisive pressure to bear on Sher Ali. At this moment, mixed messages came from England as Salisbury postponed his belligerence. Now, as foreign secretary, he was focusing on the diplomacy of the Congress of Berlin and thought the moment one of 'singular infelicity' for a showdown.[44] Lytton was told not to let the mission leave until the Russians had replied to a request to declare their position.

Much of the subsequent blame for the war has centred on Lytton's disregard of this request. However, Lord Cranbrook told him that Salisbury expected only 'specious promises'. Nor was Disraeli for compromise: 'to prove our ascendancy in Asia and to accomplish that we must not stick at trifles'.[45] Lytton may have feared a loss of prestige if a publicized mission were held back, and his primary aim for it was not so much to reach Kabul as to force the Amir to make a choice. When the mission was halted at Ali Masjid, Cranbrook secured cabinet backing for an ultimatum. No apology being forthcoming, the troops marched and Sher Ali fled to Turkestan.

The policy now was to disintegrate Afghanistan. In May 1879 Yakub Khan, son of Sher Ali, signed the Treaty of Gandamak putting foreign policy under British control and ceding the border areas of Sibi and Pishin. He was chary of a request for a British mission to Kandahar or Herat. It was here in the southern parts where rule from Kabul was historically weak that Britain's strategic interests were focused. He therefore offered to receive the envoy in Kabul where he could keep an eye on him. An impetuous officer of the forward school, Sir Louis Cavagnari, was chosen to head the embassy. In England, Lawrence predicted that 'They will all be murdered, every one of them.'[46] On 3 September mutinous troops massacred Cavagnari, his staff and 75 troopers, and Yakub Khan fled to India.

The die was cast as Lytton wrote to Cranbrook in a letter of 21 November 1878 and by mid-October General Roberts had occupied Kabul and ordered the retaliatory hangings and village burning that fuelled the *jihad* soon to be preached by local mullahs. Another column had captured Kandahar. Cranbrook shared Lytton's view that 'Afghanistan as a whole could no longer exist'.[47] He persuaded the cabinet that Lytton should avoid half-measures, so that the viceroy seemed to be accused of moderation from both London and from his own military. Only Salisbury was for caution: Lytton 'unless curbed would bring about some terrible disaster'.[48] Though the viceroy still wanted 'the undisputed supremacy of the British Power from the Indus to the Oxus', he wished to avoid occupying anywhere he would not want to hold. Ideally, puppet rulers would be found for Kabul and for Kandahar. Britain would not annex the latter unless Persia took Herat.[49]

As the military situation deteriorated, the need to find leaders with whom to negotiate became urgent. Roberts' supply line was cut during the winter; he withdrew from Kabul but was besieged at Sherpur. At this point Abdur Rahman, a nephew of Sher Ali, returned from Russia and seemed an effective claimant. Lytton told Cranbrook he had found him a 'ram caught in a thicket', though he was soon concerned that the support gathering around him might make him 'the head of a united nation, and dictate terms to us, instead of accepting them from us'. The policy of confining Abdur Rahman to Kabul and keeping the south separate did not last much longer. The change was determined by events and not by the Liberal government which came in at the end of April 1880. In May Ayub Khan, another son of Sher Ali who ruled Herat, set out for Kandahar, brushed aside the British puppet ruler and defeated a British brigade at Maiwand. Roberts reported that 'our troops were completely routed, and had to thank the apathy of the Afghans in not following them up for escaping total annihilation'. The interests of Britain and Abdur Rahman now coincided. The Amir assisted Roberts in avenging Maiwand and ending the southern breakaway, whereupon all British forces were withdrawn from Afghanistan.[50]

The outcome was that Britain now retained a border presence, especially in the Khyber Pass and, fortuitously, had found a strong and friendly Amir with whom to establish a relationship. This was important because the Russians were determined to recover lost ground, and the 'Great Game' of rivalry for influence in Central Asia was to become intense in the years ahead.

The performance of the Indian army had given grounds for concern. The supply chain had been inadequate. Eighty thousand camels, requisitioned from farmers in the Punjab, had been lost. This and other damage inflicted on north Indian agriculture coincided with famine in the south. The cost of the war, calculated at £5 million, had to be revised when Sir John Strachey resigned following the discovery that the Finance Department had not recorded a further £12 million.

Lytton's viceroyalty ended the bi-partisan approach to Indian affairs. When Gladstone, who had campaigned against the war, was returned to office, Lytton resigned. He was blamed for the war by the Indian press and most later historians, some of whom have related his poor judgement and emotional incontinence to his bizarre upbringing. The blame came first from his own party. Disraeli complained that the military leaders 'to whom we have voted Parliamentary thanks and on whom the Crown has conferred honours [were] utterly worthless'. He continued, 'As for General Sam Browne, according to Lytton, he ought to have been tried by court martial, and he goes thru' [sic] them all with analogous remarks. I begin to think he ought to be tried by a court martial himself...'[51]

Yet this was to scapegoat the viceroy who had been chosen as the instrument of a policy decided by the incoming Tory government. The object was to use Indian power as a means of putting pressure on Russia in the developing Eastern (Balkan) crisis. Details of the policy had been left to Lytton who, to circumvent opposition within his own government, stopped calling the Executive Council and dealt with members on an individual basis. But the roots of the policy lay in Disraeli's desire to project British power against the Russians in Central Asia. The Afghan policy marked a high point of direction from London.

3. Government and the Economy

The government had three fundamental concerns. The first was to maintain an army for internal security and from which expeditionary forces could be sent abroad for imperial purposes.

Second, it had to ensure that the interest would be paid on the sterling debt and on other charges which fell due in London. Government loans accounted for over half of all capital exports to India. Overall, British investments in

India were about 20 per cent of the empire total, and seven per cent of all British foreign investment. To encourage railway building, the government promised that any return below five per cent would be made up to that figure, courtesy of the Indian taxpayer. By 1900, 70 per cent of the network required this public subsidy to honour the government guarantee. Then, there were the Home Charges of government and army spending in Britain, the costs of the India Office and ICS pensions.

Third, the government was expected to ensure that the Indian market was open to British goods. During the second half of the century, more than a quarter of Lancashire textiles, Britain's principal export industry, went to India. The livelihood of 550,000 workers came to depend on this export trade and every government up to the Second World War was aware of pressure from the 60 or so Lancashire MPs to maintain the flow of textiles into India.

These expectations limited the government's room for manoeuvre. The army took about forty per cent of government income. Maintaining external confidence required a cautious monetary policy, especially from the 1870s onward as the silver rupee exchange rate fell against the gold-backed currencies. The need for revenue after the Mutiny had made a few tariffs inevitable, but resistance from Lancashire was relentless. Among most British politicians, laissez-faire was an article of faith, even after other industrialized countries adopted tariff regimes in the 1870s. Lytton moved against remaining internal barriers when he began the equalization of the salt tax by abolishing the Salt Line, the 1,500-mile hedge with its 8,000 guards which separated regions with different tax rates. In 1879 he began the removal – completed by Ripon in 1882 – of the low tariff on cotton imports. Salisbury's enthusiasm for free trade may have had a political angle. The promise of no Indian tariffs would lock Liberal Lancashire with its otherwise anti-imperialist tendency into support for British India.

The government, therefore, was under chronic financial pressure and operated on the equivalent of between five and seven per cent of national income. To the inherited debts of the Company was added the £40 million cost of 1857. In the 1860s there was an annual deficit of £10 million out of a total net income of £32 million. The land revenue constituted 40 per cent of income. Opium revenue was 16 per cent and was subject to scrutiny by humanitarian lobbies. The regressive salt tax brought in 12 per cent. The government was reluctantly dependent on these last two items, because like the empires of the early modern and ancient world, it was dependent on agricultural taxation and found it difficult or dangerous to tax the towns. Intermittent income and licence taxes were not easy to assess and provoked complaints from the upper classes. Generally, the scope for tax increases was small, though as the economy picked up between 1871 and 1893 there was a 34 per cent tax increase with a third of tax revenue coming from non-agricultural sources. Recognizing the difficulties facing a foreign government, Canning had said: 'I would rather govern India with 40,000 British troops without an income tax, than govern it with 100,000 British troops with such a tax.'[52] The choice was limited government, appropriate to the age of laissez-faire.

Yet Britain was committed to supporting the development of the country. After 1864 it began to supplement private investment in irrigation, with a preference for large works over the maintenance of local schemes. State expenditure rose from £200,000 in 1840 to £30.5 million in 1901. The other principal recipient was the railways, especially after 1869 when it had become clear that private investors and princes were not sufficient. In 1860 there were some 850 miles of track. By the eve of the First World War, India had the fourth largest railway network in the world.[53]

The railways and the opening of the Suez Canal in 1869 enhanced the export opportunities for Indian agriculture, parts of which had enjoyed a cotton boom when the US Civil War (1861–65), interrupted normal supplies. The falling rupee made Indian exports more competitive. Between 1871 and 1900 an annual population growth of 0.6 per cent underlay a rise in per capita income of about 30 per cent.[54]

At the same time the sinister shadow of famine fell across the country. Between 1860 and 1908 there were 20 famines, each affecting a wider area. The 1876–78 famine in the south was the most severe of the century and affected 36 million people. It was a rural crisis. Throughout 1877 in the columns of the *Bangalore Spectator* an argument raged between those who thought that an immense catastrophe was unfolding and those who did not; though letter-writers criticized the Municipal Committee for not removing putrefying bodies from the streets. At least 3.5 million people died in Madras, 100,000 in Bombay, and in Mysore over a million, a quarter of the entire population. Hyderabad, under Indian rule, had a lower death rate.

The immediate cause was the failure of the rains. Yet, as Lytton discovered, there was at all times food to be had for those who could pay for it. It appears that wages scarcely changed between 1860 and 1890. An all-India index for 1877 (1873: 100) shows wages at 97 and food grain prices on 166.[55] It was a classic high-price scarcity and most victims were landless labourers and weavers or providers of services the better-off could no longer afford. More than 70 per cent of the population lived on the land and there were next to no opportunities for other employment. George Couper, lieutenant-governor of the NWP – whom Lord Ripon (Viceroy, 1880–84) later got rid of – took the view that there was a surplus population that could not flourish and should not be sustained.

In January 1877, Disraeli told the Queen that the cabinet had discussed the scarcity 'which greatly exceeds the recent Bengal famine'.[56] The provincial governments, however, responded slowly. Bombay eventually had 3 million on large public works, Madras over 2 million on scattered projects. The British Commission in Mysore was slowest; as late as July 1877 the chief engineer, before his dismissal, was still refusing to employ a single extra labourer in the Public Works Department. Desperate crowds roamed the burnt landscape. Forty thousand labourers should have been coming back to the plains from the coffee estates; twice that number were going back, littering the mountain paths with their bodies. Over 200,000 square miles of the south scenes of utter horror were commonplace.

The increasing commercialization of agriculture had benefited some and made others more vulnerable. Aware of these pressures and the rising land revenue, the government repeatedly legislated to protect peasant proprietors but in doing so undermined customary tenures lower down the order. The claims of sharecroppers and landless labourers were weakened as law, not custom, mattered now. In the Western Ghats serfs were choosing the freedom of the monetized economy but lost traditional protection in bad times. The fruits of the forest were no longer available to hungry tribal people. The problem was not availability of food grains or of their distribution but the existence of millions of people living just above subsistence who were fatally vulnerable to a short-term rise in food prices.

The human consequences must have lasted for years. Survivors with their weakened physiques were vulnerable to disease and of limited use in the workforce. In 1877 cholera deaths in Madras Presidency stood at 12.20 per 1,000 and in the famine districts at twice that level.[57] For the lucky few with savings there were opportunities to purchase land. The Famine Commission of 1880 found that a third of cultivators were inextricably in debt. The landless had died or survived in relief camps; the cultivators had survived by borrowing against their land.

In the government's response, fear of the possible cost – eventually about £16 million – was clearly an important consideration in those years of deficit budgets. The Madras governor, who had initiated grain purchases, was rebuked for his lack of faith in the market, for 'not perceiving that the high prices, by stimulating import and limiting consumption, were the natural saviours of the situation'. As well as infringing free trade theory, the potential cost alarmed Lytton as he considered the unfolding scale of the catastrophe in the south. In sending Sir Richard Temple as his famine commissioner, he laid down that 'The government held that the task of saving life irrespective of cost was beyond their power to undertake.'[58] The emphasis was on relief works for the able-bodied and the 'Temple ration' which cut the daily food allowance was designed to deter applicants. The government now began to improve its statistics and drew up a Famine Code. The local governments were supposed to plan for future famines; the Supreme Government put aside £1.5 million a year for a famine fund.

The early nationalists were to make famine and poverty the focus of their critique of British rule through the theory of the 'drain' (see Chapter 2, Section 3).

Chapter 2

LIBERAL IMPERIALISM, 1880–1899

1. Different Liberalisms

The Tories had tried to legitimate British rule through the Empress of India title by offering a personalized monarchy to conservative Indians. The hopes of the western-educated were fixed on Gladstone after his victory in the 1880 General Election. Would his viceroy offer a vision for British India less imperialistic and more attuned to their aspirations? Born in Downing Street the son of a prime minister, Lord Ripon had been a radical and a Christian socialist in his youth before making another counter-establishment choice by becoming a Roman Catholic. After handling the Alabama arbitration with the USA, he had London experience of Indian government and was believed to be sympathetic to the popular and moralistic liberalism associated with Gladstone's name. But in the event, the hopes were dashed. Gladstone was not interested; Ireland, not India, was the focus of his energies.

British liberalism in the 1880s had reached the parting of the ways. Optimistic confident individualism was confronted by democratic pressures to widen the franchise and the collectivism of Irish nationalism. The Whig wing of the party, frightened by this radicalism and the risk of national and imperial disintegration, was ready to leave Gladstone for Salisbury's Conservatives, but could still see India as a field for their tradition of enlightened authoritarianism. Though there were Conservative governments in 1885–86, from 1886 to 1892 and from 1895 to1905, the appointment of the next three viceroys fell to Gladstone. He nominated the Whig Lords Dufferin (1884–88), Lansdowne (1888–94) and Elgin (1894–99), all from the Liberal Imperialist wing of the party.

There was now a keen awareness of India's importance in the empire. In 1888 Dufferin referred to the prime duty of watching 'over the enormous commercial interests of the mother country' invested 'on the assumption that

English rule and English justice will remain dominant in India'.[1] As protection spread in the western world and Britain ran a trade deficit, India's trade surplus with the rest of the world was of vital importance in maintaining Britain's overall balance of payments. The Liberal Imperialists, the men of the 1890s, Rosebery, Asquith and Grey, saw imperial service as a worthy inheritance which it was their duty to sustain in an age when British power, political and economic, was no longer unchallenged in the wider world.

Fitzjames Stephen's writings expressed a harder, more authoritarian strain of intellectual liberalism. What had been promised in the Queen's Proclamation was becoming a political reality as educated Bengalis began to demand that these pledges be redeemed. Now the mission was to be redefined. 'It was to provide for the welfare of the community…[through] peace, order, the supremacy of law, the prevention of crime, the redress of wrong, the enforcement of contracts…the construction of public works.'[2] Stephen's liberal imperialism spoke for the bureaucracy where there had never been much feeling for sentimental, political liberalism.

The approach came through strongly in foreign and princely state policy and also shaped Ripon's Gladstonian liberalism.

The North-West Frontier

The first task was to redeem the election pledge of withdrawal from Afghanistan after an 'unjust war', as Gladstone had described it.[3] Following the disaster at Maiwand, the British extricated themselves with Abdur Rahman's help, and on Ripon's orders transferred authority in the south – Kandahar and Helmand – to the former Russian protégé and withdrew from the country. Abdur Rahman was recognized as Amir, no envoy was forced on him, and he received a subsidy in return for maintaining the Gandamak Treaty which conceded British control of his foreign policy. Ripon, to the surprise of his Liberal friends in Britain, 'provisionally' occupied the border districts of Sibi and Pishin. They were annexed as British Baluchistan in 1887 during the next Liberal viceroyalty. Their strategic value on the frontier overrode Gladstonian principle.

That principle was put to another test when Calcutta was charged for the Indian contingent in the army that occupied Egypt in 1882. Ripon bargained for nearly half the costs to be returned. Gladstone held that Egypt was 'an Indian as well as a British interest', and, unlike Afghanistan, was necessary to the security of India, an argument later extended to Upper Burma.[4] In substance, if not style, Liberal imperialism was beginning to resemble Conservative policies.

In like manner, Lord Hartington (Secretary of State, 1880–82), alarmed at the Russian advance on Merv, began to press Ripon for some counteractive pressure on Afghanistan. Resisting what seemed like a return to Lyttonism, Ripon wanted to see the matter settled between London and St Petersburg. Eventually a boundary commission was set up in 1884, but as it was proceeding the Russians seized remote Panjdeh. The army was mobilized and an extra 10,000 troops were sent to India. But the war scare passed as the Russians agreed to compromise elsewhere and Gladstone asked the King of Denmark to arbitrate. The commission achieved an agreed Russian–Afghan border and Central Asian diplomacy shifted back to Europe.

The Indo-Afghan border remained problematic until Gladstone's fourth ministry which feared that Lansdowne was being pressed into a 'forward' policy by the Russophobe commander-in-chief, General Roberts. The Amir, too, had his concerns about British movement into Chitral and Gilgit. Further conflict was avoided by agreement in 1893 over the Durand Line. This recognized Indian and Afghan spheres of influence over a tribal border zone, with Britain responsible for the Afridis, Waziris, Swat and Chitral.

The new Liberal viceroy, Lord Elgin, arrived in India an admirer of the Lawrence school of 'masterly inactivity'. Soon, he was stressing the importance of British prestige in the hills, and of warning Russia off Chitral, a posture that was to the liking of the new Conservative government. Permanent garrisons were authorized in Waziristan and Chitral, and the late 1890s saw heavy fighting in parts of the tribal zone. A young participant, Winston Churchill, wrote his first book about *The Malakand Field Force* (1898). In the Khyber region, Colonel Warburton, the son of a British officer and a niece of the Amir Dost Mohammed, managed friendly working relations with the tribesmen for 18 years until his retirement on the eve of the outbreak of 1897.

The Third Burma War

Gladstone's third ministry also inherited the consequences of a war on the eastern border. Since the late eighteenth century, the Company's control of the Bay of Bengal had seemed threatened by an expansionist Burma willing to offer naval facilities to the French. The first war ended in 1826 with the Treaty of Yandabo whereby Burma ceded Arakan, Assam, Manipur and Tenasserim to Britain. But relations did not improve because the King was not prepared to sacrifice external sovereignty and become a princely state on Indian lines. Dalhousie eventually decided to send a naval force to Rangoon to support the complaints of British traders. Burmese intransigence and the 'combustible commodore' Lambert created an ugly stand-off. Remarking that 'We cannot afford to be shown the door anywhere in the East', Dalhousie ordered the conquest of Pegu which placed a continuous coastline to Tenasserim in the Malay isthmus, including the port of Rangoon, under the control of the Company. Cobden's pamphlet 'How wars are got up in India' (1853) could be shrugged off. In 1862 the various parts were amalgamated into British Burma.

The Burmese, in Upper Burma, were no more reconciled to becoming a client state than they had been after the first war. Cultural clashes continued, now centring on the removal of shoes by British envoys in the royal presence. Lytton, mindful of Cavagnari's assassination in Kabul, recalled his envoy in 1879. Mindon Min had made overtures to the USA and offered a commercial treaty to France. His successor, Thibaw Min, 1878–85, fatally refused Ripon's offer of a commercial and friendship treaty while ratifying the French agreement. Then, the Italian consul in Mandalay, who was also the agent for the Bombay-Burma Trading Company, revealed a secret letter offering French arms supplies to Burma. A fine imposed on this Bombay company was the *casus belli*. The Indian government had an invasion plan ready and Salisbury and Lord Randolph Churchill (Secretary of State, 1885–86) ordered Dufferin to move 10,000 troops to Rangoon before the ultimatum was delivered on 30 October 1885. Unprepared, the Burmese were defeated in a fortnight.

Should Britain create a client state or annex? Dufferin hesitated; he had recent experience in Egypt of the difficulties of running a protectorate. Annexation was pushed through from London. Its announcement in the Queen's speech of 12 January 1886 was in time to pre-empt the Liberals, who returned to office at the end of the month. Churchill, who still favoured the annexation of Afghanistan, observed that the trading dispute had provided 'a unique opportunity…for dealing very summarily with Burmah'.[5] Internationally, the timing was propitious. At that moment the French were tied down in Indo-China. China, which regarded Burma as a client state, needed a friend against France and was mollified by Britain's offer to send ten-year missions on a basis of equality. The Foreign Office advised that annexation would extinguish any existing Burmese treaty obligations.

The cost of taking the country using loans raised on a depreciating currency was no light matter. An official with Burmese experience, Sir Charles Crosthwaite warned that 'A considerable minority of the population, to say the least, do not want us.'[6] But, Dufferin convinced himself that the 'great mass of the people… [would be] indifferent to the future form of government'.[7] In this he was profoundly mistaken. Subsequently, five royal princes led different resistance movements, not to mention serious unrest in the extensive minority areas. The imposition of an Indian-style administration did not suit Burma. In particular, the pledge of religious neutrality in the Queen's Proclamation was held to preclude the official upholding of the Buddhist church which had been central to the old Burmese state. The post-conquest pacification tied down 30,000 troops for four years and cost ten times the original estimate for the war.

The war and subsequent annexation of Upper Burma have attracted the whole range of explanations of imperial expansion. Was the personal ambition of Lord Randolph Churchill the prime determinant? The Tory secretary knew that in the fluid state of party politics an election could come at any time. In public speeches he was playing the 'Fair Trade' card. His listeners were ready to blame the current check to prosperity on Britain's attachment to free trade in the face of spreading protectionism abroad. Business interests pressed the value of Upper Burma's raw materials and the eventual possibility of a land trade with China. Prime Minister Salisbury gave Churchill his head. He may have thought that the confident assertion of British power would look better than the Liberal fudge over Panjdeh or their failure to save General Gordon in the Sudan.

Against these metropolitan theories, personal, electoral, economic or political, can be set the pressures from India. Arguing backwards, economic considerations look strong. A dispute with the Bombay-Burma Trading Company provided the British ultimatum. Timber, minerals and oil were rapidly exploited after the take-over. Indians and Indian money flooded into the Irrawaddy delta which within a generation was producing 60 per cent of the rice traded on world markets. The Irrawaddy Flotilla Company became the largest shipping company in the world.

Strategic motives appear even stronger. Burma's eastern border was 'soft and pulpy', providing no barrier to French penetration.[8] According to this explanation what was at stake here, as with Afghanistan, was the security of India's borders. The differences between the parties' ideas regarding the defence of India were a matter of levels of enthusiasm. Gladstone, in accepting the fait accompli, regretted the necessity, but he told the House of Commons that the annexation was for 'the safety and security of our own frontier and our own people... It was not to extend trade or gratify passion or ambition, but because a door was threatened to be opened through which would have been brought into India danger, insecurity, loss of happiness and prosperity.'[9]

The 'Robinson and Gallagher Thesis' combines metropolitan and peripheral explanations. These founders of the 'Cambridge School' stressed the relentless dynamism of the metropolis. The preferred mode of expansion was informal. Nevertheless, events on the periphery might trigger the actual annexation of territory (formal empire) which 'was always a last resort... undertaken not in response to organized opinion or electoral pressures, but in response to the perceptions of a policy making elite (the *official* or *collective* mind)... Central to their thinking was India', the second centre of the empire whose 'unique political, economic and strategic value meant that Victorian statesmen were prepared...to intervene much more directly in its affairs than in other colonies...'[10] Thus, whatever the immediate French challenges, economic threats or the general strategic relevance, we should set the annexation of Upper Burma in the context of the contemporary dynamism of British expansion against weak Asian states, Ottoman, Qajar, Qing or those of South-east Asia.

Princely India

In the event, the Instrument of Transfer for Mysore's 1881 Rendition did not become a Magna Carta for the states. No Liberal vision traded the security of growing imperial control for constitutional reform by the princes. It was rather the opposite. Variety and traditional rule was thought to enhance the security of British rule in the subcontinent.

Most states were not at the mercy of the Supreme Government as Mysore had been. There were, however, ways of bringing them into line with British India. Boarding schools for young princes had been established in Mayo's time: Aitchison College for the Punjab, Daly College for central India. The government could facilitate the appointment of respected *diwans* educated in British India: S. V. Rangacarlu in Mysore; his school friend, Sir T. Madhava Rao in Travancore; Sir Dinkar Rao in Gwalior. At Hyderabad, Sir Salar Jang had more scope for manoeuvre and was probably the most important Indian politician in the empire.[11]

A minority or 'incapacity' of the ruler would normally lead to control by the British resident who would reduce palace spending, introduce versions of many British laws and arrange a western education for the young prince. Full advantage was taken of this surprisingly common opportunity. The high point came under Curzon at the turn of the century when the figures for temporary British control of states over 100 square miles – the biggest 252 states – were as follows:[12]

Year	Minority	Incapacity	Total
1898	43	18	61
1900	45	17	62
1902	47	17	64

Princes tried to keep alive appeals to international law. But the Political Department was soon sifting legal references from the records. Later editions of Aitchison's *Treaties* no longer referred to Patiala's 'full sovereignty'. The eminent jurist, John Westlake, claimed, against European tradition, that international law 'is that of…Europe, all nations outside Europe but of European blood, and Japan'.[13] But consistency was difficult to maintain.

The settlement of the border between Avadh and Nepal (an outer native state in British eyes) followed international law. An Anglo-German Extradition Treaty had a legal bearing on the states. Hyderabad was later told in 1902 when it tried to reopen negotiations over Berar that to go back on a signed agreement was contrary to the law of nations.[14]

Some court decisions encouraged princely hopes. The requirement for a state to make land available for imperial railways was a doorway through which other British claims could follow. The Privy Council declared illegal this wider use of a specific agreement in *Muhammed Yusuf ud-din v. Queen Empress* (1897). The Gaekwar, cited in a divorce case, *Statham v. Statham and the Gaekwar* (1911), was able to claim immunity as a sovereign ruler. But in high profile cases, the 1891 dispute with Manipur, for example, the government explicitly excluded international law. New legislation was always unequivocal. The Interpretation Act, 1889, replaced 'alliance' with 'suzerainty' A clarification explained that 'The paramount supremacy of the former [Her Majesty] presupposes the subordination of the latter [Native States].'[15]

The theory and practice of paramountcy were in the silent hands of the Political Department until 1894. In that year, Sir William Lee-Warner, passed over for the head of the department, went public with *The Protected Princes of India*. Theoretical clarity might be lacking but his explanation of the doctrine of the general applicability of special cases showed how paramountcy constantly developed and reflected changing British needs. His terminology lacked the conservative discretion of his successful rival, Sir Charles Tupper; a title of 'more neutral tint', *The Native States of India*, was chosen for the second edition in 1910.[16] Lee-Warner had presented princely India as being under Home Rule, when this was an explosive issue in British politics, and used 'semi-sovereign' as best describing the relationship. His title drew on a concept – protectorate – recognized in international law at the Berlin West Africa Conference of 1884–85. For Tupper, the relationship was feudal, which through its evocation of the traditions of the Rajput states – though hardly those of most other parts of India – gave the presentation of paramountcy an indigenous character, consciously aimed at in the coronation durbars of 1903 and 1911.

The variety of the states and their changing individual relationships with the government make generalization hazardous. But in the heyday of British power the trend is probably best described as 'constitutional', the description favoured by Westlake. Salisbury had thought the states might form another element in the Indian empire, a counterweight to resident Europeans, 'to all that bragging fatuity which in so many places – Jamaica, St Domingo, Cuba and the Confederate States – has induced the resident white population to dream that they can defy their own government with one hand and keep supremacy over the coloured multitudes by their side with the other'. Under Curzon, the princes were becoming, as he told them, 'pillars that help to sustain the main roof'.[17] The obligations were one way. The Imperial Service troops supplied by some states which fought in China in 1901 and in the Boer War were an obligation. They had been prefigured in the 1875 order to reduce the Muslim element in the Mysore army to a third. Instead of treating the force as outdoor relief for old Muslim families, it was to be prepared for operational efficiency. Comparisons were being drawn with indirect rule in Malaya and Africa as Tupper explained that 'native rulers may be regarded as the agents or great hereditary officers of the British Empire at large for the administration of part of its varied possessions'. As early as 1866–67, Sir Charles Dilke thought that 'There is not now existent a thoroughly native government.'[18]

The belief that British India would shine by comparison with the states' backwardness was not always borne out. Bangalore had electricity installed before Calcutta. For a time Mysore pursued a dynamic industrial policy under the *diwan* Sir M. Visvesvaraya. When Bedi, Nawanagar's new port in Kathiawar took trade away from Bombay, the ruler and famous cricketer, Ranjitsinghji, found that new dues in neighbouring British India crippled its development. Similarly, the bedizened, bejewelled style we see in portraits of the princes could be taken as a sign of their growing irrelevance or of their assimilation to British ornamentalism.

The states did form politically quiet swathes of the subcontinent. The Gaekwar and his wife and a few individuals, such as the Maharaja of Darbhanga, were helpful to early nationalists, but most preferred a quiet life. The *diwan* Sir Sheshadri Iyer could complain in 1896 that Mysorean cultivators, on account of the railways, education and contact with British India, were now showing a 'large element of upstartishness, if not of impertinence'.[19] But nationalism, Indian or local, made next to no headway. 'Mysore for the Mysoreans' had begun in the 1870s but did not transcend other divisions in the society. Their governments were not like the British, pressing on the people in ways that called new forces into life. It has been said that the English education of most princes after the 1860s began to cut them off from their peoples. Yet, in well-governed Travancore the ruling family had been educated in English since the 1820s. In the late century the ruler of a remote, small state in Chhattisgarh chose to be photographed with his elbow resting on Webster's dictionary. Even in the 'model state' of Mysore we can see from a dispute over the caste classification of the Lingayat religious community that the throne still had potency. The Lingayats rejected the Sudra status assigned to them in the 1881 census and despite a Bombay court judgement and various threats, refused to register. The young Maharaja declared that they should have a separate category of their own.[20] The dispute was over. As a local proverb had it:

> As running stops at the river bank
> Disputes stop with the king[21]

Where the British had power and were inclined to exploit divisions, Chamrajendra Wadeyar in this case had the authority to heal them.

British India

In domestic affairs Ripon wanted to signal a change of direction from Lytton's policies which had given 'an impression…that in all ways…the interests of the Natives of India were to be sacrificed to those of England'.[22] However, proposals for civil service reform, for elections to Legislative Councils and for the repeal of the Arms Act were all blocked from London. Even the Press Act, which both Ripon and Gladstone abominated, was not repealed until 1882. Hartington believed that the Indian press had become like radical liberal papers in England, and the best approach to the storm raised by Lytton's viceroyalty was quietude. His successor, the once-radical Kimberley (1882–85, 1886), became equally cautious and unwilling to provide the robust backing Ripon needed to overcome resistance within his own government.

Ripon then turned to local government, looking to widen collaboration and conscious of the financial constraints on government. In a resolution of 1870, Mayo had devolved upon provincial governments certain heads of revenue and expenditure for five-year terms. Indians, at first nominated then elected, would join these municipal and rural boards and take responsibility for education, sanitation, local public works and for raising the necessary taxes. The second quinquennial review of Mayo's scheme prompted Ripon's Resolution of 1882. The new boards responsible for areas of local administration and taxation were now to be funded by a fixed proportion instead of a fixed amount from the imperial revenues. They were to have a majority of non-official members wherever the provincial governments thought practicable. Ripon wanted official control to be external; if possible, the boards should elect their own chairmen.

This 'first-rate statesman of the second rank', as Gladstone called him, started from his leader's assumptions about the value of self-government. 'It is not primarily with a view to improvement in administration that this measure is put forward and supported. It is chiefly desirable as an instrument of political and popular education.'[23] These words of the Resolution expressed a liberalism which Gladstone himself had endorsed in a letter the year before; 'I am sure that it is better to endure the postponement of even really useful measures than to check the advance of habits of self-government among the people.'[24] Ripon wrote: 'though I am as you know, radical enough on the subject at home, I do not think that India is yet fit for a low Suffrage; I should…keep it moderately high at present. What I want to secure by the extension of Local Self-government is not a representation of the people of an European Democratic type, but the gradual training of the best, most intelligent, and most influential men in the community to take an interest and an active part in the management of their local affairs.'[25]

The Bombay and Bengal governors expressed public doubts about the Resolution but more hard-headed civilians saw the local boards and the concomitant taxation as a way of increasing revenue and avoiding the consequent unpopularity. Ripon's finance member, the future Lord Cromer of Egypt, reassured those who feared the viceroy's radicalism. 'We shall not subvert the British Empire by allowing the Bengali Baboo to discuss his own schools and drains. Rather shall we afford him a safety-valve if we can turn his attention to such innocuous subjects…'[26] The more authoritarian Liberal Imperialists had their own reasons for supporting Ripon on this matter.

Even if Ripon's idea – which he shared with more conservative Whigs – of public-spirited leadership by local gentry was found to have limited relevance to India, the 1882 Resolution was to have wide and unpredictable consequences as the government reached out to populations to whom it was previously unknown, inviting participation and posing electoral questions of who was entitled to speak for whom. Driven by the need to increase revenue, this venture, small-scale though it was, has been described by Anil Seal as part of a 'second invasion of India in the eighteen-eighties'.[27] This was the beginning, albeit modest, of a shift from local collaborative deals to the attempt at management through the manipulation of constitutional arrangements.

Race Relations: The Ilbert Bill

After two controversial years, Ripon wrote to Hartington in late 1882 'it is not likely that during the remainder of my stay here I shall give you much more trouble'.[28] However, since March a proposal had been working its way through the bureaucratic channels which would illuminate the fundamental limitation of Gladstonian liberalism in British India.

It was a clause in the current Criminal Law Procedure Amendment Bill, for which Sir Courtney Ilbert, the new law member of the Executive Council, now took responsibility. It would end an anomaly – in default of the 1833

Charter Act and the Queen's Proclamation, promising racial equality – whereby qualified Indians could try Europeans for criminal offences in presidency cities but not outside, in the *mofussil*, as it was called. Consultations within the government had produced almost unanimous assent for what was discussed as a purely technical clause in a long bill. The only warning came from Sir Henry Maine, and Hartington, having put his minute in his pocket, forgot to forward it to Ripon.

When the bill was introduced into the Legislative Council in February 1883, the storm broke. It was now a race issue. Violent denunciations came from the Calcutta bar. The previous year, Ripon, at the direction of Hartington, had reduced the salaries of the Calcutta bench to bring it into line with the other presidency courts. The chief justice had also been outraged to discover as he was about to go on leave that he would be replaced by an Indian, Acting Chief Justice Mitter. Out of this agitation a standing pressure group, the Anglo-Indian Defence Association (after 1913, the European Association), was formed. Speaking for it, the Englishman proclaimed: 'Natives of India [are not] the peers or equals of Englishmen.'[29] The head of the Criminal Intelligence Department informed Ripon that at the heart of the agitation were the Calcutta firms who owned the plantations and tea gardens and feared for the treatment of their managers in the courts.[30]

Opposition and organization spread fast. A delegation was sent to London. Angry public meetings were held in Madras. The planters of Coorg burned Ripon in effigy. In Calcutta the French, Jews, and Armenians, but not the Parsis, joined in. The new Bengal lieutenant-governor, Rivers Thompson, declaring that 'we are [not] in India simply to make our laws symmetrical and to redress the sentimental grievances of an infinitesimal minority', circularized his officials and reported that the only supporters of the bill were Indians and an American.[31]

As well as highlighting the racial divide in the bureaucracy, the controversy spread racial antagonism through the society. A play running at the time in a Calcutta theatre which ridiculed the Bengali *bhadralok* 'brought the house down'. Alternatively, one could watch the actor Dave Carson give his 'world-renowned impersonation of the Bengalee Babu'.[32] In riposte, Ardhendu Sekhar Mustafi offered derisive presentations of the English in his pantomimes. Legally, however, it was one-way traffic, as the *Saligram* case showed. Surrendranath Bannerjea was sentenced to two months' imprisonment when his *Bengalee* declared that Judge Norris, by ordering to his court 'the presiding deity of a Hindu household, had committed an act of sacrilege in the estimation of pious Hindus'.[33]

Even educated Europeans ignored the details of the bill and used the occasion to express their sense of embattled racial superiority. In a letter to the *Times*, Fitzjames Stephen wrote 'It is essentially an absolute government, founded not on consent but on conquest. It does not represent the native principles of life or government, and it never can do so until it represents heathenism and barbarism.'[34] Rougher elements publicly insulted the viceroy. The Bengal government discovered a plan to seize Ripon and put him on a ship to take him home.

Ripon turned to London for support where wider opinion seemed supportive of the bill. Kimberley, however, wanted to lower the temperature and implied that compromise would be helpful. Gladstone backed Ripon, but wanted him to take the responsibility. He refused a vote in the House of Commons which the viceroy thought would enable him to face down his opponents. Ripon had been disturbed to find that the Calcutta European police was only 60 to 70 strong. A projected public meeting and protest might therefore require European troops on the streets which he wanted to avoid at all costs.

So he modified the bill and secured its passage through the Legislative Council. Now only Indians who were district officers or sessions judges would have the power – immediately entitling only two men – though Ripon could claim he had not abandoned the principle. Then, reintroducing a racial distinction, the bill allowed Europeans to choose trial by a jury at least half of whom would be European or American. Ripon had defused a crisis, and received unprecedented goodwill from Indians. Some have argued this was undeserved because, in outmanoeuvring his opponents, he conceded, in a different form, what they wanted: a mark of racial superiority. The way the bill was resolved did nothing to heal the racial antagonism it had brought to the surface. But it did teach two political lessons: the vulnerability of the government to coordinated, determined pressure; and the ultimate importance of London. The nationalist Bipin Chandra Pal wrote that 'It burnt [sic] into the mind of the Indian politician the fateful lesson that if India is to protect her liberties and secure an expansion of her legitimate rights, she must initiate as violent an agitation as enabled the European residents in the country to compel the Government of Lord Ripon to practically throw out that proposed measure.'[35]

The home government had long recognized the dangers of racial discrimination. Salisbury told engineering graduates about to leave for India that they were 'the persons who can…deal a blow of the deadliest character at the future rule of England… No system of government can be permanently safe where there is a feeling of inferiority or mortification affecting the relations between the governing and the governed.'[36] Prejudice, though fanned by insecurity and justified in different ways at different times, was firmly based in the inequality of power. There was the brute fact that Britons ruled India, formalized by the decision of Lord Cornwallis (Governor-General, 1786–93) to exclude Indians and Eurasians from senior political posts. Initiatives from London to end discrimination had little practical effect. However, they evoked the British parliamentary tradition of free, accountable government which the western educated were studying at school.

This fundamental conflict was illuminated by a free press which reported the derisory sentences on Europeans who killed Indians. Even Lytton, whose 1878 Arms Act had permitted weapons licences to Europeans but not to Indians, was moved in such a case to suspend a magistrate for a trifling fine on an Agra barrister convicted of a killing. As late as 1925, the refusal of the Simla municipal commissioner to bow to pressure to drop the prosecution in the 'Rickshaw Cooly Murder Case' was an all-India sensation. Mohan Lal Sood stood his ground under nine hours of cross examination, and the Controller of the Army Canteen Board, who had kicked a rickshaw-*wallah* to death, received eighteen months in prison where he committed suicide.

The writings of most of the early nationalists record the sting of racial incidents or attitudes. There is a sad note of resignation from the distinguished R. C. Dutt, in many ways an admirer of British government: 'they want to shut us out, not because we are critics, but because we are natives'.[37] If the Ilbert Bill was a turning point, it was so in the way that the bureaucracy openly sided with the prejudices of the European business community. H. J. S. Cotton, a Congress sympathizer who left the ICS over such a matter, thought that 'few things are more remarkable…than the sinister growth of this commercial influence over the executive administration'.[38]

William Dalrymple and others have compared friendly relations in the eighteenth century with a bleak lack of sympathy in the nineteenth.[39] We can see from the portraits of Zoffany (1733–1810) or Tilly Kettle (1735–86) that when power relations were more equal, Indian subjects were taken seriously and not exoticized. However, this interpretation often focuses on princely states and the British officers living in and off them, rather than the British India of the Bengal famine in the 1770s. Bentinck recalled that the total removal of Indians from positions of authority was based on the current British belief in the 'utter worthlessness of the native character and of their unfitness for all charges of trust'.[40] At the end of the century, Gholam Hussein, a shrewd and not unsympathetic observer wrote in his *Siyyar al-Muta 'akkhirin* of the British as short sojourners who return nothing to the country: 'such is the aversion which the English openly show for the company of natives, and such the disdain which they betray for them that no love…can take root between the conquerors and the conquered'.[41] The growth of evangelical Christianity led to still harsher attitudes by the 1840s; but W. D. Arnold's novel, *Oakfield* (1853), suggests that for many India may always have been a dreary exile.

Whether and to what extent attitudes were changing in the later nineteenth century has been a matter of debate. K. A. Ballhatchet stressed the growing separation between Indians and Britons, emphasizing the importance of distance to maintain authority.[42] Social contact was avoided. The ability to hold a conversation in a vernacular language became rare. Sexual or marital relations, though not unknown, were unacceptable. Anything which undermined prestige was to be deplored, like the Salvation Army's 'degrading burlesque of the religion of the ruling race'.[43] Another way of exercising control through distance was to classify the vast population, as H. H. Risley's censuses tried to do, with ever more refined anthropological accuracy. The contemporary influence of Social Darwinism supported a hierarchy of racial types as it did the army's 'martial races' classification, and gave spurious substance to older prejudices like that of 'the effeminate Bengali'.

The social world of the Company and the Raj was one where status was supremely important. At the top of the hierarchy was the ICS, but by 1880 their aristocratic life-style, curtailed by the falling rupee, was being challenged by competition. Apart from the few who were able to pass the London examination, there was an increasing Indian presence in the legal services where discrimination had been less. The numbers of the highly educated made some Britons uneasy, as Ripon observed of the Bengal lieutenant-governor: 'I am quite aware of the dislike with which the educated Native is regarded by many persons, and especially by men who like Sir Ashley Eden, have a strong Philistine element in their composition.'[44] Status anxieties certainly troubled the non-official British, 63 per cent of whom were Indian-born between 1861 and 1871, and who like the 62,000 Eurasians (1881) had no direct knowledge of the 'home' country on which their claims to special prestige rested.[45]

Replying to Ballhatchet, Eric Stokes restated an older focus on these 'home' values, which had seemed to become more important with the growth of British domestic life as more wives came out. Cotton reported that 'among women...the abuse of "those horrid natives" is almost universal'.[46] Lord Northbrook told Queen Victoria that a growing separation 'arises to a great extent from the greater facility in visiting England'.[47] The steamship and the Suez Canal made Indian service seem more temporary. Indian society was judged by the standards of suburban Britain.

2. The Indian National Congress

Political hopes focused on Gladstone's Liberal Party in London. Several associations which had appeared in the civil society now flourishing in Indian cities, sent a delegation to persuade Liberal candidates in the 1885 election campaign to support more Indian participation in the Legislative Councils.

It was a bad moment. Gladstone's promise of a Parliamentary Joint Committee on the Indian constitution vanished in the current party instability and the Irish crisis. And, as Florence Nightingale, who was also interested in Indian reform, complained, Gladstone 'has never given his mind to India, and it is too late now'.[48] On their return, they found that an Indian National Congress was to meet in Bombay.

The purpose of the Congress, in the words of a circular of March 1885, was 'to enable all the most earnest labourers in the cause of national progress to become personally known to each other'.[49] Their principal objective was to obtain from London representative institutions for Indians. Seventy-two delegates met under W. C. Bonnerjee's presidency. The next year, 434 came to Calcutta with Dadabhai Naoroji as president and an annual tradition was established. The chosen town organized the four-day event over Christmas. Anyone willing to meet travel and accommodation costs could come if nominated by an association or public meeting. Proceedings were in English.

Who were these early congressmen? The young Nehru, later prime minister, remembered 'It was very much an English-knowing upper class affair where morning coats and well-pressed trousers were greatly in evidence.'[50] Appearances notwithstanding, most were the sons of low-level officials in British India or some princely state. The core members had been influenced by Naoroji in the late 1860s when studying in London for the bar or the ICS: Pherozshah Mehta; W. C. Bonnerjee; Manmohan Ghose; and Badruddin Tyabji, joined soon by Surendranath Banerjea, R. C. Dutt and Lal Mohan Ghose. In India, a key figure was A. O. Hume, an ICS officer who had retired acrimoniously in 1882. His importance lay in his knowledge of British policy making and in the mistaken belief in his influence over government.

There was early Muslim rejection of the Congress as the leading associations refused to send representatives. Syed Ahmed Khan declared 'It is our nation which conquered with its sword the whole of India.' If Congress demands were met, power would pass to Bengalis 'who at the sight of a table knife would crawl under the table'.[51] Opposing election to the Legislative Councils, he expressed the fear, reminiscent of British objections, that an inferior sort of people would get in; it was not obligatory for Muslims 'to run a race with persons with whom we have no chance of success'.[52] Similarly, they opposed entry examinations to the enlarged Provincial Service. The Muslim upper class in the NWP was a numerical minority and English education had come later here than to the coastal cities. Congress responded by taking its 1888 meeting to nearby Allahabad. The *ulema* of Deoband issued a *fatwa* against Syed Ahmed Khan and permitted political cooperation. However, despite all efforts, Congress failed to attract Muslim notables.

Congress was not a political party. It had no constitution until 1908, though a mission statement was agreed in 1899: 'to promote by constitutional means the interests and the well-being of the people of the Indian Empire'.[53] It could not offer its supporters the satisfaction of legislation, patronage or organizational tasks. There was only a Subjects Committee elected among the leaders to decide the agenda for the annual meeting. The role of standing Congress committees was exercised by the regional associations where real political activity took place. Congress had no control over these, or how they chose their representatives. On the other hand, there was the advantage that almost any organization could be drawn into the Congress. It was agreed that no motions offensive to other groups should be brought forward. The topical but contentious subject of social reform was assigned to a National Social Conference.

Congress deliberately moved around the country attracting press interest and often thousands of listeners. Banerjea claimed that his four-hour presidential address in 1895 held 5,000 spellbound. Remarkably, the tone was loyal. Banerjea and Mehta referred to the British connection as 'providential'. There was enthusiasm for the Volunteer Movement encouraged by government at the time of the Panjdeh scare with Russia. 'There are some of us yet, who would be willing to draw sword and lay down our lives for the support of that Government to which we owe so much.'[54] Significantly, the government gave in to European outrage when some Indians were enlisted in Madras. Still, as M. G. Ranade declared, 'Liberalism and Moderation will be our watchwords'.[55] Gladstonian liberalism, eclipsed at Westminster, was alive in Bombay.

Dufferin initially encouraged Congress, perhaps as a counter-balance to the Anglo-Indians. Its demands were not refused out of hand. He favoured the Whig approach of small concessions offered quickly, and a tough line with the more extreme people. In 1887 a Special Branch was set up to monitor the new movements, political, social and religious, which were coming into being. Hume's desire to draw in peasant support was not popular with other Congress leaders who were not panicked by his prediction of peasant rebellion if nothing were done. After he distributed to villagers pamphlets in the vernacular on the economic woes of India, Dufferin considered suppressing Congress and deporting 'that idiot Hume'.[56]

Dufferin's plans for the Legislative Councils were ways of meeting some of the aspirations Congress represented and at the same time checking them in a Whig balance of interests. In the provincial councils he wanted two divisions, of landowners and professionals, chosen by group elections, but overall retaining official majorities. He was prepared to allow discussion of the budget in the Supreme Legislative Council, to which some Indians would be elected from the provincial councils. The Tories, however, were in the ascendant and Viscount Cross (Secretary of State, 1886–92) was unwilling to open a door which Congress might later push wider.

Cross changed his mind in 1890 when Banerjea's paper leaked Dufferin's despatch. He did not want differences between the two governments made public. The likelihood of a Liberal return in the 1892 election convinced him that a Tory settlement was infinitely preferable to letting Gladstone handle the matter. The new Whig viceroy, Lansdowne, was enthusiastic: it would take 'the wind out of the sails of Congress'. But the Indian Councils Act of 1892 trimmed Dufferin's scheme. Election was not mentioned, being left to the viceroy's discretion. Lansdowne was keen to have men 'who will represent types and classes rather than areas and numbers'. In fact, the Whig hope for landed gentry did not materialize; 'men of property…with their oriental notions of propriety…keep themselves aloof from meddling in the Municipal and District Board elections'. In the second elections of 1895 not one such person was returned to the Supreme Legislative Council. At both levels the councillors were 'almost exclusively pleaders who have comparatively little stake in the country'.[57]

From the nineties the dominant congressmen in India were G. K. Gokhale and B. G. Tilak, both Chitpavan Brahmans from Ratnagiri district on the west coast, but quite different in their personalities and methods. Gokhale was a Moderate, cautious and constructive. Tilak, the Extremist, pushed constitutionalism to its limits and in his paper, *Kesari*, gave succour to those who would go beyond. Though hailed as *Lokmanya* (revered of the people), his practical success was no greater.

There was precious little to show for early Congress pressure on government. The Councils Act was weaker even than some Whigs had wanted. Certainly, the Aitchison Commission of 1886 had transferred 700 higher posts to the new Provincial Service designed to replace the Statutory Civil Service. Though it raised the examination age to 23 it had rejected simultaneous ICS examinations in both London and Calcutta. Then a Commons Resolution for the latter was blocked by the Indian government. The Welby Commission, 1895, on the finances of India heard submissions from Naoroji, Banerjea and Gokhale on the apportionment of charges between London and Calcutta but in the end only reduced the Home Charges by an annual quarter of a million sterling.

A younger generation was becoming restive. Aurobindo Ghose, recently returned from St Paul's School and King's College, Cambridge, writing about Congress in 1893 in his newspaper article, 'New Lamps for Old', complained of 'our cowardice, our hypocrisy, our purblind sentimentalism'.[58] Moderates and Extremists represented different tactics in the same politics of 'mendicancy', as he described pressure for greater admission to the structures of British rule.

When in 1897 the socialist H. M. Hyndman sneered that 'suave, moderate gentlemen don't get much attention', Naoroji told him 'All that you say is true. But Indians cannot yet do what you say. You should realize their position in every respect... The Government are now openly taking up a Russian attitude, and we are helpless.'[59]

Hume had earlier returned to London, where Congress put its hopes on the new Liberal government of 1892. Naoroji was elected Liberal MP for Central Finsbury, and he and William Wedderburn, a retired ICS man, formed an Indian Parliamentary Committee which, in 1893, had 150 mostly Irish and radical supporters. Congress was spending as much on its British Committee – £3,000 p.a. – as it did on its annual meeting, not to mention the costs of *India*, its British publication sent free to all MPs. After Gladstone's retirement, the Liberal Imperialist Lord Rosebery became premier and in 1895 the Liberals, including Naoroji, were swept out for a Tory decade of high imperialism.[60]

Interpretations of Early Indian Nationalism

Attempts at a class interpretation of early nationalism have not got very far. Classical Marxists have not been able to represent these congressmen as spokesmen for a fledgling Indian bourgeoisie, nor to relate changes in the economy to a new political formation. Such political consciousness as existed on a wider scale was provincial; there was yet no national economy; Indian business was fragmented and had little connection with modern politics until after the First World War.

Contemporary British critics represented Congress as speaking for an elite of discontented western-educated graduates – an approach later given scholarly form by Anil Seal's early work. The civilian, Sir Alfred Lyall, introducing the influential *Indian Unrest* (1910) by the Times correspondent, Valentine Chirol, wrote of the promotion of western education as a 'story of grave miscalculation'. Politics now appeared as a profession with Gokhale or Lala Lajpat Rai in the Punjab who declared that politics 'is a religion, and a science, much higher than both in its conception and in its sphere, than mere political agitation'.[61]

All students of Indian nationalism in the last generation have had to engage with the historians of the Cambridge School. When the term is used in historiographical debate – simplifying the range and quality of the research – it is usually taken to refer to an approach which sets India in the context of the empire, formal and informal, with a focus on local circumstances at the periphery rather than monocausal metropolititan explanations. It also prioritizes political history, especially the role of government, rather than culture or popular politics in the study of Indian nationalism. Gordon Johnson argued that 'There is no single chronological growth of nationalism in India: nationalist activity booms and slumps in phase with the national activity of the government.'[62]

As the early emphasis in Anil Seal's *The Emergence of Indian Nationalism* (1968) on western education and the formation of regional caste and professional elites 'dropped through the trapdoor of historiography', attention shifted to the vertical connections of locality and faction.[63] What forged these links above all was the growing downward pressure of government and its needs for money and collaborators. Nomination, election and potential access to local patronage all encouraged competition within the framework of government-devised categories.

Delegates came to each December's Congress from the provincial associations, and it is to these connections that historians have turned. Writing of north India, C. A. Bayly notes that 'Contemporary observers generally adhered to the official view of Congress as a product of deracine Young India, but some were clearly aware of and puzzled by the number of threads which led backwards from the new politics into the labyrinth of old city notabilities.'[64] We may view congressmen as middle-men, whose actions, in the words of D. A. Washbrook, 'were, therefore, dictated not by their own wishes, not by their desire to further the aims of their castes, classes and sects, but by their need to gain personal support from the leaders of society and from the government. Thus, it makes no sense to regard them as a permanently unified category standing against the rest of society, nor indeed as an elite in the world of politics.'[65]

The emphasis on patrons, clients and local interests being driven into an imperial net blew away some of the flimsier nationalist writing which ignored divisions or conflicts within Indian society. However, serious nationalist historians returned the charge: that the Cambridge historians themselves ignored fundamental conflicts of interest between subjects and imperial rule. If government initiatives drove nationalism, R. K. Ray has asked whether these historians suggest that India could have been kept quiet by inactive government.[66] And, did not Council reform in 1892 *follow* Congress activity in the 1880s, or the Morley-Minto reforms *follow* later uproar in Bengal? If concessions were made not to agitators but to collaborators to enhance their credibility, may not genuine opposition be treated as a form of collaboration? Tapan Raychaudhuri has expressed a common criticism: that non-rational factors have been undervalued, and that nationalism has been treated as theatre to cover the quest for material gain.[67]

The bureaucracy usually denied even the possibility of an Indian nation. Yet in the 1890s a textbook for schools, *The Citizen of India* (1897), by the civilian Lee-Warner was a best seller, and it argued that the citizen's loyalties should extend from the village to the whole of India. Yet according to Sir John

Strachey 'the first and most essential thing to learn about India [is] that there is not, and never was as an India, or even any country of India, possessing according to European ideas, any sort of unity…' Referring to the unifying aspects of British rule, he denied such 'bonds of union can in any way lead towards the growth of a single Indian nationality'.[68] Twenty years earlier, Sir Charles Dilke had drawn the opposite inference from the same premise:

> The greatest of the many changes in progress in the East is that India is being made – that a country is being created under that name where none has yet existed; and it is our railroads, our annexations and above all our centralising policy, that are doing the work…by government at home, where India is looked upon as one nation, instead of from Calcutta, where it is known to be still composed of fifty; but so rapid is the change, that already the Calcutta people are as mistaken in attempting to laugh down our phrase 'the people of India'… Whether the India which is being thus rapidly built up by our own hands will be friendly to us, or the reverse, depends upon ourselves.[69]

Confident in this process, Surendranath Banerjea wrote: 'we are making steady progress, and we are bound to win in the long run', and chose as the title for his autobiography *A Nation in the Making* (1925).[70]

3. Nationalists and the Economy: The 'Drain'

Nationalists developed a critique of British rule which focused on the economy. They could cite W. W. Hunter's admission that 'forty million of the people of India habitually go through life on insufficient food'.[71] It was estimated that the average per capita income in 1895 was £2.65 against £36.94 in Britain'.[72] The sheer visible poverty of the country highlighted by recurring famine challenged the modernizing claims for British rule, the expectations in Britain and the convictions of free traders.

Assessments of the economic impact of British rule have differed widely. Marx thought that exposure to the free market had 'produced the greatest, and to speak the truth, the only social revolution ever heard of in Asia'.[73] By contrast, a common modern view sees the Raj more in the traditions of an old Asiatic state ruling through an army, and, at this time, reaching down only to the local connections needed for stability and the collection of the land revenue.[74]

Three explanations are typically deployed to explain low growth. The *cultural charge* was that the Indian peasant was not a profit-maximizer and that religious priorities obstructed change. Officials who used this argument laid themselves open to the riposte that as foreigners they failed to understand or incentivize the peasants.

Explanation in terms of *low demand* argues that with very low per capita incomes and a preponderant agricultural sector, the market for industrial goods was too small and that very low wages were generally a disincentive to profitable investment in machinery. The nationalist scholar-official, R. C. Dutt, thought the land revenue inhibited agricultural development: its reassessments were unpredictable; the mode of collection discouraged a sense of private property; above all, it was too high – 'a bleeding process with a vengeance', as Marx had called it.[75]

The need for clothing provides a market for manufacturing even in the poorest societies. However, the upper part of this market had been captured by Lancashire. The colossal volumes produced by the latest machinery had lowered prices to the point where several saris of reasonable quality in the bright new aniline dyes could be had for the cost of a single product of the hand-weaver's art. This advantage seemed to be reinforced by the tariff to which Elgin returned in an Act of 1894 when faced by renewed deficits from the falling rupee and increased military and rail expenditure. It imposed a 5 per cent import duty – except on cotton goods. Then, this exemption was removed, but a countervailing 5 per cent excise was put on finer Indian cotton which competed with British imports. Lancashire was unhappy that cheaper goods had escaped, and eventually a 3.5 per cent excise was put on Indian woven goods. This saga of discrimination fed the nationalists' fury.

The nationalist critics of British rule came to focus on *institutional explanations*. They claimed that the modern infrastructure was inextricably linked to the needs of colonial rule to extract wealth from the country and was itself responsible for what the historian Bipan Chandra has called 'an arrested development'.[76]

It was in London in 1867 that Naoroji first put forward his idea of a drain of India's wealth to Britain which he estimated at £12 million per year or a quarter of the revenues – a figure that that he later revised sharply upwards. Under the Company in earlier times, India had paid a tribute in the form of the 'Investment', goods which the government bought in India with tax revenue and sent for sale to Britain. Now, the age of mercantilism was over and India under the Crown was supposed to be in a relationship of mutually beneficial improvement. Not so, argued Naoroji, as he pointed to the Home Charges, the cost of European civil servants and troops, the railway guarantees and the remittance of profits from foreign investment. The export surpluses of these years priced in falling rupees were another sign that India's wealth was being drained away. The charge of an exploitative relationship was at the heart of the drain argument that Naoroji summarized in *Poverty and Un-British*

Rule (1901) and which underlay the economic histories of R. C. Dutt which influenced all the early nationalists including Gandhi.

The government's defenders claimed that famine was largely the product of climatic disasters outside human control. Otherwise, India was getting good value with internal peace, a framework of law and government and a modern infrastructure of rails and telegraphs across the entire subcontinent. There had been strong growth in external trade. India was now the largest purchaser of British exports, and took about 7 per cent of capital exports from Britain, or about 20 per cent of British capital exports to the empire. In India a modern textile industry was appearing:[77]

	Cotton		Jute	
1892–93	120 mills	113,000 workers	26 mills	66,000 workers
1912–13	241	244,000	63	201,000

In 1911 Tata opened India's first steel mill. 15.7 million tons of coal were dug in 1914. By the war half a million acres of tea had been planted.

To Naoroji and his fellow nationalists, these advantages were ambiguous. Was it necessary for 23 per cent of army expenditure in 1871–72 to be placed in Britain?[78] They complained that the railways were designed to support the export trades and these – tea, jute, coal – were overwhelmingly in British hands and dealt in raw materials. By 1914, 35 per cent of foreign owned capital was in tea and jute. The railway equipment was British as were the operatives (or Eurasians); there was no manufacturing or training gains for Indians. Many believed the value of the rupee was being manipulated to serve British interests. The nationalist Dinesh Wacha called it 'the crime of 1893' when the Herschell Committee fixed the rate at 1/4d and thereby devalued the rupee.[79] Most early nationalists, except for M. G. Ranade, were averse to foreign investment and wondered why Indian capital was not being mobilized for investment.

Discussion of the drain has been bedevilled by a lack of statistical and economic clarity, as K. N. Chaudhuri has shown.[80] Drain theorists have not always made it clear whether they were talking about the effects on the welfare of the Indian people or on India's balance of payments and national income. Nor is it clear whether foreign trade, despite an eight-fold increase between 1840 and 1886, still a relatively small part of total economic activity, could have had the transformative effect attributed to it by Marx or by drain theorists. But in most historiographical traditions the drain has continued to feature, a modern estimate putting it in 1882 at 4 per cent of national income.

Paradoxically, the importance of the drain argument was primarily political. It claimed that Britain was responsible for India's poverty in both senses: as a trustee for the country's development and as the agent of exploitation. The use of 'Un-British' created a more general sense that government was not conforming to expectations of fair play. In India, the drain was not a regional or sectional claim, but a genuinely national argument. It offered an explanation of the country's poverty and a remedy: self-rule. By implication, it undermined a frequently deployed justification for British rule. If so much wealth had been drained for so long, eighteenth century India must have been a rich country and not the degraded chaos from which it had been rescued by the *Pax Britannica*. The drain avoided political language; indeed, Naoroji, Dutt and the early congressmen often praised the administrative and legal framework of British rule. Thus, the drain provided an economic rationale for an across-the-board critique of British rule without incurring the charge of overt disloyalty.

4. Communalism

Caste Associations

What mattered in most people's lives was the *jati* they had been born into, the local family community which determined the rules of life, diet, dining, marriage. Caste, or *varna* in the ancient texts, was the broad hierarchical grouping – Brahman, Kshatriya, Vaishya, Sudra, and, below, the Untouchable – to which a *jati* could be related. This now became important as the census used these categories for classifying the population. It also revealed the relative numbers of caste members, a vital matter if representation on local boards and public employment were to reflect these proportions. Sending representatives to Congress also raised the question of who should go and from which community.

The Kayasths, the writer caste of northern India, held their first conference in 1886, the year of Syed Ahmed Khan's first Muslim Educational Conference. Their concern was to see that they did not lose out in competition for public employment, and to push for Hindi, rather than the Urdu of the old Muslim elite, as the official language of the NWP. In Maharashtra, the Untouchable Mahars, the support base of the future champion of the low castes Dr Ambedkar, were getting organized to protest at their exclusion from the army under the new 'martial races' policy. However, it was especially in the middle levels of society that the lawyers and the western educated were trying to mobilize related *jatis* into provincial and regional caste associations.

The 1901 census raised the tempo. The commissioner, H. H. Risley, decided to record the social precedence of the castes 'as recognized by native public opinion', and, accordingly, sought the opinions of committees of

Indian advisors.[81] This contentious change seems to have stimulated ever more 'sanskritization' – whereby the standing of the whole group is enhanced by adopting the customs of more prestigious communities. In the 1901 census the Shanans of Madras, traditionally associated with the 'polluted' activity of toddy tapping – drawing palm sap for fermentation – adopted the more prestigious name of Nadar and claimed Kshatriya status. In east Bengal, the Namasudras, previously lowly Chandals, were later to respond to the government's promise that after the partition of Bengal jobs would go in proportion to numbers in the population. This caste would align itself in the 1920s against the (high-caste) nationalists and with the Europeans and the Muslim cultivators. The two great groupings of twentieth-century Karnataka took steps to equip themselves for the competitive world of English education. The Lingayats formed an Educational Association at Dharwar. In 1906, the main group of cultivating *jatis*, the Vokkaligas, formed a union to promote education among their members.

Made possible by the railways, press and postal service, these caste associations were enlarging the public sphere and giving experience in leadership and organization to urban professionals.

Revived Hinduism

Analogous religious changes were creating a Hinduism with novel congregational activities which appealed across the divisive boundaries of caste. At this time, the painter Ravi Varma popularized a style, still prevalent, of representing gods and goddesses, and cheap oleographs were finding their way into every home and hut.

Most dynamic of the new movements was the Arya Samaj, founded by Dayananda. It attacked polytheism, idolatry, pilgrimages, the ban on widow remarriage, the role of Brahman priests and most of the old rituals, but its core message was the fundamental superiority of original Vedic Hinduism. The emphasis on education of the Lahore Arya Sama, founded in 1877, met the aspirations of those who wanted schools for their sons safe from non-Hindu influences, yet relevant to careers in the public services. Dayananda had been alarmed at trends he found in the census and by the activities of Christian missionaries. After his death in 1883 there were disagreements about priorities in the loosely organized Samaj: education or proselytism and reconversion. Nevertheless, the basic fact was its immense and rapid success among Anglophone city dwellers in the Punjab and across northern India.

If the Arya Samaj encouraged people to think of themselves as Hindus rather than followers of one of a myriad of exclusive local and family traditions, Vivekananda made a similar appeal to self-confidence. Like some other western-educated young men in Calcutta, he had come under the influence of the mystic Ramakrishna, who preached the truth of all religions. After Ramakrishna's death he travelled through India and for four years in the USA and Britain. During this time he represented Hinduism at the 1893 World Parliament of Religions in Chicago, where he was sensationally effective in establishing the perception of Hindu spirituality as one of the world's great religious traditions. Vedantic societies were formed in San Francisco and elsewhere, and financial support was forthcoming. Yet, though international recognition was important, Vivekanada had no doubt that the West, for all its achievements, was materialistic and selfish. By contrast, he proclaimed the glorious past of Hinduism and the spirituality of its ancient Vedantic form. Now the tables were turning. 'This is the great ideal before us, and everyone must be ready for it – the conquest of the world by India – Up, India, conquer the world with our spirituality.'[82] Vivekananda's message helped resolve the anxieties of educated Indians caught between two worlds and through the Ramakrishna Mission, an organization combining social service with the idea of a monastic order, forged wide social and geographical contacts.

Christophe Jaffrelot has seen in these two movements the origins of Hindu nationalist strategies: stigmatization – western materialism, Christian missionaries, assertive Muslims; *emulation* – copying what was best and useful in western civilization; and *evoking a Golden Age*, which anticipated western scientific knowledge and restored ethnic pride.[83] Marxists have seen the beginnings of communalism as a false consciousness propagated by a section of the traditional elites to counteract the forces of nationalism and democracy.

Some highly westernized congressmen joined the ranks of cultural nationalists and wrote historical studies or romances – Ranade's *Rise of the Maratha Power* (1900), or Dutt on Shivaji – which began to create national histories for their regions. Bepin Chandra Pal testified to the power of the historical novels of Walter Scott and those of Bankim Chandra Chatterjee (d. 1896) which called to life recent struggles against Muslim rule in his native Bengal and deplored the divisions in Hindu society. The *Times* correspondent, Chirol, believed that it was not merely a case of westernized men rediscovering their roots but of a deeper continuity coming through in modern dress, what would now be called a primordial nationalism.

The Theosophical Society belonged to this revivalist world, and provided a forum where some early nationalists could mix with Europeans like Hume. Madame Blavatsky and Colonel Olcott had founded it in New York in 1875 and later moved to India where by 1884 there were a hundred branches. Believing that only Hinduism and Buddhism still taught the truths of the Ancient Wisdom, Madame Blavatsky claimed to be in touch with the

Mahatmas who lived in Tibet. Her special powers had enabled her to find
in a Simla garden a lost brooch belonging to Mrs Hume. Hume soon fell out
with the Society when it rejected his leadership. Despite revelations of fraud,
its appeal continued. When Annie Besant, a later Congress president, read
The Secret Doctrine (1888), allegedly dictated by the Mahatma Koot Hoomi,
she swung from atheism to ardent theosophism. In India its increasingly
uncritical celebration of everything Hindu caught and fuelled the mood of
returning self-confidence.

The early tone of critical self-examination in the Brahmo Samaj began
to change. Founded in 1828, it had presented Hinduism as a voluntary
association, theist, anti-idolatrous and founded on the ancient texts of
the Vedas and Upanishads. Now the main wing of the Samaj became less
puritanical and more associated with devotional experience. Its charismatic
leader Keshub Chandra Sen made a strong positive impact in public speeches
in Britain and well-publicized meetings with Queen Victoria, Gladstone and
Dickens.

The changing attitude to social reform appeared in the reaction to the
Parsi reformer Malabari in 1888. He pressed the government to raise the age
of consent for marriage to 12 in the Age of Consent Act (1892) and was
supported by those who thought that improving the status of women was at
the heart of the enterprise. 1857 had seen the launch in Bombay of *Stri Bodh*,
the first women's journal. Satyendranath Tagore seems to have translated
Mill's *Subjection of Women* (1863) into Bengali for his family and friends as
soon as it was published. His wife Jnadadebi pioneered the modern style,
suitable for public life, of wearing the sari with blouse and petticoat. The
1872 Civil Marriage Act recognized marriages outside the traditional codes
of Hinduism, Islam, Sikhism and Christianity.

Now, Tilak voiced the outrage felt at this invitation to foreign rulers to
change marriage customs sanctioned by scripture and ancient usage which
weakened India by exposing divisions and shortcomings to a western audience.
Shortly after, he instituted the Ganpati festival, a religious celebration which
was no longer a domestic occasion but involved public processions with
young men marching in paramilitary style. Something similar was developing
in Bengal with English-educated youths from the *akharas* (gymnasiums).
Tilak was cautiously exploring the link between regional nationalism and
these movements in which religious and social identity were being redefined.
British rule had abandoned the religious and cultural patronage expected of a
ruler, and this vacuum was now being filled by new patrons.

First, there was an indication of what the changes could mean for British
rule. The late 1890s were grim years. Famine returned in 1896 and by
1909 had taken at least six million lives. In the same year plague reached

Bombay from Karachi. There was cholera, and a severe earthquake in Assam. Meanwhile, London and Calcutta, alarmed at the impact of plague on India's foreign trade, ordered strong action on public and domestic hygiene. In Poona the brutal methods of Commissioner Rand backed by British troops created outrage and despair. On Jubilee night Rand and Lieutenant Ayerst were assassinated by the Chapekar brothers. They were hanged after their terrorist cell was identified.

Tilak had tried to upstage the celebrations for Queen Victoria's jubilee in 1897 by launching his Shivaji festival to commemorate the great seventeenth-century Maratha ruler's defence of his homeland against the Mughal Empire. For this he had written rousing articles asserting that 'hero worship' was at the root of 'nationality, social order and religion'.[84] He was also associated with a campaign to encourage peasants in famine areas to withhold the land tax. The government used the opportunity to arrest him. He was tried for sedition, the judge telling the jury that 'disaffection' meant absence of affection.[85] Convicted by the European majority, he was sentenced to eighteen months in jail, and his wealthy backers, the Natu brothers, were detained for two years without trial. Other editors were prosecuted and in 1898 a tougher law of sedition was introduced. However, acknowledging the changing mood, the government avoided any social legislation in the period between 1892 and the Sarda Act which regulated minimum ages for marriage in 1928.

Second, and more threateningly, there were the communal implications. The Ganpati festival came just after Mohurram where Hindus had traditionally joined this Muslim festival. Now there was separation, tension, and complaints that music was disturbing prayers in the mosques. Tilak warned that Hindus should not 'purchase peace with Mohammedans with dishonour to their own religion or loss of self-respect'.[86] For Lajpat Rai, the Arya Samajist from the Punjab, friction with Muslims would make the fragmented Hindus appreciate their common Hindu identity. The new Punjab Hindu Sabha was the forerunner of the All-India Hindu Mahasabha of 1915. Revivalist Sikh sabhas were also being set up. At this time cow-protection societies were challenging the Muslim custom of butchering and eating the revered animal. In 1893 riots spread from Bombay to Rangoon. As they died down, the campaign shifted to replace Urdu with Hindi as an official language, as happened in 1899 in the NWP. Responding to this challenge the Anjuman-i Taraqqi-i Urdu was formed in 1903 to promote the language. The frequent public recitations from Hali's famous poem *Musaddas* (1879) reflected Muslim nostalgia for lost power, and returning self-consciousness. There were clear indications that nationalism was taking a communal form.

Chapter 3

THE CONSEQUENCES
OF LORD CURZON: INDIA OR
THE EMPIRE, 1899–1916

1. Lord Curzon

Curzon's aim was to revive British imperialism in the East. In the late nineties the Indian government seemed to have been merely reacting to the difficult times. In Britain the triumphalism of the Queen's Diamond Jubilee in 1897 was tinged with intimations of mortality. US and German economic power were rivalling that of Britain. The continent was now in two alliance systems and a powerful group in the cabinet believed that Britain could no longer base its foreign policy on 'Splendid Isolation'.

In the event, Curzon's success was limited. There was no room in his imperial vision for other points of view, least of all for nascent Indian nationalism. His dynamic foreign policy raised the question of priorities: India or the empire? Above all, the partition of Bengal overshadowed everything and permanently changed the relationship of rulers and ruled.

At 38 years old, Curzon had super-abundant energy, self-confidence to the point of arrogance, high administrative capacity, though not the ability to delegate, and detailed knowledge from his travels, publications and spell as Under Secretary at the India Office. Efficiency was the goal. Curzon declared: 'I am in favour of sweeping out every gutter, whatever the stink it causes.'[1] His determination to seize the initiative threatened the secretary of state's primacy in policy making which had been growing steadily since 1858. Tact, however, was not his forte; nor that of his wife who described Lord George Hamilton (Secretary of State, 1895–1903) as 'a small-minded, ferret-faced, roving-eyed mediocrity'.[2] A similar intolerance of lazy or routine-laden officials meant that the viceroy was feared and admired, but not loved. A German governess is supposed to have asked him: 'Tell me, Mr Curzon, what is the meaning of the English word "bounder" which I sometimes hear you called?'[3]

Curzon's programme was that of a Liberal Imperialist – rule of justice, bringing peace and order and good government – but was in his case informed by a genuine imperial vision. He was more than ready to follow the advice which Queen Victoria sent to Lord Salisbury at the time of his appointment:

> [T]he future Vice Roy must really shake himself more and more free from his red-tapist narrow-minded Council and Entourage. He must be more independent, must hear for himself what the feelings of the Natives really are, and do what he thinks right and not be guided by the snobbish and vulgar, over-bearing and offensive behaviour of our Civil and Political Agents...[4]

There seems to have been an upsurge in racial incidents at this time, and Curzon was not intimidated by the unpopularity that came with his collective punishments of army units where justice had been stifled, such as in a case of group rape in Rangoon in 1899; or in the 1902 beating of a cook to death by men of the 9th Lancers in Sialkot. He ordered a re-trial where the jury had condoned atrocities by a planter in the Bain case of 1903. He seems to have been more outraged by their failure to rise to their imperial responsibilities than by the racial inequities of the jury system. In 1903 the cabinet asked for 20,000 coolies for railway work in the Transvaal. Rejecting the terms of the proposed indenture, he telegraphed St John Brodrick (Secretary of State, 1903–1905): 'the name of South Africa stinks in the nostrils of India'.[5] With his strong sense of Britain as the custodian for India's ancient glories, he revived the Directorate of Archaeology, passed an Ancient Monuments Act in 1904, and took a personal interest in the restoration of the Taj Mahal as well as lesser sites. However, his imperial vision was one-eyed. He lacked sympathy with Indian political aspirations, and was prone to provocative rudeness. In his Calcutta University Convocation Address of 1905 he said: 'I hope I am making no false or arrogant claim when I say that the highest ideal of truth is to a large extent a Western conception.'[6]

He was fortunate to arrive to a period of surplus budgets when the rupee rate was stabilizing, which permitted reductions in the salt and incomes taxes. Famine abated after 1900, though plague claimed a million lives in 1904. But the 1901 Famine Commission pulled no punches: 'In no province were well-considered programmes of public or village works ready at the beginning of the famine.'[7] Dutt's published famine letters to the viceroy blaming the lack of a permanently settled land revenue outside Bengal stung Curzon into an official reply in the Resolution of 1902, which attributed the principal cause to the failure of the rains.

Two areas of admitted weakness were addressed. The Police Commission of 1902–1903 sought to increase numbers and raise the pitifully low wages, and a Department of Criminal Intelligence was set up to deal with political crime. Much trumpeted was the desire to raise educational standards, especially through grants-in-aid to private ventures at the primary level. However, the available resources, as always, were puny. In 1903–1904, Rs 20.46 million were spent, and in 1905–1906, Rs 24.49 million, about 2.5 per cent of the total budget. In 1911 the literacy percentage for British India was only 11.3 for men and 1.1 for women. For higher education, the unpopular Universities Act of 1904 which shifted the emphasis from universities as examining bodies towards postgraduate teaching eventually led to good things under Calcutta University's vice-chancellor Asutosh Mukherji.[8]

More interventionist government paralleled the contemporary National Efficiency movement in Britain. A Board of Scientific Advice was established, and, in 1905, a Department of Commerce and Industry. A duty was put on the import of subsidized European sugar. More railways were built – 6,100 miles – than in any other viceroyalty. Irrigation received more investment; credit schemes were promoted by the 1904 Co-operative Societies Act; in the Punjab in 1900 the policy of restricting land sale was taken further than ever before.

2. Foreign Policy

Late in 1903, Curzon, escorted by warships of the East India Squadron, made a ceremonial tour of the Persian Gulf. Two years earlier the cabinet had vetoed such a visit. They did not wish to challenge other powers' claims to influence at a time when the Boer War had left Britain diplomatically isolated. Now, the splendour of the durbars and the warmth of Curzon's reception by the Shaikhs, if not by the Persians, made French pretensions look insignificant. No doubt, the rulers of Muscat, Sharjah, Bahrain and Kuwait feared closer claims from the Ottoman Empire or Persia, rendering Curzon's implied recognition of their domestic sovereignty attractive. For Curzon, they were outer native states in a strategically important area; the Gulf and the Arabian Sea were Indian spheres of interest. The development of oilfields was about to make them British spheres as well.

Curzon shifted his attention to the northern border. Nepal's reliability was cast-iron, but routes through Kashmir to its west and through Sikkim, Bhutan and Assam to its east were potentially soft areas. In the Great Game of rivalry with Russia, there was a dearth of geographical information about Central

Asia and Tibet whose capital, Lhasa, was a forbidden city to non-Buddhists. For some years the Army Intelligence Department had been training enterprising Indians, 'the Pundits', in the skills of surveying. They were taught a measured step, whether on the level or climbing, which they counted and recorded in a modified prayer wheel. Disguised as Buddhist pilgrims and often assisted by Indian business communities in Central Asian towns, they carried ingeniously concealed scientific instruments. For the terrible dangers of these journeys, rewards were meagre: a small civil service pension or, for Kishen Singh, a gold watch from the Royal Geographical Society. One of the bravest, Sarat Chandra Das, 'a hardy son of soft Bengal', was probably the model for Huree Chunder Mookerjee, the secret agent in Kipling's *Kim.*[9] Despite the surveyors' achievements, Tibet was still largely unknown. The 1890 and 1893 border and trade agreements were, in British eyes, not being honoured, and Curzon's letters to Lhasa were returned unopened.

The viceroy wanted this border settled by bringing Tibet into a subordinate relationship, and found that 'It is really the most grotesque and indefensible thing that at a distance of a little more than 200 miles from our frontier, this community of unarmed monks should set us perpetually at defiance.'[10] His counterpart in Lhasa was the remarkable Thirteenth Dalai Lama who had come of age in 1895, the year of China's humiliation in the war with Japan. Taking advantage of this weakness to promote the resurgence of Tibet, he sent a diplomatic mission to the Tsar. Curzon's fear of Russian involvement was further inflamed by reports of Dorzhiev, a Buriat Mongol with Russian connections, who had come to study in Lhasa in the 1880s and was said to be the Dalai Lama's tutor. To the prime minister Arthur Balfour, Curzon's approach was unwelcome. It was not in the interests of Britain to risk further trouble with Russia, whose attention was clearly focused on Manchuria which, after 1902, was threatened by Britain's ally Japan. In addition, taking any part of the Chinese Empire would reopen the scramble of the 1890s. Britain supported the US policy of calling a halt to the 'slicing of the Chinese melon'.

The arrival of a new Chinese resident in Lhasa in December 1902 moved things forward. Curzon's 1903 despatch took up his offer of talks but insisted that they be held in Lhasa and that a Tibetan representative must be present. However, the instructions he received from Hamilton were more limited: the talks should take place over the border at Khamba and be confined to trade relations, the frontier and grazing rights. On 11 December 1903 a force of mostly Gurkhas entered Tibet by the pass of Jelap La at 14,390 feet. They were commanded by Francis Younghusband who had dreams of liberating the Tibetans from their ignorant superstition. He found, however, they were no more to be intimidated than the Afghans; no Tibetans came to Khamba.

Direction of policy now became fragmented. Curzon, on leave in London, insisted on a representative in Lhasa, a trade agreement and the frustration of Russian designs. Brodrick authorized nothing more than a punitive thrust to Gyantse, half way to Lhasa, followed by withdrawal. Lord Ampthill, the temporary viceroy, and Kitchener, the commander-in-chief, both favoured limited action which would not upset Russia.

In one respect the expedition belonged to an earlier age. Twelve days away from a London telegram, Younghusband could use his initiative. At Guru on the Gyantse road a confused skirmish led to the death of 700 Tibetan soldiers; their equipment was pathetically inadequate, but as the *Manchester Guardian* reported, they 'all died game'.[11] The army pushed on and Younghusband led them into the Forbidden City in August 1904 past crowds of people clapping – to dispel evil spirits, as was later discovered. Nepal, which had provided 4,000 yaks for the expedition, did not want Tibet hopelessly weakened and pressed them to settle. Finally, with Chinese assistance, Younghusband was able to pull off a remarkable treaty: trade arrangements; no fortifications on the Indian road; no foreign relations without British consent; a British agent at Gyantse with access to Lhasa; and an indemnity.[12]

Who made policy? The trend, reinforced by the telegraph and the Suez Canal, had for long been strongly in favour of London. Curzon, with his imperial vision and prodigious powers of work, clawed back some freedom of action for Calcutta. Whatever their difference in outlook, Curzon and Younghusband were 'forward' men and that policy prevailed. Brodrick was all too aware that the viceroy looked on him 'as his representative at the Court of St James...and an unprofitable servant' at that.[13] Curzon paid a high personal price for this perception; and succeeding viceroyalties saw a reversion to type.

For whom was policy made? Curzon might believe that it was in India's interest to fight the Great Game against Russia in Central Asia, and assert Indian paramountcy from the Red Sea to the Malacca Strait. Yet in London during the years of his first term a profound realignment in foreign policy was taking place. With the perception of a growing German threat, the priority now was the defence of Britain itself. Colonial disputes needed to be settled: with the USA in 1901–1903; France in 1904; and Russia. Russian power temporarily collapsed in the 1905 Revolution, but in the long run only she had the manpower to stop the German army. Curzon's outlook was beginning to look old-fashioned and India-centred. Balfour feared Curzon 'would raise India to the position of an independent and not always friendly power'.[14]

With the 1907 Anglo-Russian Entente, the Great Game was over: Afghanistan and southern Persia were recognized as British spheres of influence, and the scene was set for supporting anti-Ottoman positions which would be anathema to India's Muslims. The scene was set, too, for a later Great Game between India and China. A useful outcome of this focus on the northern border was the 1910 treaty with Bhutan. At last friendly relations were established and Bhutan accepted British control of its foreign relations. Tibet, however, was leaderless after the flight of the Dalai Lama to China in 1904 and on to Darjeeling in 1911. Though it was under an informal British protectorate, the Chinese were careful not to relinquish their claim to suzerainty. China provided the money for the indemnity and in 1908 moved into Chambi following the British evacuation. They also used a revolt in eastern Tibet to annex large areas to China proper. In the longer run, Tibet existed in limbo, guaranteed by British power, but unprepared for any other future.

3. The Partition of Bengal

Congress had been in the doldrums since the early 1890s and the decade of Tory dominance, 1895–1905, offered them nothing. The wrangle in the nineties over tariffs had helped to propagate ideas of exploitation, but also left a sense of helplessness. The congressman P. Ananda Charlu complained that India 'is defenceless where the Indian and English interests clash and where (as a Tamil saying puts it) the very fence begins to feed on the crop'. Curzon wrote that 'Congress is tottering to its fall, and one of my greatest ambitions while in India is to assist it to a peaceful demise.'[15] Pressure was first applied to the Bengali critics of government. The seat on the Legislative Council normally occupied by a lawyer was reserved for a *zemindar*. From 1899 the elected membership of the Calcutta Corporation was cut by a half. The university legislation drastically reduced the elected element in the Senate. The 1904 Official Secrets Act threatened the local press.

More important was the proposal published in December 1903 to break up the cumbrous province of Bengal, which had a population greater than the USA. The plan was to create an East Bengal and attach it to Assam. The port of Chittagong would help European export interests in tea, coal and oil, and at the same time reduce the power of the planter lobby in Calcutta. Curzon also thought that a shake-up would invigorate the out-of-touch Bengal government.

It was not a new idea; in 1874 Assam and Sylhet had been separated from Bengal. Now other reorganizations were taking place. The Punjab lost the frontier to a new North-West Frontier Province (NWFP) which maintained peace by the cheaper expedient of paying tribal levies. The NWP was renamed the United Provinces (UP) in 1902. In the same year Curzon settled the 50-year-long dispute with Hyderabad over Berar by convincing the Nizam that the proposition of a permanent lease with a substantial annual rent was the best deal he would ever be offered. Berar was assigned to the Central Provinces. The Marathi speakers there may have expected to go to Bombay, but the government had no wish to strengthen that nationalistic bloc. Similarly, there were suspicions that the break-up of Bengal was not purely a matter of administrative convenience.

Until July 1905 planning proceeded without any public information or consultation. In a speech in February, Curzon had raised the temperature by declaring that it would be wrong to make any concessions to the manufactured opinions of an unrepresentative minority. He ignored protests. A 'native gentleman' had told him that Bengalis 'always howl until a thing is settled: then they accept it'.[16] During this period political considerations became more important as Risley and the lieutenant-governor, Sir Andrew Fraser, redrew the 1903 proposals. Fraser's aim was to separate Calcutta *bhadralok* from *bhadralok* in Dacca and Mymensingh districts, the latter being 'the hot bed of the purely Bengali movement, unfriendly if not seditious in character'. 'Bengal united', thought Risley, 'is a power; Bengal divided will pull in different ways.'[17]

The charge of also encouraging Hindu-Muslim tensions gains credence from Curzon's speech at Dacca in February 1904 promising east Bengali Muslims 'unity which they have not enjoyed since the days of the old Mussulman viceroys and kings'.[18] Muslims stood to gain from their majority position in the new province where in 1901 they held 41 public appointments compared with 1,235 held by Hindus. Muslim notables were thin on the ground so the government welcomed support from Nawab Salimullah of Dacca and provided him with financial assistance. Nevertheless, even Curzon's sternest critics agree that the main official attraction of partition had become the prospect of dividing the nationalist Hindus.

In July 1905 the new province of East Bengal and Assam was announced. It had a population of 31 million with a Muslim-Hindu ratio of 3:2. Bengal, with 50 million, was overwhelmingly Hindu. Brodrick, despite grave doubts, backed Curzon.

Swadeshi (*Home Produce*) and Swaraj (*Self-Rule*)

The advice of the 'native gentleman' proved wrong or misunderstood. As the explosion of protests broadened in focus from partition to a vociferous anti-British Bengali nationalism, the big landholders of the British Indian Association hastily withdrew. Banerjea's Indian Association kept up the public meetings, but did little in the way of real organization. *Samitis* (associations) sprang up throughout the province; soon they had 10,000 'volunteers'.

In October after the Carlyle Circular threatened to withdraw grants from institutions whose students were involved in protest, an Anti-Circular Society was formed and within a year had 75 branches. The consequent National Education Movement did not get very far because disaffiliation from Calcutta University led to loss of funding. Nevertheless, other boycott proposals were in the heady air. The cry was *Bande Mataram*, the first words of a hymn from Bankim Chatterjee's novel *Anandamath* (1882):

> I revere the Mother! The Mother
> Rich in waters, rich in fruit
> Cooled by the southern airs
> Verdant with the forest fair[19]

Rabindranath Tagore composed many patriotic songs at this time, notably 'Amar sonar Bangla' (My Golden Bengal), now the national anthem of Bangladesh. In Kishoreganj, Nirad Chaudhuri recalls in his *Autobiography of an Unknown Indian* (1951), 'We thought we had no right to live any other life but a dedicated life. Our country was waiting for us to rescue and redeem her.'[20] In another eastern town, Barisal, a local zemindar, Ashwini Kumar Dutt, alarmed Governor Fuller by drawing Muslim cultivators into organized protests. When Banerjea arrived for the 1906 Bengal Provincial Conference he found police ready to ban chants of *Bande Mataram* and break up the meeting. Soon, Gurkhas sent to intimidate Barisal by Fuller 'had become a formidable bogey to child and grown-up alike'.[21] *Yatras*, popular theatres, were spreading the message of Bengali nationalism and even national symbols – a flag of red, green, orange – were appearing. Moderate leaders were finding matters passing beyond their control.

Those involved were mostly *bhadralok*, western-educated Hindus from the higher castes. They were typically 'intermediate tenure-holders' with bitter memories of the Bengal Tenancy Act of 1889 which had weakened the already weakening position of the landlords. Sub-division through inheritance had reduced their rent income from often-resistant cultivators. Entry to the professions, which they dominated, had become intensely competitive. Those now in East Bengal found their access to Calcutta University impeded and, at first, had no high court of their own. The horizon of public employment was shrinking. Before partition, *bhadralok* from Dacca held a tenth of all posts in Bengal; now in their smaller world they would face positive discrimination in favour of the Muslim majority. It was even said there were family disadvantages for a bride to marry east to 'backward' Assam.

At first, *swadeshi* campaigns with their emphasis on self-improvement displayed familiar encouragement to Indian production. In 1878 Tata had opened his Swadeshi Mills. The Punjab government had long been encouraging support for local produce. Tagore, who was also a zemindar, promoted schemes in the 1890s for autonomous rural development based on ideas of Armenian nationalists. In the tariff arguments with London in the 1890s both the government and local British business had been, albeit less stridently, on the same side as the nationalists.

However, in the storm centres of the east, Mymensingh, Kishoreganj and Tangail, *swadeshi* meant a boycott of British goods. The popularity of drain theory through Dutt's *Economic Histories* was enhanced by the effect of sharp price rises, partly fuelled by an export boom.[22] Businesses selling *bideshi* (foreign) goods were picketed and often attacked. Since Indian businesses stood to gain from these protests, we might see evidence here for a bourgeois class-based interpretation of Indian nationalism. In fact, it appears that the Bombay mill owners, busy with a huge surge in Chinese demand from 1903 to 1905, did not compete at the upper level of the market held by Lancashire, and, when opportunity arose, found the profits too low to interest them. They were also dependent on the goodwill of the British government for a variety of services including consular assistance in the Far East, concessions for new mining ventures in India, and the importation of British machinery.[23]

Boycott was no longer just the refusal to buy British textiles. It became a political weapon. Aurobindo Ghose, editor of *Bande Mataram*, had been impressed by the achievement of Gandhi under much more difficult conditions in South Africa. Boycott in a more general sense, passive resistance, would break the illusion of British power and call for sacrifices to be made, presenting an appeal to idealism which the petitioning, the 'mendicancy', of the Moderates never could. *Swadeshi* was turning into *swaraj*. 'The movement is not primarily against bad government – it is a protest against the continuance of British control', declared Aurobindo, 'whether that control is used well or ill, justly or unjustly, is a minor and unessential consideration.'[24]

Congress

Congress opposed the partition, but soon found the campaign an embarrassment. Mehta and Gokhale had steered the 1904 Bombay Congress into a decision to focus on London, where the decline of the Tories promised opportunities. Gokhale was in London in 1905–1906 and did not want to negotiate with a background of disorder and violence. The temperature rose at the 1905 Benares Congress where Tilak and Lajpat Rai challenged the Moderate leadership in their demands for boycott. Adroitly, Gokhale ensured that Congress support for boycott would be confined to Bengal alone.

However, when the new Liberal secretary of state, John Morley (1905–11) declared partition to be 'a settled fact', the initiative at the next Congress in Calcutta passed to the Extremists: Lajpat Rai, Tilak and Bipin Chandra Pal – Lal-Bal-Pal as they were called. Anil Seal has seen them as trying 'to reverse at the top the defeats they had suffered in the localities'.[25] Tilak had been outmanoeuvred in his own Maharashtra by Mehta and Gokhale. In Bengal, where Banerjea was still a force, partition had stymied the Extremists. After 1907 in the Punjab, Congress support fell away as the government reversed its policies on revenue collection and payment of canal duties. By contrast, Sumit Sarkar has argued against this interpretation, pointing out that Congress was still just an annual forum, scarcely worth capturing. Though he conceded there were moves afoot to make it more: a 1906 resolution to create district associations for continuous political work; and industrial conferences began to be held along with Congress sessions after 1905. Nationalist historians have stressed different nationalist visions rather than personal and factional struggle.[26]

Tilak's speech at the Calcutta Congress, 'Tenets of the New Party' drew a distinction between Extremists and Moderates: India not London: boycott not petitioning. The 1906 president, the elderly Naoroji, postponed the showdown with a skilful closing speech which promised 'a clear goal...of self-government or *swaraj* like that of the UK or the Colonies'.[27] Congress was moving in a tougher direction, but definitions and time-scales for *swaraj* were flexible.

The split came at Surat in 1907. After the disastrous venue of Calcutta, Mehta brought Congress to the Bombay Presidency where he had more influence and where, according to the rules which excluded local men, Tilak could not be president. As Banerjea was speaking at the opening session, a shoe flew through the air and chaos brought proceedings to a close, and victory for the Moderates. Discretely managed by Mehta, they had been alienated by the rising tide of violence in Bengal, and the Extremist leaders were, or were about to be, under arrest. Moreover, there was still hope for reform from London. When legislation was announced in 1908, Gokhale could rejoice in government recognition: 'Hitherto, we have been engaged in agitation from outside: from now we shall be engaged in what might be called responsible association with the administration.'[28] The Extremists were virtually excluded by the constitution drawn up at the 1908 Allahabad Convention. All now had to sign up to 'the attainment by the people of India of a system of government similar to that enjoyed by the self-governing Members of the British Empire', to be pursued through constitutional means.[29] Congress had ensured that it was no longer dominated by the politics of Bengal; but the price was a political vacuum.

4. Curzon's Departure

Curzon's resignation in November 1905 is often represented as the outcome of a clash between two titans who could never work together. Kitchener came out in 1902 as commander-in-chief, the senior member of the Viceroy's Executive Council, and quickly proposed the abolition of the second army member, the military secretary, who was responsible for finance and administration. He wanted neither second opinions nor any discussion, as the latter was not his forte. The viceroy resisted on the principle of upholding civilian control of the military, an issue which had been simmering, on and off, for a century. Kitchener had told a friend that he would dominate the next viceroyalty; some thought he wanted the position himself. When he heard in August 1903 that Curzon's term was to be extended, relations became acrimonious. On the military secretary question, Curzon was outmanoeuvred, and he went.

An alternative interpretation would emphasize the role of the home government. Apart from some army resentment at Curzon's disciplinary measures, official opinion in India backed the viceroy. In London things were very different. Brodrick was smarting from Curzon's disdain, and Balfour was uneasy at his wilfulness over Tibet. A master of intrigue, Kitchener was going behind the viceroy's back to the British press, and to his admirer, the future Lady Salisbury, whose husband was Balfour's cousin. More important were the political considerations. Balfour did not wish to lose the commander-in-chief when an important item on the domestic political agenda was the reorganization of the empire's military resources. After Sudan and the Boer War Kitchener was an imperial hero in the eyes of the public. The Conservatives were disintegrating on the issue of free trade. In the first ten months of 1905, they lost seven by-elections, and the government fell the day Curzon arrived home at Charing Cross station. If one resignation had to be accepted, it was the viceroy's.

5. The Morley-Minto Reforms

The expectations of the Moderates were high after the Liberal landslide victory of January 1906. The elderly John Morley was a Gladstonian Liberal but like his master had never developed a detailed and sympathetic grasp of Indian affairs. Domestic politics were currently less focused on empire than the challenges of trade unionism, Irish nationalism and Imperial Germany. Morley, cautiously anxious to discourage appeals to London, disappointed the Bengalis by confirming the partition in March. When he took two Indians on to his council in 1907, he described it to the new viceroy, Lord Minto (1905–10) as 'the *cheapest* concession that we can make. It would leave the executive power as strong and as absolute as it now is…to my mind the cardinal requirement of any reforming operations that we may undertake.'[30] Minto was also prepared to take an Indian member on his council – the lawyer Sir S. P. Sinha was appointed in 1909 – but, believing that only some form of authoritarian government was appropriate for India, suggested rallying the conservative forces in society with a Council of Princes. However, Morley's five meetings with Gokhale in 1906 convinced him that something constitutional had to be offered to the Moderates. As the Calcutta government dragged its feet, he feared being 'laughed out of court for producing a mouse from a labouring mountain'.[31] Finally, the bill was introduced into the House of Lords in time for the 1908 Madras Congress, the first since the expulsion of the Extremists the previous year.

The Indian Councils Act, 1909, extended the nomination and election of Indians to enlarged councils. On the Viceroy's Council, 27 out of 60 members were non-officials. The provincial councils now had non-official majorities, though some non-officials were nominated and would side with the official members. The case of the two Bengals where, uniquely, there were elected majorities, illustrates the problem for the nationalists. Seats awarded to European business interests would in practice be part of the official bloc, which would then number 30 out of 53 seats in Bengal and 27 out of 41 in East Bengal and Assam. In Bengal there were only 12 seats to which nationalists could hope to be elected and most of these covered non-Bengali speaking parts of the province, Bihar and Orissa, thus leaving only four for the Bengali *bhadralok*.

The Act had two distinctive features. First, it established the principle of election, which was no longer left to the discretion of the viceroy. However, the latter decided electoral qualifications and could disallow 'unsuitable' candidates. The largest electorate had 650 voters. In the Imperial Legislative Council there were only 4,818 electors for the 27 elective seats. Two thousand four hundred and six were landowners, 1,901 were Muslims.[32] The threshold payment was Rs 3,000 per annum in land revenue or the equivalent in income tax. Second, and momentously, there were separate electorates for Muslims, despite Morley's reluctance.

Nothing came of Minto's suggestion of a Council of Princes but Curzon's interventionism was replaced by a policy of non-interference, announced by Minto at Udaipur in 1909. The foreign secretary, Harcourt Butler, wrote: 'We are only, I take it, at the beginning of an anti-British movement which is a permanent factor now in Indian politics. Surely it is beyond measure to strengthen the position of the chiefs and attach them to our side.'[33]

The aim was still to represent interests, either through direct election as with Muslims and landowners, or indirect election, through, for example, universities and trade associations Yet the extension of links between higher and lower councils enlarged the political world. Councillors could consider the budget and frame questions. Their entitlement was a small advance on the 1892 Councils Act; but this was not responsible government. Most historians would now doubt Stanley Wolpert's belief in Morley's far-sightedness and prefer Stephen Koss's sceptical conclusion that we should not anachronistically assume that these were distant preparations for Indian self-rule.[34] In December 1908 Morley told the House of Lords 'If I were attempting to set up a parliamentary system in India, or if it could be said that this chapter of reforms led directly or necessarily up to the establishment of a Parliamentary system in India, I for one would have nothing to do with it.'[35]

The Muslim Initiative

The most striking aspect of the reforms was the success of the Simla Deputation which presented its petition to Lord Minto on 1 October 1906. Thirty-five notables led by the Agha Khan had been organized by Mohsin-ul-Mulk, the political heir of Syed Ahmed Khan. Though they came from all provinces except the NWFP, their petition represented the fears of the Muslim elite in the UP, where the recent Nagri resolution had ended the dominance of Urdu. Responding to news that extension of the Legislative Councils was under consideration, they repeated their fear that Muslims would lose out under an elective system and asked for recognition

> not merely [of] their numerical strength but also [of] their political importance and the value of the contribution they make to the defence of the Empire, and…[of] the position which they held in India a little more than a hundred years ago, and of which the traditions have naturally not faded from their minds…[36]

The same Aligarh group was the driving force behind the creation at Dacca in December 1906 of the All-India Muslim League out of the Mohammedan Educational Conference. In 1907 the Karachi constitution limited membership to 400. It was a party of 'men of influence and property', financed by the Agha Khan and the Nawab of Arcot. At this stage it was a platform for putting pressure on the British; it had no common position for the council elections. 'The new movement had been forced on them' thought the Nawab of Dacca; 'only those who shout loudest had a chance of being heard.' The League would maintain the pressure of the petition; by 1909 there were provincial leagues in all provinces and in London.[37]

Outside the UP, especially in the Muslim-majority provinces, trends seemed favourable to Muslims. In the new state of East Bengal and Assam by 1911 there were 20,729 Muslim students in English middle schools where in 1906 there had been only 8,869. The Punjab Land Alienation Act had been seen as disproportionately benefiting Muslim cultivators. By 1901 30 per cent of civil service appointments in that province were reserved for Muslims. The local government had introduced communal representation in elections to municipal boards after 1882, to which practice the petition referred when it sought to represent all Muslims, even in the new majority East Bengal province, as in need of government protection.

The League persuaded the government to treat Muslims as a unity, as 'an absolutely separate community, distinct by marriage, food and custom, and claiming in many cases to belong to a different race from the Hindus'.[38] In a draft despatch of October 1908, Morley, despite misgivings, granted separate electorates for every council and increased Muslim representation in the Imperial Legislative Council from the existing two elected and two nominated members to five elected members. As Morley responded to further pressure the number rose to eight seats. Muslims could also vote in mixed electorates, where they gained two more seats in the first election. There were four extra seats for Bengal, as well as four in Bombay and three in East Bengal. Muslim representation exceeded their proportion in the population in the UP and Madras.

Why was there such a favourable settlement? It was pressed on the Liberals by Lord Minto, the Conservative choice to replace Curzon. Minto had arrived to head a government shaken by what was widely seen as Hindu opposition in Bengal and Bombay. Influenced, perhaps by his secretary, James Dunlop Smith, who was the go-between in the negotiations, he feared the possibility of additional Muslim resistance: 'though the Mahomedan is silent he is very strong'.[39]

Such public opinion as there was in Britain was pro-Muslim, primed by Chirol at the *Times* and many retired civilians. The London representatives of Congress, Lajpat Rai and R. C. Dutt, had a weak hand and did not wish to undermine the reforms in general. In the House of Lords, which retained the veto until 1911, opinion followed Curzon and Lansdowne who supported the proposals. Morley neither wanted the legislation bogged down in the unfolding constitutional crisis nor, like his predecessors, did he want party divisions revealed over Indian legislation.

Some historians, such as M. N. Das, have stressed the divide-and-rule character of the policy; others like S. R. Wasti have downplayed this interpretation. But, as Francis Robinson has argued, the communal approach reflected British assumptions that 'Indian society lives, thinks, acts according to castes, races and religions'.[40] This was how India was governed, and the Punjab in particular.

6. Terrorism

As zeal for *swadeshi* died down by 1908, terrorism was rising. There were several assassination attempts in 1907 including the first of four on the lieutenant-governor. In April 1908 at Muzaffarpur two Englishwomen were killed by a bomb intended for an unpopular magistrate. Bomb attacks were being made on the East Bengal Railway where the future communist leader, M. N. Roy, was active. In 1908 a weapons cache was found in north Calcutta in the Maniktola Garden House Raid at the headquarters of the Yugantar group.

The Rowlatt Report recorded that of the 186 convicted of terrorist crimes between 1907 and 1917, all were Hindu and 89 per cent from the high castes. Almost all were *bhadralok* from small landholding families in the east, many from among the 40,000 educated unemployed. The two main groupings were the Calcutta Yugantar party and the Dacca Anushilan Samiti which was inspired by Bankim Chatterji's conception of *anushilan*: 'development of all human faculties in the service of the country and of a rejuvenated Hindu faith'.[41]

The religious dimension was important to most of the activists. Aurobindo insisted that oaths be taken on the *Bhagavad Gita*. The Yugantar newspaper proclaimed that 'Without bloodshed the worship of the goddess will not be accomplished.'[42] Vivekananda was another influence: 'In Europe political ideas form the national unity. In Asia religious ideas form the national unity.'[43] The implications are even clearer in Tilak's formulation: 'The common factor in India society is the feeling of *Hindutva*...we say that the Hindus of the Punjab, Bengal, Maharashtra, Telengana and Dravida are one and the reason for this is only Hindu *dharma*.'[44]

Within a few years, terrorism declined sharply. Attacks by Europeans on Bengalis had, it was said, ceased overnight, but otherwise the terrorists had no obvious achievements to show. Government repression had less to do with the decline than their own socially isolated position as *bhadralok*. Mostly from small *rentier* landholder families and articulating their ideas with a Hindu religious vocabulary they could make little or no appeal to the Muslim peasant majority. They had no programme of agrarian reform to offer the poor cultivators, many of whom engaged in rent strikes during the disturbances. Shopkeepers, Muslim and Hindu, might have had their stocks of foreign goods seized by *swadeshi* enforcers. For the Muslims, partition was not self-evidently bad. Tagore has caught the tensions of those years in his novel *Ghare Bhaire* (*The Home and the World*) (1915).[45]

The same social exclusiveness prevented the exploitation of labour unrest. There were about a quarter of a million industrial workers in the province, almost all Hindi-speaking immigrants from Bihar. Under the 1881 and 1891 Factory Acts the working day for 9–14-year-olds had been restricted to seven hours, and for women to eleven hours with no night work. Nevertheless, conditions in that oppressive climate remained harsh; the normal day in the jute mills was 5am to 8pm. Strikes flared during the years of high food prices, and not just in Bengal. They also occurred in the Rawalpindi railway engineering workshops in 1907 and the next year in Bombay – the latter, a strike which Lenin noticed. All this troubled the government, but coordination was lacking.

The revolutionary mood had an international dimension. A Parsi, Mme Cama, unfurled the flag of independent India at the 1907 Stuttgart Conference of the Second Socialist International.[46] Lala Har Dayal was preaching a revolutionary message to Sikhs struggling with discrimination in British Columbia and in California's Sacramento Valley. The government had no wish for his newspaper, *Ghadr* (Revolt, or Mutiny) to spread the contamination back into the recruiting ground of the Indian army. In 1905 Shyamaji Krishnavarma founded an Indian Home Rule League, and chose Highgate, London 'which has the lowest death-rate in the UK' to open his India House.[47] Here boarded 25 Indian students, among them the future revolutionary historian V. D. Savarkar and Madan Lal Dhingra who assassinated the civilian Sir Curzon Wylie at the Imperial Institute in 1909. Krishnavarma had left that cradle of the ICS, Balliol College, Oxford with glowing references, later returning the compliment by endowing the university with a Herbert Spencer lectureship. He published the *Indian Sociologist*, 'an organ of Freedom, and of Political, Social and Religious Reform', and, after its suppression in Calcutta, *Bande Mataram*.[48] His contribution to the 50th anniversary of the Mutiny was the republication of *India* (1857) by the positivist Richard Congreve which had called for British withdrawal under international guarantees. In 1909, anticipating arrest, he moved to Paris where he had the Marseillaise translated into Indian languages, and defended terrorism – the policy of frightening the British out of India.

Repression

Morley had to tell Minto that there was no 'howl' in Britain at the assassination of British officials; strikes seemed more of a threat. He expressed his revulsion at a sentence of seven years imprisonment for a seditious pamphlet and of 30 strokes, reduced to 6, for Kalamchand Dey, a 7-year-old boy. Senior officials seemed to have no idea of Parliament or of British opinion; 'what utter simpletons they must be...'[49] Nor was Morley happy at the prosecution of Tilak in 1908 with a 'most obviously packed jury', and his subsequent sentence to six years imprisonment. The number of political prisoners in the Andaman Islands Penal Colony, with its Benthamite Cellular Jail, was soon to surpass 14,000. Morley worried about American opinion, and the effect that pure repression might eventually have on the army.[50]

Despite Morley's private anguish and appeals for restraint, repression rather than reform was arguably his more important legacy. The extent of Extremist encouragement for terror was a matter of conjecture. Tilak's journalism stressed the value of action. Pal's 1907 Madras lectures argued that self-government under British paramountcy was a contradiction in terms. From August 1906 *Bande Mataram* was calling for passive resistance. The government was taking no chances and revived Regulation III of 1818 which allowed detention without trial. The *samitis* were targeted especially. There were high-profile uses of the regulation in 1907 with the deportation of Lajpat Rai for encouraging land protests in the Punjab. Next year Aurobindo followed. To general astonishment, he and 16 others of the 36 accused had been acquitted in the sensational Alipore Bomb trial, during which the Public Prosecutor, Ashutosh Biswas, was assassinated. The censorship of the 1908 Newspaper Act was toughened into the 1910 Press Act, though judicial appeal was allowed. Similarly, the 1911 Seditious Meetings Act hardened an act of 1907. The trend continued in the viceroyalty of Lord Hardinge (1911–16) who was seriously injured in an assassination attempt as he entered the new capital of Delhi in December 1912, culminating in the wartime suspension of most civil rights in the 1915 Defence of India Act.

7. New Delhi and the Lucknow Pact, 1916

In the Bengals the reforms had failed to rally the Moderates, most of whom followed Banerjea in boycotting the councils. Minto, though gratified 'to see the "King of Bengal" sitting on my sofa...inveighing against the extravagances of Bepinchandra Pal', nevertheless felt something must be done to heal the wound, especially in view of the continuing strength of the now underground revolutionary *samitis*.[51] King George V was pressing for the revocation of the partition of Bengal and the new team of Lords Crewe (Secretary of State, 1911–15) and Hardinge made it easier to overturn Curzon's decision and announce a new province of Bengal proper. The non-Bengali-speaking parts of the old provinces, Bihar, Chota Nagpur and Orissa were hived off under lieutenant-governors and a chief commissioner for Assam.

Simultaneously, George V announced at the coronation durbar of 1911 that the capital would move to Delhi. This would lift the Supreme Government above the maelstrom of Bengal politics, and signal a decisive move towards decentralized government in India.[52] However, the Mughal resonance of Delhi no more pacified Muslim leaders outraged at the loss of their new province than the offer of a new university at Dacca. They recalled the virtual dismissal of the pro-Muslim Governor Fuller of East Bengal, noted Britain's failure to help the Ottomans in the Italian and Balkan Wars, 1911–12, and Hardinge's rejection of a proposed Muslim university at Aligarh.

Expressive of the feeling that the government had betrayed Muslim interests a Young Party arose from an Urdu-speaking small landowning background, more Islamic than nationalist, and pushed aside the older League leaders. Though they gained no seats in the 1913 provincial elections, they were firmly in charge, and moved the League's headquarters from aristocratic Aligarh to the city of Lucknow. There was the charismatic Oxford graduate Mahomed Ali and his brother Shaukat, owners of two newspapers and full-time politicians, as well as Fazlul Huq in Bengal. A resolution which they pushed through the League in March 1913 for self-government by constitutional means brought them into line with the aspirations of Congress.

There, rising young men like Jawarharlal Nehru from Allahabad, disappointed by the Morley-Minto reforms, called for something more purposeful than the elderly Moderates offered. Though Mehta rebuffed Tilak's attempt at reconciliation on his release from prison in 1914, all changed the next year with the deaths of Gokhale and Mehta himself. Extremists and Moderates were reunited through the good offices of Annie Besant, president of the 1915 Bombay Congress, and talks were opened with the Muslim League. The go-between was Mohammad Ali Jinnah, Naoroji's former secretary, and in 1916 the Lucknow Pact was sealed. Congress and the League called for immediate self-government and dominion status. Congress accepted the League's demand for separate electorates. A deal was struck over the distribution of seats which would have an immensely important future effect: over-representation in Muslim minority states and under-representation in majority states.[53] The government was faced with a united nationalist front.

8. Diaspora

The history of Chinese nationalism can hardly be written without reference to the overseas Chinese. In different ways the Indian diaspora was comparably important. From Africa across the Indian Ocean to the Pacific and North America the growth of Indian settlement slowly strengthened the claim of nationalists to speak for one of the principal peoples of the world. From the First World War political lobbying in the United States became a factor which no British government could ignore. And from South Africa, in the form of Gandhi and his methods, came the nemesis of the Raj.

India's part in Britain's worldwide empire, formal and informal, had a human side. In the seventeenth and eighteenth centuries, a million Britons had emigrated, the majority of them as indentured labourers. It was this form of emigration, in the 75 years before its abolition in 1920, that also drew perhaps a million Indians abroad. In signing an agreement, the implications of which must often have been unclear, they consigned themselves to a sort of slavery for a fixed term, usually four or five years.

What drew them out was the need for labour in the European sugar plantations, and poverty and dislocation at home. After slavery was abolished in the British Empire in 1833, John Gladstone, father of the future prime minister, decided in 1838 that importing indentured Indian labourers to British Guiana was the way to make his fellow planters 'independent of our Negro population'.[54] Of the West Indian islands, Trinidad took the most labourers: 51,000 by 1882. In 1869 a law there offered a land grant to any labourer who had worked for ten years. As West Indian migration declined, Mauritius became the most important destination. By 1867 the island was home to 341,000 indentured labourers, 261,000 male and 80,000 female. The Dutch consul-general in Calcutta also oversaw recruitment to their West Indian sugar colony of Surinam where the abolition of slavery in 1863 had created a labour shortage on the plantations. A recent work has estimated that in the mid-century half a million coolies passed through the French port of Yanam in the Godaveri delta.

Voluntary emigration from British India may have been on an even bigger scale than the trade in indentured labourers. There were also later specific schemes of emigration, for East African railway construction, or to recruit Sikhs for police forces in British colonies from Hong Kong to central Africa. Some, no doubt, were joining Indian communities who had lived around the Indian Ocean for centuries. When Zanzibar came under British influence in 1861, it was said that foreign trade was in the hands of the local Indian community then numbering 5,000–6,000. Of the 10,000–12,000 *lascars* (seamen) in British merchant ships, at least sixty per cent were reckoned to be Indian.

The eastern indentured migration possessed some different features. The quarter of a million who went to Malaya between 1844 and 1910 showed a high propensity – 82 per cent – to return, and generally seem to have accumulated some savings. In Fiji the creation of sugar plantations was encouraged by the British authorities who needed to raise revenue after annexation in 1874. About 61,000 migrants arrived between 1879 and 1916.

The British Indian government's attempts to regulate and ameliorate the traffic was nominally strengthened by a law of 1864. The labourers went out through Calcutta, Madras and Bombay. The ratio of men to women was supposed to be at least 10:4, and emigrants were required to show evidence to a magistrate that they were being recruited in their home district. The greatest number of migrants through Calcutta came from the tribal population of the Chota Nagpur hills and from impoverished districts of Bihar and the eastern NWP, where the revenue demand was particularly heavy. Despite the law, it seems that many had already left their home villages in search of work. Though they were often described as being from the lowest classes and castes, research suggests that in both the NWP and Tanjore, the main district for Madras emigration, the proportion of high caste Brahmans and Rajputs was about the same as in the general population.

Though opportunities arose for individuals and groups, there seems to have been little to offset the misery and degradation of so many people. Indentured labour helped to prolong the existence and high profits of the plantations where, as a historian has written, 'estate discipline was maintained by the whip and the stocks'.[55] As numbers of immigrants built up, tensions arose with indigenous Fijians and, in the West Indies, with the African population. Belatedly, the British Indian authorities took their responsibilities more seriously. However, the abolition of the indentured system in 1920 really followed from the consequences of the shipping crisis in the First World War.

Mohandas Karamchand Gandhi

By then, from the Pacific to the Atlantic, the Indian diaspora in the British Empire was significantly large, 2.5 million by some accounts. It was not, however, accepted as on an equality with the British diaspora. Lord Crewe observed in 1907 that Indians could not go to some dominions 'without undergoing vexatious catechisms',[56] as Gandhi discovered in 1896 when he narrowly escaped with his life from a demonstration in Durban against Indian settlement. This London-trained barrister, finding employment difficult in India, had gone three years earlier to Natal. He was soon engaged in campaigns on behalf of the Indian population over the franchise, immigration control, registration and the many humiliations to which they were subject. Indians had come to South Africa mostly as labourers and traders. In the face of European political control and brutality their claims to be treated as citizens of the British Empire were difficult to uphold. During 20 years Gandhi developed a range of remarkable political skills in organization, journalism, fund raising, and symbolic action in drawing together a varied Indian population divided by religion, social custom and language.

Passive resistance was not new – British suffragettes employed it – but Gandhi's positive version, *satyagraha*, required a spiritual and ethical transformation of his followers and of himself. It implied 'the conquest of the adversary by suffering in one's own person'.[57] Since his time in London, his inner life had become increasingly important to him. His Hinduism, focused on the theism of the *Bhagavad Gita*, was broad and tolerant, but conservative. He deplored the inequalities of the caste system, but had no desire to overturn the social order. From the Jainism of his native Gujarat, he appreciated the many-sidedness of truth. The ethical teachings of Jesus appealed to him strongly, and he corresponded with the Russian novelist Tolstoy on themes of peace. Among the lessons he learned from John Ruskin was the equal value of all contributions to society, especially of physical work. He founded small communities, Phoenix Settlement and Tolstoy Farm to work out his ideas of the good life in practice. It is probable that western experience brought to the surface influences from the Hindu-Jain world of his childhood. All his ideas seem to be rooted in an Indian past except for the emancipation of women and the dignity of manual labour.

His emphasis on small peaceful communities recalls anarchist methods prevalent in the West at the turn of the century. From that milieu, Max Nordau, who warned of the degeneracy of modern civilization, impressed Gandhi and may have left his mark on his seminal work, *Hind Swaraj*, which he wrote on the way back from London in 1909. Here was the 'mighty message of *ahimsa* [non-violence]' which was 'in answer to the Indian school of violence' of Krishnavarma and Savarkar, with whom he had been arguing in London. Quoting Mazzini, he tells the reader that the way to freedom is through purifying the self. 'It is *swaraj* when we learn to rule ourselves.'[58] Then, unified by a common language – he argued for Hindi in both Persian and Nagri scripts – India will not need British rulers, 'who are at present in India because we keep them'. He agreed with Tolstoy that 'Indians... have enslaved themselves'.[59] *Hind Swaraj* struck a new note, a turning away from western civilization with its corrupting materialism of cities, railways, machinery and hospitals to the 'ancient civilization of India which, in my opinion, represents the best that the world has ever seen' and which is 'sound at the foundation'.[60]

Nevertheless, he had not yet given up on hopes for the British Empire. As a citizen he had thought it his duty to offer himself to the medical services in the Boer and Zulu Wars. Though his sympathies were with the other side, he had accepted British medals for his philanthropy. His most important link was with Gokhale, who, despite differing views of the West, returned his reverence by telling the 1909 Lahore Congress that Gandhi's name could not be mentioned 'without deep emotion and pride'.[61] Partly through his influence, Gandhi became so well known in Congress circles that his name was mooted for the presidency in 1911. Morley less charitably thought he was 'aiming less at claiming rights in Africa, than in finding fresh fuel for the smouldering fires in India'. When he left for India in 1914, the South African minister J. C. Smuts wrote 'The saint has left our shores, I sincerely hope for ever.'[62]

9. The Illusion of Permanence

Disraeli's description of India as 'the jewel in the crown of England' never seemed more apposite than on the eve of the First World War.[63] By then, India had taken a tenth of Britain's overseas investments, and 17 per cent of iron and steel exports for its railways. It was still Lancashire's biggest market, and financed two-fifths of Britain's balance of payments deficit with Europe and North America. The civilian Sir Richard Temple in *India in 1880* (1881) had listed a number of reasons why 'England, then, must keep India': including, 'because a vast amount of British capital has been sunk in the country on the assurance of British rule being, humanly speaking, perpetual…'[64] In an empire that expanded by 3.5 million square miles between 1884 and 1900, India was the second centre, safeguarding vast interests in South-east Asia, China and Australasia. Possession of India made the difference between being 'a first rate power and a third rate power', thought Lord Mayo. Britain should be 'determined as long as the sun shines in heaven to hold India… Our national character, our commerce demand it…'[65] Permanence had become a necessary illusion.

The lofty isolation of the rulers reinforced an assumption of permanence. During the seven and a half months Ampthill acted as viceroy, he could not recall meeting socially with even a dozen Indians. Dunlop Smith was shocked to find that even 'the more sober-minded' Indian students he met in London wanted the British to leave the country.[66] When Edwin Montagu, the Indian under-secretary, visited India, he rejected the social illusions of Simla. 'At a time when the very poor masses are beginning to think', the growing luxury and separation spelt future danger.[67] In retirement. Curzon's private secretary Walter Lawrence recalled the working illusions of a civilian: 'Our life in India, our very work, more or less, rests on illusions. I had the illusion, wherever I was, that I was infallible and invulnerable in my dealings with Indians. How else could I have dealt with angry mobs, with cholera-stricken masses, and with processions of religious fanatics?… the idea is really make-believe – mutual make-believe. They, the millions, made us believe that we had a divine mission. We made them believe they were right.'[68]

Great attention was given to the symbolism of permanence. Curzon checked every detail of the 1903 coronation durbar, even prohibiting the hymn 'Onward Christian Soldiers' because of the passage 'Crowns and thrones may perish,

Kingdoms pass away'. In 1877 the princes had been spectators; they were now to be participants. Pageantry and modernity were juxtaposed. The princes, as on all official occasions, were required to wear Indian dress: the ancient grandeur of the Red Fort was illuminated with electric light for the banquet. The presence of George V made the durbar of 1911 even more auspicious, and much use was made of photography and film to propagate images of authority and permanence. The Gaekwar incident, however, showed that the new media could not be controlled, outside India at least. The *Illustrated London News* printed a page of still frames to allow readers to decide for themselves whether the demeanour of the prince had been deliberately insulting.

At the turn of the century architectural statements of the grandeur of an empire at its apogee were being made in India as well as in London and the dominion capitals. After the death of the Queen, Curzon planned a Victoria Memorial in Calcutta to impress the world and, through the exhibits and internal murals, draw Indians and Britons together in the celebration of a common modernizing past. Shivaji, Tipu Sultan, the Rani of Jhansi and Keshub Chandra Sen all appeared with the names of famous Company men. Yet, the viceroy told the architect, William Emerson, that he would have no hybridity in the design. He rejected the Indo-Saracenic style of much British building in the subcontinent. The St Pancras-inspired Gothic architecture of Bombay's Victoria Terminus was out, too. The imperial style should be a chaste Palladian classicism. Though, somehow, Indian corner towers appeared in the final design.

Lord Crewe declared that the monumental scale of the new capital planned for Delhi represented 'an unfaltering determination to maintain British rule in India'.[69] A letter to the *Times* in 1910 signed by a number of art critics and historians, has been identified as a turning point in the British appreciation of Indian art. However, the architects, Sir Edwin Lutyens and Herbert Baker, rejected any stylistic compromise. They dismissed the orientalizing classicism of the Gateway of India, then building in Bombay, and declared that to 'embody the idea of law and order which had been produced out of chaos by the British Administration' a pure western classical style was required.[70] Yet, here, too, thanks to the lobbying of E. B. Havell, that champion of Indian art, Indian influences crept back into the final result: *chujjas* – deep cornices – for the sunlight and rain; *chattris* and Buddhist domes and railings; and the Mughal Garden. Lutyens was responsibile for the overall design and for the viceroy's house, Baker for the two secretariat buildings which flanked the approach to it. A great controversy arose when Lutyens discovered that the viceroy's house on Raisina Hill, the axial point of an ordered symmetry, was not, as intended, always visible from the approaching King's Way. Though the two men only spoke through intermediaries for five years, the vast enterprise went on. The government departments moved into their new offices in 1926–27 and the inaugural ceremonies took place in 1931. By then a new world had come into being. A legislative building had to be added after the Montagu-Chelmsford reforms.

Calcutta seemed indifferent to the changing international order and the consequent realignment of British foreign policy. Morley had to tell Minto: 'You and Kitchener talk of an Anglo-Russian Entente as an open question. It is not: it is policy.'[71] Perhaps it would have been considered weakness to exploit Britain's 1902 treaty with Japan, a country whose rise was followed so closely that a Bengali paper was running a subscription fund for Japanese soldiers wounded in the Russian war. With the growing international tension, the illusion of Britain as the solitary superpower could no longer be sustained. Critical remarks by the American Populist leader W. J. Bryan, after a tour of India in 1905 drew attention to a superpower in the making. Morley asked Minto to maintain a reputation for fair and constitutional government. He feared a tide of American opinion akin to critical British attitudes to Austria in Italy or the Ottomans in the Balkans.[72]

British observers did not always share the illusion. Visiting MPs had always been the bugbear of the bureaucracy.

Pagett, M.P. was a liar, and a fluent liar therewith...
As I thought of the fools like Pagett who write of their 'Eastern trips',
And the sneers of the travelled idiots who duly misgovern the land...[73]

There were now more of Kipling's Pagetts. The visit of Keir Hardie in 1907 was a pointer. Though he committed the new Labour Party to Indian self-rule, there was for the moment no follow-up, yet as Morley remarked 'It brings into sudden and full view the great riddle how a parliamentary democracy is to govern India'.[74] British politics was convulsed with the constitutional crisis over the House of Lords, Irish Home Rule and trade union power. For the moment, the bi-partisan approach to India still held, and the Morley-Minto reforms were debated in an empty chamber.

Even within the Indian establishment, there were doubting voices. Sir Denzil Ibbetson, who, as lieutenant-governor inherited disturbances which arose from his own 1900 Punjab Land Act, 'does not take hopeful views of the durability of the Raj'.[75] Reporting this to Minto, Morley wrote 'how intensely artificial and unnatural is our mighty Raj. And it sets one wondering whether it can possibly last. It surely cannot...' It was hardly reassuring that, when he was talking at Windsor with the visiting Kaiser about 'the impossibility of forecasting British rule in the Indian future, he hit his hand vehemently on his knee, with a vehement exclamation to match, that British rule would last forever. When [Morley] told this to Lord Roberts, he laughed and said "the Emperor doesn't know much about the facts".'[76] In the same way, some modern historians now view the mighty Raj as a weak state; not weak technically, as Aurobindo recalled when reviewing the terrorism of his youth, 'At that time the military organization of the great empires was not so overwhelming and apparently irresistible as they now are', but weak in the sense of being an alien structure with a low income and shallow roots in the country.[77]

Some historians have remarked on signs of discouragement among civilians, as when John Beames (retd. 1893) in his *Memoirs of a Bengal Civilian* (1961) complained of 'almost insoluble problems...[and] the apparently unconscious and unintentional, but for that reason all the more unconquerable obstructiveness of the whole population'.[78] Theodore Morison, former principal of Aligarh College who served on the councils in Calcutta and London, was not alone at this time in asserting that India required and responded to authoritarian government.[79] British rule was now being justified in more passive ways: as authorized by treaties with Indian rulers; as the outcome of rescuing the country from the supposed anarchy of the eighteenth century; and as necessary to preserve the peace amid the complex antagonisms of this huge and varied country. There was an awareness that the era of government 'without politics', in Kipling's words, 'that wonderful time between the post-Mutiny reconstruction and the coming of the New Age', was drawing to a close.[80]

Imperial self-confidence was not only challenged on the outside by the Indian 'other'. The 'other' was on the inside, too. Anxiety about the quality of ICS entrants was commonplace; not just about the choices young men were making but about the possibility that the national character was deteriorating. The 1905 Aliens Act checked the immigration into Britain of 'undesirable aliens'. However, as improved communications made Britain, like France and Italy, more unified, it was clear that there were 'undesirable aliens' within the country. The Boy Scouts and other such movements could address problems of character, but current interest in Social Darwinism and social pathologies raised the possibility that some elements in the population constituted a permanent drag or threat. Fear of national degeneracy was fed by the growth of democracy, socialism and anarchism. As Lord Salisbury had asked in his 'Disintegration' article of 1883, faced by these threats, 'how long can the final disintegration of the Empire be postponed?'[81] At the time of the 1897 Jubilee there were warnings in Old Testament language in Kipling's 'Recessional'. Without humble thought and action:

> Lo, all our pomp of yesterday
> Is one with Nineveh and Tyre![82]

Chapter 4

THE FIRST WORLD WAR, 1914–1922

1. The Strains of War

Imperial strategy had assumed that troops would have to be sent to India on the outbreak of war. Yet the opposite happened and India's contribution to the war effort was a massive 1.4 million men sent overseas, of whom 53,500 were killed and 66,400 wounded.[1] On 25 August 1914 four Indian divisions sailed for Europe, where they helped defend the channel ports until Kitchener's New Army arrived. During that winter nearly a third of the British force was from India. Casualties were heavy; in the Second Battle of Ypres, when poison gas was used for the first time, the Lahore Division lost 3,889 men, or 30 per cent of their complement. The loss of British officers created leadership problems only belatedly addressed in 1917 with the announcement of the limited King's Commission for Indians. Letters sent home from the western front, and read by the censor, give a sense of the soldiers' political education. Nationalist language was absent, but many were struck by India's poverty by comparison with Flanders or Sussex, and by the importance of education for both men and women in Europe. References to individual British officers were rare; the name most mentioned was the King-Emperor, to whom there was clearly a sense of personal loyalty.

By the end of 1914 six expeditionary forces had left India. Eventually, as well as to France and Belgium, there were deployments to East Africa, Cameroon, Egypt, Somaliland, Gallipoli, Mesopotamia, Palestine, Salonika, Aden and Persia. The experience on some of these fronts was grim. In November 1914 at Tanga in East Africa 8,000 troops were defeated by 1,200 Germans. Deplorable leadership and lack of machine guns made for a fiasco which, even with strong South African help, was not reversed by November 1918 when the Germans, acknowledging the outcome in Europe, finally surrendered.

Worse still was the Mesopotamian campaign. The original occupation was designed to cover the Anglo-Persian oilfields. It was then decided to move inland and capture Baghdad for the prestigious effect it would have on Indian public opinion after the bad news of Turkish victory at Gallipoli. Between November 1915 and April 1916 the army was defeated at the battles of Ctesiphon and Hanna and finally surrendered at Kut el-Amara. Half of the Indian prisoners, and 70 per cent of the British, died in captivity. The victorious thrust from December 1916 onwards could scarcely erase these memories. When the Mesopotamia Commission of 1917 revealed the bungling of the campaign and called in question the effectiveness of Kitchener's centralizing of authority without developing a general staff, Austen Chamberlain (Secretary of State, 1915–17) resigned and would have taken Hardinge with him had the latter still been viceroy.

Despite all the stresses of battle and of religious affiliation, the Indian army, unlike the French or the Russian, did not crack. There was recognition of Muslim reluctance to fight the Turks and recruitment of Pathans stopped in late 1915. Letters from the Western Front revealed a knowledgeable interest among soldiers in the revolt of the Sharif of Mecca in 1916. But the war had not stopped the *hajj*, though numbers were low. The Indian army was still sending men in batches in 1917. The 15 or so mutinies which have been identified between the 1880s and 1930 were by no means concentrated in the war years.[2]

The only mutiny in the whole period which involved lethal violence occurred outside India in a Singapore denuded of British troops in February 1915. While the Chinese celebrated their New Year on part of the island, the 5th (Punjabi) Light Infantry seized the rest. Some crossed into Johore where the Sultan ordered their capture and came in person with his troops to Singapore. Other aspects of the pacification prefigured events of three decades later. Signals to Japanese cruisers produced a landing party which recaptured the barracks. A Japanese journalist noted 'consternation and panic among the Europeans until recently so arrogant'.[3] An enquiry found that poor leadership was the determining cause. From a local mosque pan-Islamism influenced Muslim troops whose commanding officer had not made it clear that the next move was to Hong Kong not to the Middle East. British prestige had suffered locally when the German cruiser Emden, after shelling Madras, had sunk shipping in the Penang roads in October 1914. The troops had also been allowed to supervise German prisoners of war who had sown doubts about the war's likely outcome.

Armies can be defeated by news coming from their families, so the government had a particular reason to be concerned about the home front. There were revolutionary threats, and in late 1914 only 15,000 British soldiers were left in the subcontinent. Four thousand Ghadrites who had returned from North America to challenge British rule were arrested. Plans for a general rising in north India in February 1915 by the Bengali revolutionary Rashbehari Bose misfired and he fled to Japan. In December a Provisional Government of Free India headed by Raja Mahendra Pratap and with German backing was proclaimed in Kabul. However, British success in enlisting the support of neutral governments kept the revolutionaries under cover and on the move. Within India, these political threats were hugely offset by the public support of many leading nationalists. The princes added practical help with 22,000 Imperial Service troops on the outbreak of war.

The economic effects of the war came through slowly. Businessmen complained of the war taxes and restrictions. Only a fifth of the railways were regularly available for ordinary traffic. Yet, as external trade fell with the shipping shortage, import substitution benefited the Tata Iron and Steel works at Jamshedpur. The Bombay cotton industry, stoked by large government orders and the absence of Lancashire competition, boomed. But for tens of millions of consumers the increased money supply, from Rs 660 million in 1914 to Rs 1530 million in 1919, brought inflation with rising prices and shortages of cloth and kerosene for cooking.

Price Index

1873	1910	1913	1914	1915	1916	1917	1918	1919	1920	1921	1922	1923
100	122	143	147	152	184	196	225	276	281	236	232	215

Source: Sarkar, *Modern India*, 170.

By 1916 Hardinge thought that the country had been bled 'absolutely white'.[4] The lower levels of government employment were among the worst hit, as widespread strikes at the war's end showed. Food grain prices had doubled and in 1917–18, the year after harvest failure across the northern hemisphere, two million tons were exported to Britain and Mesopotamia. For the poor, misery turned to desperation in 1918. The monsoon failed, from June onwards perhaps twenty million succumbed to the flu pandemic, and in early 1919 cholera was killing 800 a day in Bombay.[5]

The war also damaged the prestige that was so important to British rule. Its duration and reports from the battlefields brought home to Indians that Britain was just one power among a number fighting for their lives. Some derived satisfaction from the humbling of their masters. Nehru recalled that 'There was little sympathy with the British in spite of professions of loyalty. Moderates and Extremists alike learnt with satisfaction of German victories.'

Loss of confidence spread to the 'masses' who, in Tagore's recollection 'refused to accept as true every news of success of the allies that came to them from the English sources'.[6]

At the same time self-confidence and expectations rose, encouraged by tributes like that of the *Times*: 'The Indian Empire has overwhelmed the British nation by the completeness and unanimity of its enthusiastic aid.' Early in the war Gokhale wrote: 'I'm not sure that the Indian army won't do more for us Indians than all the Royal Commissions in the world.'[7] In 1918 Tilak and Gandhi were still supporting recruitment and in their different ways looking for recognition of India's claims to equality within the empire. As Gandhi wrote to Jinnah: 'Seek ye first the recruiting office and everything will be added unto you.'[8] Tilak recommended the purchase of war bonds as 'title deeds of Home Rule'. Britain's claim to have been fighting to defend the rights of small nations increased the pressure, as did President Wilson's support for the principle of national self-determination. In 1917 Curzon warned the cabinet that with 'free talk about liberty, democracy, nationality and self government… we are expected to translate into practice in our own domestic household the sentiments which we have so enthusiastically preached to others. The Russian Revolution has lent an immense momentum to this tide…'[9]

2. Wartime Politics: The Loss of the Initiative

The pressures of war raised expectations in India, but in Britain they retarded the development of pre-war initiatives. Hardinge's despatch of 1911 proposing to move the capital to Delhi had indicated a shift to the devolutionary tactics which would be used until the end of British India:

> [I]t is certain that , in the course of time, the just demands of Indians for a larger share in the government of the country will have to be satisfied, and the question is how this devolution of power can be conceded without impairing the supreme authority of the Governor-General-in-Council. The only possible solution of the difficulty would appear to be gradually to give the Provinces a larger measure of self-government, until at last India would consist of a number of administrations, autonomous in all provincial affairs, with the Government of India above them all, and possessing power to interfere in cases of misgovernment, but ordinarily restricting their functions to matters of Imperial concern.[10]

In the House of Lords, Curzon, the champion of the strong centre, had denounced this as a federal vision which would lead to 'Home Rule all round' for the provinces, leaving the British in Delhi, puppets cut off from the political life of the country like the last Mughals. Crewe insisted that this was a trend not a policy, but he was undercut in a speech by his more radical under-secretary, Edwin Montagu, who hailed it as a welcome policy.

Indian hopes for a British initiative were jolted in 1915 when the House of Lords rejected a proposal for an executive council for the UP overruling the legislative council, governor, viceroy and secretary of state on the grounds that the proposal represented the wishes of a microscopic minority and that personal rule was better suited to the East. Moderate Congress leadership more or less went with the deaths of Mehta and Gokhale. Sinha, as president, made what sounds in retrospect like a final appeal for a policy statement, 'so that hope may come where despair holds sway and faith where doubt spreads its darkening shadow'.[11]

Montagu was also pressing for change, but his chief in the coalition formed after the Liberal government fell in May was the cautious Conservative, Austen Chamberlain. When a reform despatch was at last sent in November 1916, the effect was spoiled by the insistence on a distant time frame. There had been other priorities in British politics: the ammunition crisis; Gallipoli; and in 1916, the Easter rebellion in Ireland, and the ouster of Asquith as prime minister climaxing in December.

The second half of 1916 saw a transformation of the situation in India. Pre-war politics had been strongly regional and even sectional. Bengal had been convulsed by the partition, but most Bengali Muslims did not share the outrage of the bhadralok. Nor did it have the same resonance in Maharashtra where the nationalist leadership was divided between Mehta and Gokhale in Bombay and Tilak in Poona. In the Punjab, urban Hindus, roused by the Arya Samaj, claimed discrimination in the 1900 Land Act, just as canal colonists were fighting the changes that threatened them. Madras was still quiet, as was the UP. In the latter, what D. A. Low has called the 'husk culture' of a Muslim elite still held, as did the British–taluqdar alliance presided over by its staunch champion, the governor Sir Harcourt Butler.[12]

Suddenly, a national campaign was launched in September 1915 – and got underway a year later – for self-government. Taking advantage of the vacuum in the nationalist leadership, government delays and the changing mood brought on by the war, Mrs Besant united factions in a Home Rule League. A supportive league was founded in the USA and Lajpat Rai, who was then living in America, appeared before the Senate Foreign Relations Committee. Tilak threatened a league of his own if he were not readmitted to Congress, and developed an organization in Maharashtra with a slightly bigger membership of over 30,000. Home Rule was a national campaign, with a national organization that used the agitational style of politics which

Congress was later to adopt. It drew in fresh areas of the country, especially the south, and new supporters, providing them with a political education. The simplicity of its demand was also its weakness. The difficulty of satisfying the followers in the short run and the repudiation of passive resistance which had been briefly encouraged built up frustrations which Gandhi was to harness in 1919.

In December the Extremists re-entered Congress, and the Lucknow Pact sealed the alliance with the Muslim League. The government now faced a united demand for full self-government and dominion status. The latter was encouraged by India's representation in April 1917 on the Imperial Council in London.[13] To regain the initiative Chelmsford (Viceroy, 1916–21) pressed Chamberlain who in May told the new viceroy: 'I am coming round to your view that a statement of our object is necessary.'[14] At last, Montagu (1917–22), who had replaced Chamberlain, made his historic declaration in August 1917.

> The policy of His Majesty's Government, with which the Government of India are in complete accord, is that of the increasing association of Indians in every branch of the administration, and the gradual development of self-governing institutions, with a view to the progressive realization of responsible government in India as an integral part of the British Empire.[15]

It had been held up by Curzon's insistence that 'self-government' be replaced by 'responsible government', though ironically this was soon interpreted as a commitment to introduce parliamentary self-government on the British model. The declaration was also taken to point to India's future as a dominion. In retrospect, this has been called the end of the 'two empires', one of white, self-governing colonies and one, Indian, non-white and dependent – the beginning of what has been called the Third British Empire.[16]

When Montagu visited India in November, Congress impressed on him the urgent need for concrete steps towards self-government. Though the Extremists were in control, their response to the Montagu-Chelmsford Report in August 1918 – 'disappointing and unsatisfactory' – was not wholly negative. At its Delhi session in December, Congress decided to work with the coming legislation 'so as to secure an early establishment of full Responsible Government'.[17] There was uncertainty over what steps to take, but widespread agreement that now was the moment somehow to redeem India's wartime sacrifices.

The radical pressure to go outside constitutional channels was already driving the Moderates to form a party of their own. In June 1918 the National

Liberal League was established in Bengal with Banerjea as president; then in November in Bombay an All-India Moderates' Conference met and agreed, in Banerjea's words to 'co-operate when we can; criticize when we must'.[18] At the second conference in Calcutta in 1920 the name National Liberal Federation of India was adopted, and the aim clarified as one of constitutional progress in co-operation with the British government aiming at dominion status within a British Commonwealth. Then, Montagu's resignation in 1922 dashed their hopes. They were a party without an organizational base; most resigned from provincial governments that year. Some were to serve on the Executive Council in the inter-war period; a few, such as Sir Tej Bahadur Sapru, had a future as influential behind-the-scenes facilitators.

3. Gandhi and the Rowlatt *Satyagraha*

Having returned to India in 1915, Gandhi followed Gokhale's advice to avoid the limelight for a while. At the end of the war he was drawn into three local disputes which brought him and his methods back to public attention. Champaran was an indigo-planting district in north Bihar where peasant grievances had a long history. In 1917 in this caste-ridden backwoods area he launched a personal *satyagraha* against the local magistrate. This challenge to the legitimacy of government was balanced by his readiness to compromise and the other practical skills soon in evidence on an all-India stage: the ability to raise funds and to build up a local team of dedicated workers, here including the lawyer Rajendra Prasad, later president of independent India. Intervention on his behalf by the government of India secured a success for the cultivators.

This was not forthcoming in Kaira where the different layers of government stood together. However, Gandhi's use of the press in this campaign for land tax remission on behalf of Patidars, richer cultivators, made him better known in his native Gujarat which had hitherto been outside the mainstream of nationalist politics. As president of the Gujarat Political Conference he spoke to hitherto excluded groups by insisting on the Gujarati language.

Urban conflicts such as the Ahmadabad millworkers' strike in 1918 presented another challenge. Wartime disruption of the railways had limited the flow of coal needed by the factories, so the mill owners were facing cutbacks anyway. They reduced wages and ended the 1917 plague bonus designed to keep workers in the city, and were prepared to sit out the strikes. For the workers the huge price rises had affected kerosene and cloth as well as food. Gandhi promoted arbitration and used the reproach of fasting for the first time. The outcome – a 35 per cent wage increase instead of the 50 per cent claimed – established Gandhi as someone the workers could turn to and also offered the promise of social harmony to capitalists, some of whom became important supporters in the future.

What propelled Gandhi onto the national stage was the Rowlatt Committee, appointed to investigate 'seditious conspiracy'. Noting the continued low-level terrorism in Bengal, it recommended the extension of the Defence of India Act for a term of three years. Gandhi felt that a 'satanic' bureaucracy was using this 'black act' to pre-empt whatever reforms were coming from the Montagu-Chelmsford Report.[19] At Benares University in 1916 he had stressed that freedom had to be taken, not received, and that the force of truth was the means:

> We shall never be granted self-government…the British nation freedom loving as it is…will not…give freedom to a people who will not take it themselves… Learn your lesson from the Boer War. Those who were enemies of that empire only a few years ago have now become friends.[20]

On 24 February 1919, he took the *satyagraha* pledge: to 'refuse civilly to obey these [Rowlatt] laws and such other laws as a Committee hitherto appointed may think fit and we further affirm that in this struggle we will faithfully follow truth and refrain from violence to life, person and property'.[21] In protest at these laws, which in the event were never used, he called a *hartal* – a day of 'humiliation and prayer' – for 6 April.

With Congress leaders sceptical, Gandhi had no organization except what help was offered by the Home Rule Leagues and the Khilafat committees being formed to protest at the treatment of the Ottoman Empire in the Treaty of Sèvres. The *hartal* received mostly urban support, especially in northern and western India. The response was less to the ideals of the movement than due to a variety of local grievances and the distress of the times. Gandhi, who was orchestrating the campaign from his Bombay base with his colleague Vallabhbhai Patel, was shaken by the crowd violence that spread through the city.

The Punjab was even more of a tinder box. The business and professional classes who had done well since British rule was established in 1849 had found that the 1900 Land Alienation Act prevented their investing their wealth in agricultural land. The attitude of the governor, Sir Michael O'Dwyer, confirmed this lack of sympathy for the urban classes, and he was suspected of some responsibility for the 1913 financial crash in which many had lost their savings. Even some of his favourite peasants were antagonized by the 1906 Chenab Colony Act which attempted to solve problems of subdivision by establishing primogeniture. War with the Ottoman Empire had raised pan-Islamic ideas among the Muslim population. There was also the misery of plague which had killed 2 million by 1910 and returned to the province in 1915.

Because of the 'martial races' policy, recruitment had fallen disproportionately on the Punjab, especially the rural north-west, which supplied 40 per cent of the wartime total. Punjab's population of 20 million provided 447,000 soldiers, against 59,000 from Bengal's 45 million. By late 1916 the number of volunteers, as in Britain, was insufficient. Coercion replaced reliance on voluntary service, though O'Dwyer won a libel case against the accusation of using 'terrorist' methods to find recruits. From June to November 1918, 99,000 men were enlisted; by then one Punjabi in 28 was in the army. O'Dwyer, heading a militarized bureaucracy, had been the strongest supporter of the Defence of India Act (1915), which gave draconian wartime powers to the government.

On 9 April Gandhi was arrested while speaking in Lahore, but despite O'Dwyer's declaration of martial law, disorder spread to the neighbouring city of Amritsar where several Europeans were killed and the police fired into crowds. On 13 April General Dyer took 50 Gurkha and Baluchi soldiers to an illegal meeting in the Jallianwala Bagh, a walled area surrounded by housing near the Golden Temple of the Sikhs. Dyer's estimate put the number of people in attendance at 6,000; an official enquiry raised the figure to 10,000–20,000. Without warning the crowd, Dyer ordered the soldiers to begin firing which only ceased ten minutes later when 1,650 rounds had been expended. Estimates put the dead at 379 and the wounded at over 1,500. Had the narrow entrance not obstructed the armoured cars, Dyer would also have used machine guns, as he later admitted.[22] He explained to the official enquiry that his action was not simply aimed at this unarmed crowd.

> Q: I take it that your idea in taking that action was to strike terror?
> A: Call it what you like. I was going to punish them. My idea from the military point of view was to make a wide impression.
> Q: To strike terror not only in the city of Amritsar but throughout the Punjab?
> A: Yes, throughout the Punjab. I wanted to reduce their *morale*; the *morale* of the rebels.
>
> ...
>
> Q: Did this aspect of the matter strike you that by doing an act of that character you were doing a great disservice to the British Raj?
> A: I thought it would be doing a jolly lot of good and they would realize that they were not to be wicked.

Horrified by the violence, Gandhi called off the *satyagraha* on 18 April. Both parties needed to reassess their positions. The viceroy had left the governors to decide how to handle the campaign in their provinces, and their response ranged from O'Dwyer's severity to the judicious restraint of Sir George Lloyd in Bombay. If the aim of government policy was to rally the Moderates to work the coming reforms, the previous few months had been a disaster.

Gandhi had not achieved the repeal of the Rowlatt Act, but it was clear that if the Montagu-Chelmsford reforms were to succeed, it could not be invoked. He acknowledged that the country was not yet ready for non-violent passive resistance. But despite weak support in Bengal and the south, it was remarkable what had been achieved. Gandhi's name was known throughout the subcontinent, and in May he secured editorial control of the weekly *Young India*. Muslims had participated in a campaign which, for all its patchiness, was truly national.

4. The Montagu-Chelmsford Reforms

With the 1919 Government of India Act, the old policy of decentralization was sharply accelerated. Whatever Montagu may have intended, most London politicians saw it not as a reward for the war effort, nor as part of the evolution of British policy, but as a defensive measure. As Curzon said: 'if the government does not take charge of the operation, someone else will…and there may easily grow up a disaffection that would soon become dangerous'.[23] Responsible government had arrived, but partially and at three levels.

'Local bodies' became locally responsible. Since the electors of municipalities and local boards also elected the provincial councils, the reforms were linking locality and province and facilitating future nationalist politics.

At the provincial level there was 'dyarchy' or divided responsibility. Local government, public health, agriculture, public works and education were 'transferred' to Indian ministers responsible to the Legislative Councils. Revenue, finance, irrigation, justice and law and order were 'reserved' to the governors. However, there was one purse for both 'transferred' and 'reserved' matters, and the council had the right to pass the budget and so could exert pressure on 'reserved' subjects.

The Government of India would keep control of foreign policy, military matters, income tax, currency, communications and criminal law. The Executive Council of six plus the commander-in-chief was to be enlarged with three Indians. A bi-cameral arrangement replaced the Imperial Legislative Council: the Central Legislative Assembly (CLA) and the Council of State. The CLA could only pass resolutions. For matters considered vital by the viceroy or in cases of emergency, legislation could be re-routed through the Council of State. The Government of India and the 'reserved' ministers remained responsible to Parliament, to which a commission would report and advise on progress to full responsible government in ten years time.

The Islington Commission on the Public Services, 1912–14, had recommended that a quarter of the ICS be recruited in India. This was raised to a third, with an annual 1.5 per cent increase. Now, however, the problem was not keeping Indians out but Europeans in. Young men who had chosen war service were not coming back to the ICS and even before the Lee Commission of 1924 improved the terms of service nearly half the entrants were Indian. Thereafter, 40 per cent of places were designated for Europeans, 40 for Indians and 20 for promotion from the Provincial Service. There were reserved places for candidates nominated from minorities, principally Muslims. For Europeans unable to come to terms with the post-war world, an early retirement scheme was introduced in 1922, the year when examinations were first held in India. To stiffen falling European morale, the prime minister, Lloyd George, declared, to nationalist anger: 'I can see no period when they [Indians] can dispense with the guidance and assistance of this small nucleus of the British Civil Service... They are the steel frame of the whole structure.'[24]

The creation of an advisory Chamber of Princes was a natural corollary of the general policy of decentralization, and followed from the Conference of Ruling Princes and Chiefs held in 1916 in recognition of their help in the war. The first of the annual meetings in Delhi was in February 1921. There was a chancellor and a standing committee of seven. One hundred and twenty-seven states, with eight million people, elected 12 members to join the 108 who sat in their own right. Three hundred and twenty-seven states with a total population of about one million were unrepresented. Montagu's 1917 Declaration of the aim of British policy had referred to India, not British India. This had alerted the bigger states to potential threats to their sovereignty, and, anxious to be taken seriously in their own right, they played no part in the Chamber which was run by middle-sized states like Bikaner and Patiala.

Franchise and constituency arrangements were worked out by the Southborough Committee. There was a huge extension of the vote, to more than 5 million people. Women had been explicitly excluded in the Morley-Minto reforms, but this time there was pressure from women's suffragist organizations in India and especially Britain. Now the question was left to the provinces; about one per cent were enfranchised except in Madras where the figure was considerably higher. The provincial councils were doubled in size and had elected majorities chosen by substantial electorates: 1.5 million in the UP; 1 million in Bengal and Madras; 500,000 in Bombay and the Punjab. There was a bias towards rural areas in an attempt to draw in richer peasants, many of whom were illiterate. The CLA had 140 members of whom 26 were officials and 100 elected by smaller, more affluent electorates: 180,000 in

Bengal and 20,000 in Assam. The Council of State of 60, including 25 officials and four nominated non-officials had a small higher-taxpaying electorate of a few thousand in the big provinces.

The Montagu-Chelmsford Report of 1918 had criticized communal representation in principle, recommended no extension and that Muslim reservation should not be kept where Muslims were already in a majority. In the event, entrenched pressure ensured that communal representation was retained and enlarged. The Muslim League pushed hard to retain the Lucknow Pact ratios; the Depressed Classes now had a share; non-Brahmans did notably well in Madras; and Sikhs who were 11.1 per cent of the Punjabi population received 17.9 per cent of the region's seats.

The reforms aimed to keep matters of real substance in British hands and pass some local powers to friends and collaborators. Nevertheless, in the context of the changed post-war world they fuelled beliefs in England and among princes that 'we regard our mission in India as drawing to a close [and] that we are preparing for a retreat'. Montagu assured Lord Reading (Viceroy, 1921–26) that 'If such an idea exists, it is a complete fallacy...'[25] At the opening of the CLA in 1921, Chelmsford's expectation of 'complete self-government within the Empire' was significantly qualified by the phrase 'in the fullness of time'.[26] The royal message referred to dominion status for India, little thinking that this status would soon mean independence in external relations.

Other changes reinforced the impression of weakening control from London, where the secretary of state was now to be paid by the British taxpayer. From 1920 the Indian government was represented in London by a high commissioner. The Council of India was reduced in scope, its members, a larger proportion of which were now Indian, on short appointments. India was represented at the Peace Conference and hence was a founder member of the League of Nations and also of the International Labour Office as one of the eight most industrialized countries. This fed through later to the agencies of the United Nations. In 1944 an Indian director was on the founding board of the International Monetary Fund.

Military Implications

The disintegration of the Ottoman Empire had provided the opportunity of guaranteeing the security of India in an unprecedented way. Yet no sooner had most of the Middle East fallen into the triumphant British Empire than alarms sounded on all sides. After the proclamation in January 1919 of the Dail Eireann, 30,000 British troops were tied down in Ireland, and by 1921 the General Staff was warning that 200,000 might be needed. In March came the rising against the British protectorate in Egypt, 'the nodal point of our whole imperial system'.[27] Simmering behind all this was the continuing crisis with Turkey. Then it suddenly appeared that the old assumption that the Indian army could be deployed when needed anywhere in the empire no longer held. Awareness of the changed situation in India and the interconnectedness of events dawned. Concessions in Egypt, for example, would have a knock-on effect in India. The empire was overextended and faced by American rivalry which had to be appeased because it could not be matched.

The army was now set at 228,000, but internal demands became pressing. The Kuki Chin rebellion kept troops tied down in Burma from 1917 to 1919. In the Punjab the challenge was not only from Indian nationalism. In 1920 the Connaught Rangers mutinied and raised the Irish Republican flag over the fort of Jalandhar. Shortly before, the Afghan army had crossed the border and begun the Third Afghan War/Afghan War of Independence. Fear of a simultaneous uprising in Peshawar, which the Afghans claimed, added to the sense of crisis. The fighting which lasted from May to June 1919 ended with RAF bombing raids on Jalalabad and Kabul. The subsequent Treaty of Rawalpindi in 1919 was ambiguous on the central issue of Afghan control of its foreign policy. After renewed pressure this was conceded by the Treaty of Kabul in 1921, in which year fresh fighting flared in Waziristan. Unsurprisingly, Chelmsford opposed Montagu's request in September for troops to suppress the revolt in Mesopotamia, and demanded the end of India's financial contribution to the cost of the South Persia Rifles.

There were now severe financial constraints on the use of the Indian army. Despite tax increases there was a deficit of Rs 34 *crores* in 1921–22. Though the rupee fell briefly to one shilling, exports did not pick up. Dyarchy had been launched at the time of a world trade depression. More important still was the constitutional constraint. To keep the new provincial politicians sweet, 6 million pounds a year were being transferred from the centre, where both military affairs and the budget were outside the control of the CLA. However, general taxation was not. So, indirect pressure could be brought to limit military spending and bring it below the current level of 32 per cent of the budget. The nationalists and the hard-pressed government had a common interest in refusing London's requests. London could wonder whether the security of India brought by the post-war settlement was worth having. The parody of the music hall song was well and truly redundant:

We don't want to fight; but, by Jingo, if we do,
We won't go to the front ourselves, but we'll send the mild Hindoo.[28]

Fiscal Implications

The war greatly hastened changes already evident before 1914. The 1860s were long past when a third of Lancashire's exports accounted for 90 per cent of India's cotton imports. The war allowed the take-off of Indian production from 400 million yards at the beginning of the century to 4,000 million yards on the eve of the Second World War. Wartime disruption, Japanese competition and the rise of Indian mills saw an abrupt change from 1913 when India took 37,000 million yards from Lancashire to 1921 when the former was only taking in 1,000 million yards. British exports to India halved in value between 1913 and 1918. Government policy followed the trend. The Industrial Commission of 1916 had recommended state intervention to promote Indian industry. Disruption of shipping had revealed the helplessness of an isolated India unable to meet basic industrial needs even in an emergency. Industry would also, it was hoped, reduce nationalist militancy by providing work for the educated. The difference between Bombay with its indigenous businesses and Calcutta with its European business dominance pointed the moral.

The war made free trade impossible, broke its spell and ended Lancashire's unique position as a pressure group in British politics. Inflation and the new demands of war led to a massive increase in government spending which required new sources of income. Land revenue ceased to be the mainstay of government finances and was supplemented by income tax and surpassed by customs duties. The India Office in London realized two years into the war that India's external financial contribution was relatively small, because it was limited to the 'normal costs' of Indian troops overseas. The request for a £100 million Indian donation to the war effort was sweetened by allowing the cotton tariff to rise from 3.5 to 7.5 per cent. After another increase in 1921, Delhi's proposal for a 15 per cent duty in 1922 brought huge pressure from Lancashire on Lloyd George and was a reason for Montagu's dismissal that year. However, the CLA voted down this last increase because they thought it would be used for military expenditure. The government's willingness to offer tariffs was designed to anticipate nationalist demands and manage the Assembly. London accepted this and was moving towards a system of imperial preference whereby British exports to India would pay a lower rate than foreign ones.

Underpinning this new world was the Fiscal Autonomy Convention of 1919 which laid down that the secretary of state should not interfere with Indian tariffs so long as the viceroy and Executive Council were in agreement with the Indian legislature. Whether the Joint Select Committee on Indian Constitutional Reform understood the implications of their measure in the context of the constitutional changes is an open question. Curzon told the House of Lords 'that I am amazed at the little attention it has attracted in this country... Among the powers you are handing to India, this particular one is in many respects the most important of all.'[29]

5. The Khilafat Movement

The travails of the Ottoman Empire in the Balkan Wars and its collapse in 1918 fanned a pan-Islamic politics voiced by the Ali brothers in Lucknow and in Delhi by Dr Ansari who had led the Indian Medical Mission to Turkey. Such feelings seem to have been much stronger in India, among both Sunni and Shia, than elsewhere in the Islamic world. As Fazlul Huq, president of the Muslim League in 1918, put it, 'Every instance of a collapse of the Muslim powers of the world is bound to have an adverse influence on the political importance of our community in India.'[30] Attention was specifically focused on the plight of the Ottoman Sultan and Khalifa (successor to the Prophet Muhammad), and his guardianship of the Holy Places, threatened by the revolt of the British-backed Sharif of Mecca. Suspicion of the government's good faith was confirmed by the publication of the Treaty of Sèvres which reneged on a promise in President Wilson's Fourteen Points and a recent pledge by Lloyd George: 'Nor are we fighting to deprive Turkey of its capital, or of the rich and renowned lands of Asia Minor and Thrace.'[31]

When an All-India Khilafat Committee met in Lucknow in September 1919, it was decided that a day of protest should be held. Gandhi, who had cultivated links with leading Muslims, took this up and proclaimed a *hartal* for 17 October. Khilafat participation was vital in allowing Gandhi to draw the scattered protests into something national in scale. He realized that the movement with its spreading organization could help to achieve the '*swaraj* in one year' he was to promise Congress in December 1920. As he himself said, 'My language is aphoristic. It is therefore open to several interpretations.'[32] He later claimed that he was talking of a parliamentary *swaraj*, but in *Hind Swaraj* he had written that 'It is *swaraj* when we learn to rule ourselves.' For that, Hindu-Muslim unity was essential. As he told the Ali brothers on their release from prison in December 1919, 'In the proper solution of the Mahomedan question lies the realization of *Swarajya*.'[33]

Not all Congress leaders to whom this union was presented as a *fait accompli* agreed. C. R. Das in Bengal and Tilak especially objected to an alliance with Muslims on a religious issue. Even some Khilafat leaders were concerned at the growing radicalism and accompanying violence as control passed to the Ali brothers, radical journalists and the *ulema* from the hands of Bombay business sponsors – who feebly declared that 'the coolie class was not to cease work [for a *hartal*] for more than an hour at the time of midday prayer'.[34] The movement appealed to poor Muslims normally outside even parochial politics. An Urdu ballad put into the mouth of the saintly mother of the Ali brothers was said to be on everyone's lips:

> Even if I had seven sons,
> I'd sacrifice them all for the Khilafat.
>
> ...
>
> This is the way of the faith of the Prophet,
> Son, give your life for the Khilafat.[35]

To make the campaign attractive to Hindus, Gandhi linked it with the 'Punjab wrong' which his recent *satyagraha* had failed to right. The Rowlatt Act was unrepealed, and the Hunter Commission reported on the Amritsar massacre in May, the same month that the Sèvres details were revealed. The reception of the report in England did more damage in India than had the immediate news of the massacre. It revealed details which had previously been little known: the numbers affected; the 'crawling order' and other humiliating punishments; aerial bombing of the disturbed district of Gujranwala; and disagreement among committee members as to whether the disorders constituted a rebellion. A vocal minority in the Commons did not take kindly to Montagu's repudiation of Dyer's methods as 'terrorism, Prussianism, racial humiliation'. The coalition government, now predominantly Conservative, only survived thanks to a powerful speech by Churchill. Rejecting the claim that another 1857 had been averted, he denounced the shooting of an unarmed crowd as 'an extraordinary event, a monstrous event, an event which stands in singular and sinister isolation...absolutely foreign to the British way of doing things'.[36] Yet the House of Lords supported Dyer, and a public subscription for him raised £26,000.

6. Non-Cooperation

At the Allahabad meeting of the Central Khilafat Committee in June 1920 a four- stage programme of Non-Cooperation was adopted which promoted the boycott of titles, government service, the police and the army as well as the non-payment of taxes. Gandhi, who had been present, launched a national Non-Cooperation movement on 1 August, the day Tilak died. There was strong opposition from Congress bosses. Nevertheless, its ratification at a special Congress in Calcutta in September was certain after Gandhi mobilized his new support and won a narrow victory in the Subjects Committee. Gandhi had by then, perhaps following Lajpat Rai, become a convert to the boycott of the imminent council elections. Both Rai and Motilal Nehru probably feared that Congress would not do well in the elections. In Maharashtra and Bengal the opposite was the case, and C. R. Das seems to have struck a deal for just one year's Non-Cooperation at Nagpur, the biggest Congress ever held. He received approval for pushing on with all four levels of Non-Cooperation and not staging them as Gandhi wished. Jinnah – 'the Muslim Gokhale' – found his motion for *swaraj* 'within the British Commonwealth'[37] shouted down and Gandhi's version for *swaraj* by all legitimate and peaceful means upheld by 14,000 votes to two. Muslim demands for complete independence as the only way to force British withdrawal from the Middle East, were side-stepped.

The operation of these boycotts was patchy, but in the succeeding months all manner of local discontents rose to the surface. A million industrial workers were on strike, and in October the first All-India Trade Union Congress met. From August violence was flaring up in many parts of the country. The governor of the UP warned: 'My ministers think that a Mussalman rising is imminent.'[38] In the rural UP landlords were being challenged by Kisan Sabhas (Peasant Unions). Significantly, Gandhi made it clear that rent boycotts – unlike tax boycotts – were no part of Non-Cooperation.

The most serious trouble was in Malabar (northern Kerala), where the Moplahs, a Muslim community of mostly poor cultivators and landless labourers, constituted a third of the population. Their numbers had trebled since 1831, partly by the conversion of many Cherumars, who as local Hindu slaves, had shared their resentment at the way British rule had strengthened the property rights of landlords and upper peasants. Between 1836 and 1919 the Moplahs had risen violently against their Hindu landlords 28 times; as they were shot down they considered themselves martyrs to their Muslim faith. A fresh wave of tenancy agitation was launched in the harsh economic climate of 1919. Shortly after, the local Khilafat/Congress organizations sought, successfully, to recruit Moplah support. 'Khilafat, tenancy and *swaraj*' was the slogan of the revolt which broke out in 1921. If British rule were broken, they would be able at the very least to assert their old customary rights against the Nair landlords. When the leaders were arrested, the campaign was left in the hands of committees who quickly turned to violence. After six months, government forces had killed 2,000–3000 and arrested 45,000. Millenarian expectations of a new order collapsed leaving nothing but strained communal relations.[39]

All this and serious rioting in Bombay in November tested to the limit the government policy of holding back and letting the campaign run out of steam. Lord Reading kept control in his own hands, a policy unlike Chelmsford's during the Rowlatt *satyagraha* of leaving matters to the provincial governors. Although Moderates were working the councils, nerves were beginning to give way. In December Reading offered Gandhi a round-table conference if he would call off Non-Cooperation. He did this without cabinet approval, and had Gandhi agreed it is difficult to see how the government could have avoided conceding full responsible government at the provincial level. Gandhi has been blamed for missing an important opportunity but he was preoccupied by the violent evidence that society was not yet ready for his methods, In February, after a mob burned 22 policemen in the UP village of Chaura Chauri, he shocked many of his followers by announcing an end to the campaign.

The Khilafat Movement was also disintegrating. Moderate support was weakened by the publication of a despatch in March 1922 which revealed that the government of India opposed British government policy and shared the core Khilafat demands: the evacuation of Constantinople; the Khalifa's (Sultan) suzerainty over the Holy Places; and the restoration of Smyrna (Izmir) to Turkey. Without consulting the cabinet, Montagu acceded to Reading's request that it be published; and was promptly dismissed. By then, the Khilafat leadership, disrupted by imprisonment, was divided over council entry and allegations of embezzlement. Among the rank and file, communalism was becoming more important than pan-Islamism, which lost its focus after action by the new Turkish republic. Ironically, it seems that Indian Muslim support for the Khilafat brought on the crisis that led to its abolition in 1924.[40]

In 1923 a bumper harvest brought down food prices, Gandhi was in prison, Congress divided and the Khilafat alliance dissolving. Lord Birkenhead (Secretary of State, 1924–28) observed: 'Poor Gandhi has indeed perished, as pathetic a figure with his spinning wheel as the last minstrel with his harp, and not able to secure so charming an audience!'[41] Even if this had indeed been the end of the Mahatma, his legacy would have been remarkable in at least four respects.

First, at his behest a constitution was adopted at Nagpur which transformed Congress from an annual platform from which English-speaking lawyers from a few politically active provinces could make representations to London and Calcuttta to, in Gandhi's words, a 'parallel Government to the Raj'.[42] The British Committee was closed, and a standing executive was created, the Congress Working Committee (CWC), which would meet once a month. There was still no party bureaucracy, but where there had been a haphazard presence in about half the districts in the 11 provinces of British India, there was now a hierarchy of organizations throughout the country from village and town sending, ideally, one delegate per 50,000 of the population from 21 provinces defined by language.[43] By 1921 membership of more than 2 million paying four annas provided a stable financial base. Gandhi's talent for fundraising helped find Rs 10 million in three months in 1921 for the Tilak Memorial Swaraj Fund for promoting social work, *khaddar* (home-spun cloth) and Hindi. Instead of requesting further admission to the magic circle of government, Congress challenged the very legitimacy of British rule with its exclusive claim to represent the Indian nation.

Second, with the Khilafat alliance Gandhi had mobilized resistance across religious communities and drawn into national politics previously excluded provinces such as Gujarat and Bihar. Judith Brown warns against the assumption that Gandhi was successfully appealing to the 'masses', rather than to new urban classes and some richer peasants. However, the Khilafat committees drew in many poor Muslims. Gandhi's symbols – *charkha* (spinning wheel) and *khaddar* were a reminder of and an appeal to the excluded millions in the countryside among whom there were many autonomous movements of protest. An official report noted a 'spurious divinity' attaching to Gandhi's name which raised millenarian expectations that under *swaraj* 'payment of rent and revenue would no longer be required of them'.[44]

Third, there was the restraining influence of his doctrine of *ahimsa*. Critics from the Left have accused him of betrayal, of calling off Non-Cooperation not only on account of Chauri Chaura but because of the growing anti-rent movement from Kisan Sabhas in the UP. This check to class conflict appealed not only to landlords but also to businessmen from his own western India, who also responded to his religious message. The shift of Indian business towards support of Congress was a significant consequence of the war. Also, the appeal of non-violence had a historic significance. 'Khaddar was a less abrasive invocation of India's past than was Kali. It was during these years that the issue was settled whether India's path to independence was to be trodden in argument or in blood.'[45]

Fourth, Gandhi offered an uncompromising leadership. He expected to be followed and when Tilak and Lajpat equivocated over the Khilafat alliance, he told them bluntly: 'conditional assistance is like adulterated cement which does not bind'.[46] Clearly the style was charismatic, but the extent to which other modes of leadership were present reflects the divergent interpretations of the man. Those who have seen him as a religious conservative – albeit sometimes as an anarchic populist – can point to elements of traditional leadership. His rejection of technological modernity was because modern materialism drove human exploitation. To the extent that his critique of modern India *and* the West was a moral one, it was a universal and not a nationalist message.[47] Gandhi's anxious desire to negotiate, convince and, above all, compromise led S. Gopal to represent him as a legal or rational type of leader, as sharing the Moderates' strategy of negotiating with the British for concessions, though seeking to build up greater mass pressure.[48] Judith Brown has also emphasized that Gandhi's effectiveness in each case was proportional to the willingness of the British authorities to deal with him.

Despite Gandhi's tactical adroitness, it would be difficult to deny the importance of his vision of an alternative social order and a power structure responsive to self-reliant villages linked in voluntary cooperation. As Ramachandra Guha has written: 'Mahatma Gandhi was not so much the father of the nation as the mother of all debates regarding its future.'[49]

The political initiative had passed from London to Delhi, and from Delhi to the provinces. The age of laissez-faire was over. India had ceased to be the great market for Lancashire textiles, as the mills of Bombay and Ahmadabad were expanding behind a tariff barrier. The Indian army was no longer at the disposal of the British government. Just when Britain was introducing limited responsible self-government, nationalist politicians were turning away from constitutional politics. Hitherto excluded regions and populations were being drawn into a national politics. And a charismatic leader had emerged capable of focusing protests and aspirations and representing them with novel skills to the British rulers.

The years 1918–22 had presented British India with its greatest challenge since 1857. The mobilization of populations around the world to fight the war, the expectations raised by President Wilson's Fourteen Points and by the Russian Revolution and the new wealth of a few and the distress of many had fuelled a myriad of discontents. The fault-lines had been recognized before the war by the governments of Minto and Hardinge both of whom acknowledged the need to re-state the aims of British rule. Through delay and distraction, the initiative was lost and Congress and the Muslim League came together in the Lucknow Pact. The Treaty of Sèvres provoked the Khilafat Movement into mass backing for Gandhi's attempts to coordinate the multitude of protests into a national campaign. Then, Montagu-Chelmsford was launched in the middle of a political and inflationary crisis. Was it only a tactic – decentralization – to retain British control, or a vision – responsible government – heavily qualified by definitional imprecision and long time-tables? The new fiscal and military relationship raised fundamental questions for imperial policy makers. Was India Britain's greatest asset, or greatest liability? Serious introspection was not likely in the aftermath of victory.

Chapter 5

DYARCHY AND DEPRESSION, 1922–1939

1. Provincial Politics

Congress remained divided on tactics after the Khilafat and Non-Cooperation movements. The 'no-changers', followers of the imprisoned Gandhi, would have no truck with the councils. However, as the reforms had devolved politics from the centre to the provinces, so provincial circumstances suggested varied responses. C. R. Das in Bengal, Motilal Nehru in the UP and Lajpat Rai in the Punjab decided to enter the councils and wreck them from within in pursuit of full responsible government. The Swaraj Party, formed for this purpose, had considerable success in the 1923 elections. When Gandhi was released from prison due to ill health the next year, he maintained his personal position of Non-Cooperation and devoted himself to countrywide tours promoting *khaddar* and social work. Nevertheless, he reached a compromise whereby the new party could remain within the Congress fold. Within a couple of years the failure of Swaraj Party tactics became clear. In most councils the government could still find allies and where that failed there was the side-route of legislation through 'certification' by the governors and, at the centre, by the Council of State.

In Bengal it had seemed that the Swaraj Party might be successful. The 1923 election had seen the Grand Old Man, Surendranath Banerjea, then a Liberal minister, lose his seat. That year he had passed the Calcutta Municipal Act which made the city a great political prize for its prestige and patronage and an arena for Das's brilliant disciple, Subhas Chandra Bose. Going against the trend elsewhere, Das strengthened links with the Muslims of the province. The 1923 Bengal Pact raised the Muslim allocation of seats from 40 to 55 per cent and guaranteed Muslims a generous allocation of places in the Calcutta Corporation. However, Das's lack of success in paralysing the council showed the futility of his approach as the governor responded by 'certification'. Forced to change tactics in 1925, Das was making unsuccessful attempts to negotiate when he died – 'the most brilliant opportunist in Indian politics, virtuoso of agitation, broker between irreconcilables, gambler for glittering stakes'.[1] Thereafter, the Muslim majority began to assert itself and between January 1927 and December 1936 there were six ministries all either led by Muslims or dependent on Muslim votes. The dominant party from 1929 was Fazlul Haq's Krishak Praja Party (KPP) representing Muslim and Namasudra (lower-caste Hindu) cultivators. Congress and the Swaraj Party were dependent on landlords, and the 1923 Bengal Tenancy Amendment Act had sharpened already acute resentment in the countryside.

In the Punjab, the other Muslim-majority province, Fazli Husain, a Cambridge-educated lawyer, laid the foundations of his Unionist Party. Montagu-Chelmsford had skewed the franchise heavily to the countryside, the more so after parliamentary pressure for votes for former *sepoys*, and his party rested on rural Muslim support with some Sikh and Hindu help.

All this posed difficulties for Jinnah as he tried to revive the Muslim League, summoning it to Lahore separately from Congress in 1924. His politics had been based on representative not responsible government, direct access at the centre to the British rulers, with the reserve weapon of a communal veto. Following the passage of Montagu-Chelmsford, all that had gone and with it the dominance in Muslim politics of the aristocratic-led minority in the UP. Numbers mattered now: and the Muslim-majority provinces of Punjab and Bengal were coming into their own, and they were not especially interested in politics at the centre.

At the centre Jinnah tried to maintain the political cooperation with Hindus which was dissolving elsewhere in the country. In the CLA, his Independent Party held the balance between the government forces and the Swaraj Party, with whom in 1924 it formed a joint Nationalist Party. Together, they presented a National Demand, hoping for a sympathetic hearing from the first Labour government in London. However, it was a minority government and, taking the pragmatic view that Montagu-Chelmsford should be given a longer run, rejected appeals for a round table conference to prepare for full constitutional government.

The next year, with the Tories returned to office, Lord Birkenhead announced that there could be no constitutional review unless the parties were participating in the councils. In protest, Nehru returned to Non-Cooperation for the 1926 elections and so broke with Jinnah. Jinnah took part but when his party was wiped out he quickly tried a personal recovery with his Four Proposals in March 1927. He offered to abandon separate electorates if the Muslim majority provinces were expanded to five – Sindh to be cut out of Bombay and Baluchistan and the NWFP to be upgraded to full provincial status. Pressure on Congress from the Hindu Mahasabha as well as Fazli Husain's lack of interest undermined Jinnah's constitutional proposals.

In Madras the reaction to the Home Rule movement had proved helpful to British rule in ways that were an indicator of developments elsewhere in the 1920s. The main Congress group, known as the Mylapore clique, had begun as critics of the government, but since the 1892 Councils Act, they had been insiders working the system so well that Congress had become moribund. Then, during the war, Mrs Besant's Home Rule League healed rifts between Mylapore and the Egmont clique and other Extremists excluded by the Allahabad Convention.[2] Used to a quiet life, the Madras government was shocked by the coordinated attack led by the Home Rule League and Congress and was horrified to discover that local finances were being used to serve nationalists needs. The British official presence in the presidency was lower than elsewhere. This meant that the 761 municipalities and 906 rural boards were relatively unsupervised. Yet their expenditure – a seventh of total provincial spending – made elections well worth fighting for the patronage.

There was no part of India where Brahmans, between three and four per cent of the population, so dominated education and public employment. In 1912 a non-Brahman movement had appeared which launched its Justice Party in 1916 with a manifesto opposed to any move 'to undermine the influence and authority of the British Rulers, who alone…are able to hold the scales even between creed and class…'[3] It was strongly supported by senior Madras civilians as a counter to a re-united and invigorated, and overwhelmingly Brahman, Congress. It succeeded in getting separate representation for non-Brahmans in the Montagu-Chelmsford settlement, though the Meston Award reduced its claim for 60 per cent of the seats to 50. To the incoming governor, Lord Willingdon, this was baffling: 'Why the d—l they were allowed the most unfair advantage which they are most unfairly exploiting, I can't think.' Faced with Non-Cooperation and the Congress boycott, he saw the light and in 1920 appointed a justice ministry even though that party had only won 15 of the 65 general constituency seats. 'Politically, the non-*Brahmin* is the most steady of our politicians' he told Montagu, 'and this should keep our presidency all right.'[4] The ministry lasted until 1926, but it was soon clear that the Justice Party was struggling to maintain links with the localities which Congress had long exploited and Gandhi had for a time coordinated.

There is agreement that the Justice Party benefited from official support, that 'the non-*Brahman* category carried inside it the hopes and fears of the Madras ICS'.[5] Eugene Irshchick, however, has put the movement into wider context, stressing the growth of education among non-Brahmans and the role of southern Dravidian revivalism. Washbrook has argued that the former is not supported by the figures, and that no evidence for social change can be found: the Tamil revival was also promoted by Brahman scholars. Similarly, Robert Hardgrave's linkage with the non-Brahman movement of the late 1920s or with the post 1947 DMK party finds no favour with the Cambridge School historians who treat the Justice Party as a purely political phenomenon. For Washbrook the Justice Party was a new formation prompted by the success of the Mylapore clique and by British caste definitions of Indian society.[6]

By the mid-1920s the government's strategy seemed to have worked well. Politics had been decentralized and the government had found new allies in the provinces. In Delhi with the help of Liberals, British control seemed more secure than it had been for years. It had weathered the storms of the Rowlatt *satyagraha* and of Non-Cooperation. The Khilafat Movement had wound down, and much local Hindu-Muslim unity had been shown to be ephemeral. Gandhi and the Ali brothers were no longer co-operating, nor were Nehru and Jinnah. There was no love lost between the Mahasabha and the Swarajists, and the latter were on the point of turning to the government.

There were other blows to nationalist morale. Lloyd George's 'steel frame' speech in 1922 praising the British ICS was designed to rally ICS morale, but also raised doubts about promises to recruit more Indians. In the same year London rejected Delhi's proposal to Indianize the army by 1955. The advantages of the Fiscal Convention seemed checked by the revaluation of the rupee – to 1/6d – in 1926 after the Hilton Young Commission. This damaged exports and favoured those who wished to remit money to Britain. Above all, Congress had lost its way. Gandhi and other leaders had been imprisoned, and disagreement about tactics had fractured the party.

2. Communalism and Civil Society

The communalism of the 1920s had roots stretching back to the 1880s or further. David Page has seen the deepening divisions of this decade as the *Prelude to Partition* (1982) in 1947. In the UP between 1923 and 1927 there were 91 communal outbreaks; in the Calcutta riots of 1926, 138 people died. After the 'magic moment' of Hindu-Muslim unity in the Khilafat Movement, the subsequent alienation of the two groups from each other has been blamed on Gandhi's use of religious language, or British 'divide and rule' tactics or, variously, as the 'false consciousness', the promotion of communal feeling, which suited certain elites.

Mushirul Hasan and Page have related this trend to the framework of politics shaped by separate electorates as groups organized to compete for patronage. The competition was heightened by the uneven development of different communities, the growing numbers of Muslims seeking a western education and the lack of job opportunities in a stagnant economy. Provincial governments were unable to meet rising expectations. The allocation of financial resources through the 1920 Meston settlement left no flexibility and land revenue, the main source of income, could not be raised, especially when the Depression arrived.[7]

With the promise of mass politics and the mobilization of Muslims in the Khilafat Movement, a sense of vulnerability was voiced by Savarkar in his *Hindutva: Who is a Hindu?* written in Nagpur in 1923. For the ideologue Savarkar, the religious element in *Hindutva* (Hinduness) was minimized in favour of geographical unity, racial features and a common culture: Hindus were a nation. In 1915 M. M. Malaviya had helped establish a national Hindu Mahasabha, and in 1916 inaugurated the Benares Hindu University. Less sectarian Hindu *sabhas* also sprang up dedicated to the reform and integration of the deeply divided Hindu world. These were predominantly high caste movements supported by conservative notables and princes.

Two pressures were driving Congress in this period towards the Hindu Mahasabha for support. The British were cultivating Muslims and ignoring the divided Congress. Then there was the Hindu backlash in Muslim-majority provinces against the deal on separate electorates in the 1916 Lucknow Pact. As Peter Hardy has written: it was a 'post-dated cheque upon a bank that, after 1922, had failed, namely that of Hindu-Muslim co-operation at the all-India level against the British'.[8] In 1923 when Banerjea's Calcutta Municipal Bill continued the principle there was an outcry which grew even louder in the same year over Das's Bengal Pact.

The Punjab was especially affected. Fazli Husain, like Fazlul Haq in Bengal, had left Congress over Non-Cooperation. The former's Unionist Party with its rural base drew opposition from urban Hindu professionals and merchants, especially as Fazli Husain extended separate electorates to local bodies and educational institutions. Like Fazlul Haq, he was seeking to raise Muslim representation to the level of the Muslim proportion in the population rather than in the electorate where property and education were favoured. As early as 1923 a Congress deputation reported that 'we found [in the Punjab] that the relations between the Hindus and Muslims were so greatly strained that each community had practically arrayed itself in an armed camp against each other'.[9]

A more militant organization, the Rashtriya Swamyamsevak Sangh (RSS) was founded at Nagpur in 1925 by K. B. Hedgewar. Influenced by the *akharas* and the Bengal revolutionary societies, the RSS network had a paramilitary style with an oath, uniform and marching drills. Its members escorted Hindu processions and clashes with Muslims were frequent. By 1939 there were 500 branches and over 60,000 members. There was a strong appeal to youthful idealism and, in the closing days of British rule, numbers leapt to 600,000.

Similarities with contemporary anti-liberal movements in the West have led to accusations of fascist tendencies. The RSS did have contacts with Mussolini's Italy, and Hedgewar's successor, M. S. Gowalkar, was influenced by German nationalist thought. But there was no European-style racism, no leadership obsession and no great concern with the role of the state. Hedgewar left Congress in 1930. He wanted to create a new man; the RSS's concern with nationalist social reform took priority over the anti-colonial struggle. From a day-to-day point of view it was curiously unpolitical, standing apart from the Quit India Movement (see Chapter 6). In addition, its fundamentally Brahmanical view of Hinduism limited its appeal in the south.

The Self-Respect Movement founded by E. V. Ramaswamy Naicker in 1925 also operated mostly outside formal politics. It was another movement of the 1920s whose propaganda and huge public meetings evoked and broadened social identities. The Justice Party was associated with high-caste Hindus and *zemindars*, whereas Ramaswamy's atheist vision of a reformed Dravidian society was aimed at low-caste Tamils in the Madras Presidency. It was particularly successful in raising the self-confidence of Tamil Muslims who had hitherto responded, as with the Khilafat agitation, to the leadership of the less numerous Urdu speakers. Ramaswamy, keeping his atheism in check, supported Muslim leaders in attacking 'irrational' customs in the local practices of Islam. Between 1927 and 1935 he ran virulent campaigns against (high-caste) Hindu society urging his low-caste listeners to convert to Islam where, he told them, their claim to human equality would be recognized. The legislation in Madras to allow temple entry to previously excluded castes was probably a response to this. In 1937 the movement found political expression when the Brahman Congress premier, Rajagopalachari, introduced compulsory Hindustani in 125 schools as a first instalment in a programme to draw the south into all-India politics. A reactive outburst of Tamil nationalism followed. Muslims were prominent in the demonstrations which led to the order being rescinded on the eve of the war. Hundreds, including Ramaswamy, went to prison in a movement where language and ethnicity meant more than religion.

By the end of the decade the Muslim search for political identity was bearing fruit. In the Punjab, the Ahrars and the Khaksars were active movements for radical social reform, the latter favouring Direct Action. In 1930 the poet Sir Muhammad Iqbal in an address to a poorly attended Muslim League called for the creation of a Muslim India, a north-western state incorporating Sindh, Baluchistan, the Punjab and the NWFP. He stressed that 'within the body-politic of India, the North-West Indian Muslims will prove the best defenders [of] India against foreign invasion, be that invasion one of ideas or of bayonets'.[10] Less influential at the time was the proposal by a Cambridge student to the Muslim delegates at the Round Table Conferences. It was more radical because it envisaged a state separate from an India which had been artificially united by Britain. Chaudhuri Rahmat Ali coined 'Pakistan': the *pak* (pure) land made up of the Punjab (P), Afghanistan/the NWFP (A), Kashmir (K), Sindh (S) and Baluchistan (tan).

Culture[11]

The inter-war years saw a great extension of civil society. Despite the dismal economic conditions, both new and reconfigured patterns of association and expression flourished providing a social counterpart to the growing linkages of political life. Even the habit of tea drinking, spreading after the First World War and even more after the second, no doubt facilitated wider patterns of social interaction.

Film also brought together people who would not normally have engaged in any shared activity. Concerned at the wider implications of this, the Imperial Conference of 1926 raised the possibility of Empire films to convey the 'right tone'. Nothing came of this despite the misgivings of the Indian Cinematographic Committee of 1927. The dominant Hollywood films of this period took the viewers, some paying only one *anna*, into the private spaces of European lives. In that year there were only 265 theatres and by 1939 there were 1,265 and an unknown number of travelling shows. Censorship had been introduced in the 1920s but the conservative conventions that were to ban on-screen kissing in the 1940s were not yet in place. Political controls, relaxed in 1937, returned during the war, and it became compulsory for cinemas to show the official Indian News Parade, dubbed in Indian languages, and Information Films of India.

Just as these government films, albeit from a government viewpoint, enlarged the public arena, Indian productions also built up a sense of shared cultural heritage. Even before the First World War, D. G. Phadke's historical and mythological films were being shown in cinemas from east Africa to Singapore. The 1920s saw social films; the 'modern woman' appeared in the hit of 1925, *Gun Sundari (Why Husbands Go Astray)*. By the late 1930s, Hindi films were becoming important with other regional productions, like the Bengali hit *Devdas* (1935), appearing in that language. A total of 283 films were made in 1947.

By contrast, broadcasting lagged. Listening was not cheap. By 1930 there were only 8,000 licences at Rs 10. By 1940 there were 85,000, but a radio set cost Rs 500. Nationalist leaders refused to broadcast until independence had been promised. Officials, impressed by the Soviet example, urged upon the government the potential benefits of broadcasting for rural development, but under the 1935 Government of India Act broadcasting remained a provincial subject. Eventually, the centre became concerned that local politicians might exploit the possibilities, or that Russian and German short-wave broadcasts might make an impact. Thus, the creation of All-India Radio set the scene for the vast expansion during the Second World War with broadcasts in 22 languages to the Far East, Middle East and Europe. The BBC began broadcasting to India in English in December 1932, mostly for expatriates or those with the literary tastes to enjoy George Orwell's wartime programmes.

The national pride of the middle classes was fanned by the achievements of Indian scientists. In the mid-nineteenth century B. N. Bose, the first Indian doctor trained in London, had returned to an unrecognized career in the public service. A government resolution regretted that Indians had not taken to modern science. A senior official considered that 'an Indian was temperamentally unfit to teach the exact method of modern science'.[12] Ronald Ross's ground-breaking work in Calcutta on malaria does not seem to have engaged local doctors. Yet, in the next generation remarkable figures overcame formidable obstacles. The brilliant mathematician, Srinivasa Ramanujan, once a clerk at Madras port, became a Fellow of the Royal Society in 1918 and a Fellow of Trinity College, Cambridge the next year. Though the government supported Marconi's work rather than J. C. Bose's on electric telegraphy, his election to the Royal Society brought belated official recognition in India. Another great scientist, Satyendranath Bose is remembered today as a co-founder with Einstein of quantum statistics. In 1930–31 the physicist Venkata Raman became the first Asian Nobel Prize winner in a science.

Nationalist aspirations were appearing in painting as Abanindranath Tagore sought to express *swadeshi* values in art. There was British encouragement for this, some unwitting. The Indian Museum in Calcutta dated from 1814. In the Great Exhibition of 1851 the Indian Court had been one of the most sumptuous. At the end of the century E. B. Havell, the politically conservative superintendent of the Calcutta School of Art, replaced the European casts and copies with an Indian fine art collection and supported artists trying to re-work indigenous styles. In Jamini Roy, India produced a modern painter of international interest. Rabindranath Tagore's school (1901) and university (1921) at Santiniketan sought to encourage the imagination, and the appreciation of local craft and design. His Nobel Prize for Literature in 1913 was a matter of national celebration as well as international recognition.

Western-educated nationalists led the music revival, also bringing and moderating dance traditions from the temple to the concert hall. Apart from C. R. Day, European musical appreciation was exceedingly rare. Congress began all-India music conferences in 1916, the first at Baroda. On an ancient base, new traditions of Karnatak as well as Hindustani music arose. Congress inspired a Madras Music Academy in 1927 and four years later there was a music course at the university.

Sport, in the form of cultivating indigenous traditions of wrestling, had appealed to the early nationalists. Western sports would also build up strength and give opportunities for confident self-assertion in an international context. Vivekananda told his followers that they would be nearer to heaven through football than the study of the Gita. It was a day never to be forgotten when Mohun Bagan of Calcutta, with ten of their players barefoot, beat the East Yorkshire Regiment in the Indian Football Association Shield in 1911. Bengal's preference for football has been variously attributed to the climate, the collectivist appeal of the game and the European racism associated with cricket.

Ironically, it was Lord Harris, the reactionary governor of Bombay, who encouraged Parsi cricket. This presidency match led to the Triangular Tournament (Parsis, Hindus, Europeans) in 1907, to the Quadrangular (with Muslims) in 1912 and finally to the Pentangular (with the 'Rest') in 1937. Although this reflected the communal trend of the inter-war years, there were also strongly integrative elements in the game which had become a national obsession by 1918. Baloo, the great spinner and Untouchable, eventually captained the team which had once left him outside the pavilion. A national side toured England in 1932 with C. K. Nayudu scoring a century on the first appearance at Lord's; and Douglas Jardine led a notably popular tour of India the following winter.

3. Constitutional Initiatives

The Simon Commission

When nationalist fortunes at the centre were at their lowest ebb, Birkenhead appointed a Statutory Commission of seven parliamentarians under Sir John Simon. A review of the constitution had been promised after ten years, but he called it early in 1927 fearing an incoming Labour government. 'You can readily imagine what kind of commission would have been appointed by Colonel Wedgwood [Benn] and his friends.'[13]

The all-British membership of the commission provoked the main parties and leaders to declare a boycott, thus achieving the unity which had eluded Gandhi and the other leaders since 1922. This decision came from the new viceroy, Lord Irwin (1926–31), who took the advice of officials from the Punjab where there was a strongly communal way of looking at Indian politics; individual Indians, they claimed, could only speak for their own region or community and not for the country as a whole. The government was now left looking for support from various minorities: Liberal ministers who had been working the councils; some Muslims, though not Jinnah; non-Brahmans; Anglo-Indians (as Eurasians were now called); Sikhs and Christians. The responses to the commission brought the question of legitimacy back to centre stage. Demonstrations on the theme of 'Go Home Simon' followed the commissioners around the country. After police dispersed a crowd in Lahore, Lajpat Rai died of his injuries.

The boycotters called an All-Party Conference and, responding to Birkenhead's taunt that they could never agree, formed a committee to draw up a constitution themselves. The (Motilal) Nehru Report, with important contributions by Sapru and the young Jawaharlal Nehru, was published in 1928 – 12,000 copies sold in six weeks. However, its aim of full dominion status under a unitary government dissolved the momentary unity and opened the communal divide with Muslims. Jinnah's debate with M. R. Jayakar, the conference president and Mahasabha leader established that there would be no concessions on communal provinces or provincial autonomy. There were to be joint electorates and reservations for Muslims only in minority provinces and at the centre. To many Muslims this sounded like a Hindu *raj*. Jinnah was reported to have called it the parting of the ways. The report's assumption that paramountcy over the states would pass to the envisaged Indian Commonwealth also alarmed the princes.

The younger generation in Congress represented by Jawaharlal Nehru and Subhas Chandra Bose was becoming restive. In 1927 Jawaharlal had attended the Brussels Congress Against Colonial Oppression and Imperialism and found himself made honorary president of the League Against Imperialism. The sense of international socialist solidarity made a deep impression on him, reinforced by a visit to the USSR on the eve of the great economic plans. At the Madras Congress in 1927, in Gandhi's absence, he and Bose passed a resolution to seek 'complete independence' from Britain. The following year at Calcutta, Bose was narrowly defeated when he returned to this goal. On the other hand, Malaviya secured an amendment to the report which guaranteed all titles to personal and private property. Challenges from the Left, Right and communalism were threatening to fragment Congress. Motilal persuaded Gandhi to return from social work to help restore unity.

Lord Irwin's Declaration

Irwin realized the importance of taking the political initiative. Gandhi was fresh from his success in the Bardoli *satyagraha*. In this district of Gujarat a campaign with V. Patel on behalf of the dominant Patidar farmers against a raised revenue assessment had just succeeded. There was widespread labour unrest in the country and the Depression was beginning to bite. The viceroy, therefore, secured the support of the Labour government and of the Conservative leader, Baldwin for his declaration of October 1929:

> I am authorised on behalf of His Majesty's Government to state clearly that in their judgement it is implicit in the declaration of 1917 that the natural issue of India's constitutional progress…is the attainment of Dominion status.[14]

The declaration provoked an outcry at Westminster from Churchill, Birkenhead and Austen Chamberlain supported by Liberals like Reading, and voiced through the *Daily Mail* and the Beaverbrook Press. A further ground for complaint was that the Simon Commission had not yet reported. The viceroy explained that that would be 'policy'; his statement of 'purpose' was justified by the urgency of the situation. He told Benn (Secretary of State, 1929–31) 'The big stake for which we are playing [is] the retention of India within the Empire.'[15]

Churchill now broke the bi-partisan approach to Indian politics. He believed that the promise of dominion status was tantamount to that of independence, and he could point to the definition of equality in the empire formulated at the Imperial Conference of 1926, soon to be enshrined in the Statute of Westminster (1931). Churchill's part in the recognition of the Irish Free State in 1921 may have troubled his conscience and provided ammunition for critics within his own party. He accepted the movement towards provincial self-government in India, but insisted on British control at the centre. He was alarmed at 'the growing lack of confidence at home in the reality of our mission' to rule India and protect the peasants and workers and minorities. Churchill resigned from the shadow cabinet in November 1930 and joined the Indian Empire Society, a new pressure group of retired civilians and imperial champions like Kipling, to warn 'of the dangers which now lie directly ahead of us'.[16]

Irwin's hopes that the declaration would draw the Congress leaders and Jinnah to London for a Round Table Conference (RTC) on constitutional progress were dashed. He believed that the hostile reception of his declaration in London had damaged confidence in India, reminiscent of the 1920 Hunter Commission.

In fact, Gandhi was briefly inclined to attend the RTC but the rising unrest in the country and divisions in Congress, whose presidency he had declined in 1929, probably changed his mind. Jawaharlal predictably found the declaration 'ingeniously worded' so that it 'could mean much or very little...the latter was the more likely contingency'.[17] Seeking to preserve Congress unity and focus the unrest, Gandhi demanded immediate dominion status, which the viceroy could hardly accept. Under Gandhi's guidance, the December 1929 Congress in Lahore voted for the achievement of *purna* (full) *swaraj* and authorized 'the All-India Congress Committee, whenever it deems fit, to launch upon a programme of Civil Disobedience including non-payment of taxes'.[18]

The First Round Table Conference

The first RTC gathered in London in October 1930. In the absence of Congress, there was Sapru and other Liberals, M. R. Jayakar of the Mahasabha, 16 Muslims led by the Agha Khan and including Jinnah, minority delegations – Sikhs, Parsis, Christians, Eurasians, Anglo-Indians, women, and the Justice Party – and another 16 speaking for the states. They now had before them the Simon Commission's recommendations for a full transfer of power in the provinces and, at the centre, an indirectly elected federal assembly to replace the CLA. This left the executive intact but restructured the legislature, and rejected the existing system of separate electorates. Irwin doubted that this would be workable and also came under strong pressure from Fazli Husain the Muslim *eminence grise*, who was not in London. A Reforms Despatch from Irwin in September 1930 modified the recommendations by proposing to restore some separate electoral arrangements and offering responsibility at the centre for all matters, except those held to be vital for British control: defence; foreign relations; internal security; high-level finance; and protection of minorities.

Before the delegates could come together to press for dominion status, there had to be agreement on the electorates. Yet the communal question could not be resolved. Simon had offered Muslims separate electorates everywhere on a population basis, or general electorates in the Muslim-majority provinces of Bengal and the Punjab with separate electorates and weightage in the minority provinces. Jinnah had been ready to trade the abandonment of separate electorates in return for representation by population in Bengal and the Punjab, a guaranteed third of the seats in the central legislature, and new provinces in Sindh, Baluchistan and the NWFP. At the first Round Table Conference Jinnah was trying to find a universal Muslim position that would be acceptable to the Muslim minority as well as the Muslim-majority provinces. As a consequence, according to the *Manchester Guardian*, 'Hindus thought he was a Muslim communalist, the Muslims took him to be pro-Hindu, the Princes deemed him too democratic, the British considered him to be a rabid extremist...'[19]

Fazli Husain was obdurate. He feared Jinnah would trade away separate electorates which were needed because of the narrow Muslim majorities in Bengal and the Punjab. He was determined that there should be no change at the centre before provincial self-government was fully established. To strengthen the Muslim position in an India of loose provinces, he also wanted Sindh, Baluchistan and NWFP, though here the British were not being very helpful. Referring to the NWFP claim, the Nehru Report said 'The inherent right of a man to smoke a cigarette must necessarily be curtailed if he lives in a powder magazine.'[20] The Mahasabha leaders, Jayakar and B. S. Moonje, would not accept the full Muslim claims and would not negotiate unless the Muslims first supported the demand for dominion status. The Muslims would not do this without prior agreement on the electoral provisions.

Civil Disobedience (CD)

Gandhi now launched the unifying symbolic initiative of naming 26 January as Independence Day. He announced that CD would only be called off on the fulfilment of 11 points embodying a spectrum of grievances: prohibition; reduction of the sterling/rupee ratio; reduction of land revenue; and abolition of the salt tax. In connection with the latter, he set off on 12 March 1930 to walk 240 miles to the sea at Dandi where he would heat some sea water and break the law by making untaxed salt. Irwin understood that this small elderly figure in a *dhoti* walking through a salt-producing area in his own province was aiming 'to shatter the psychological roots of collaboration on which the *raj* stood'.[21] However, he underestimated the scale of the impact. By 5 April when Gandhi reached the sea, the news cameras of the world were on him and at least 5,000 other breaches of the salt laws were taking place.

Violent news came from eastern India in mid-April with the Chittagong Armoury Raid by a group of Yugantar revolutionaries. In the north-west on the 23rd Abdul Ghaffar Khan was arrested in Peshawar and in the ensuing disorder the government faced a mutiny by a detachment of Garhwal Rifles and the loss of control of the city for a week. Ghaffar Khan was the leader of the Khudai Khitmatgars (KKs) of the NWFP, the only substantial Muslim group to join in CD and, notwithstanding the events in their capital city, to heed Gandhi's message of non-violence. The KKs were a Pathan nationalist movement reacting to British interference in Afghanistan where so many fellow-Pathans lived. They aimed at a reformation of their society disfigured by violent feuds which they partly attributed to the distorting effects of encroaching British rule. Since 40 per cent of the population who lived in the tribal areas paid no tax, the burden fell relatively heavily on the KK strongholds around Peshawar. For support they looked to Congress which 'is a *jirga* and not a Hindu body. It is a *jirga* composed of Hindus, Jews, Sikhs, Parsis and Muslims.'[22]

The conflict intensified. Gandhi's *Young India* carried 'Weekly War News'. Press censorship was tightened on 27 April. Most Congress leaders were arrested, including Gandhi on 5 May. On 15 May the CWC resolved on a complete boycott of foreign cloth and to continue the salt *satyagraha* but left new forms of CD, including non-payment of the land revenue, to local committees. In June Congress itself was declared unlawful. By the end of the year 90,000 people had been arrested and government had broken down in many patches of the country.[23] Except in the NWFP where the RAF had been used, the armed forces had not been required. Yet the level of repression was severe. Unsurprisingly, the 200,000 police escaped the 10 per cent cut in wages imposed on other public servants during the Depression. Hindu voters boycotted the September council elections. In Bombay province the turn-out fell to 8 per cent from 36 in 1926.

The Communal Award and the Poona Pact

On 26 January 1931 Gandhi and the CWC were released unconditionally as both Irwin and Benn wanted to reopen negotiations. Initial Muslim and princely support for some sort of federation made moves towards constitutional change seem possible. Gandhi, encouraged by business supporters, may have wanted to act before the declining CD weakened his hand. At the beginning of March Gandhi and Irwin reached an agreement. Both parties had difficulty selling this Delhi Pact to their supporters. Irwin agreed to the release of prisoners, though Gandhi did not press the case of the condemned Bhagat Singh (see below). The government made compromises over rural complaints and Gandhi accepted that land seized for non-payment of land revenue which had been sold would not be returned. CD was called off and, at the high point of his influence, Gandhi got the Karachi Congress to ratify the agreement. Many – the KKs, Congress Muslims, and Jawaharlal Nehru and the radical wing – were nonplussed by what they regarded as a sell-out. Despite this, there was a wide sense in India of victory. The viceroy and Gandhi had met as equals in the Delhi Pact, as an outraged Churchill recognized:

> It is alarming and also nauseating to see Mr Gandhi, a seditious Middle Temple lawyer, now posing as a fakir of a type well-known in the East, striding half-naked up the steps of the viceregal palace, while he is still organising and conducting a defiant campaign of civil disobedience, to parley on equal terms with the representative of the King-Emperor.[24]

Gandhi then went to the second RTC as Congress's sole representative and, as he told Prime Minister Macdonald, 'the sole genuine representative of the people'. He thought 'he could represent the Muslims and the Depressed Classes better than those who purported to do so'.[25] He explained: 'Congress claims to represent all Indian interests and classes…represents in its essence, the dumb semi-starved millions…in its 700,000 villages, no matter whether they come from what is called British India or Indian India.'[26] However, the Karachi resolutions by which he was bound made it difficult to negotiate fruitfully. They demanded the transfer of financial, military and foreign affairs. As before, the Muslims insisted on first clarifying the provincial position which meant agreeing on electorates. They and all the minorities except the Sikhs, who suggested dividing the Punjab, demanded separate electorates.

MacDonald broke the deadlock with his Communal Award which had less to do with population percentages than with Britain's political need to conciliate Muslims and keep them away from an anti-British front. Samuel Hoare (Secretary of State, 1931–35) stressed 'one of the basic principles of imperial policy was agreement…with the Moslem world'.[27] Fazli Husain had his way in the Punjab with 49 per cent of reserved seats for Muslims, 30 for Hindus and 18 for Sikhs who comprised 13 per cent of the population. In Bengal, Hindus had previously had 46 per cent to the Muslims' 39; this was reversed with Hindus at 32 and Muslims at 48. Muslims now had an interest in either a British centre or a weak centre while Congress sought the opposite.

The Award had granted separate electorates to Untouchables. These impoverished communities, 60 million strong, suffered exclusion from public facilities on the grounds of ritual uncleanness, and all manner of other social discrimination. They found a champion in Dr Ambedkar who, uniquely for someone of his background, had received higher education both in the USA and in London. He believed the fault-line in Hindu society was not between the high and low castes, but between the 'touchables' and the 'untouchables'. The extent of the challenge facing a reformer can be seen from Gandhi's efforts at Vaikom in Travancore in 1924–25. Though his campaign to open a road beside the temple to Untouchables succeeded, the temple itself remained closed to them until 1936.

Consultation by the Southborough Committee encouraged Ambedkar to mobilize his community, and his recommendations to the Simon Commission bore fruit with a quota of seats. The Nehru Report ignored them. At the first Round Table Conference, Ambedkar repeated the demand for reserved seats and universal suffrage – a property franchise was no good for the poor. This belatedly alerted Congress and the Mahasabha to the dangers of a split in the Hindu position. An All-India Depressed Classes Congress was called and

G. D. Birla, the wealthy businessman and Gandhi's friend, donated a fund to be devoted to social uplift. In order to undermine Ambedkar, a deal was struck – the Rajah-Moonje Pact – with Untouchable politicians who would stay within the Hindu fold.

At the second RTC, Gandhi challenged Ambedkar's right to speak for Untouchables and made his opposition clear to any sort of special treatment. When the Communal Award recognized them with 71 separate constituencies, Gandhi began a fast, the only time he used this weapon against an Indian politician. With Gandhi's health deteriorating, the pressure on Ambedkar became intense and he finally withdrew his claim for separate electorates. In the 1932 Poona Pact agreed between them, Ambedkar received instead 148 reserved seats, though they could not now benefit from political representation proportional to their numbers. Gandhi had won, but he acknowledged that Ambedkar 'has every right to be bitter, that he does not break our heads is an act of self-restraint on his part'.[28] He began to devote himself to the cause of those he now called *Harijans* (People of God). Attitudes needed changing and society reforming, but of the fundamental soundness of caste he had no doubt. He told Ambedkar that 'in accepting the Poona Pact you accept the position that you are Hindus'.[29] To the dismay of the secular-minded Tagore and Jawaharlal Nehru, he expressed confidence that:

> [N]ature will, without any possibility of mistake, adjust the balance by degrading a Brahmin, if he misbehaves himself, by reincarnating him in a lower division, and translating one who lives the life of a Brahmin in his present incarnation to Braminhood in the next.[30]

Ambedkar struggled with the hope of a new religion or identity which Untouchables could adopt. His greatest problem was that in looking for British support at such a time he opened himself to the charge of being a traitor to the nationalist movement. His constituency was divided. When Ambedkar founded his Independent Labour Party for the 1937 elections, he aimed to include numerous deprived groups, but most candidates were from his own Mahar community.[31] Literal untouchability was found in Bombay and the south, but extreme discrimination existed elsewhere; he pressed unsuccessfully on the 1932 Franchise Committee the idea of 'notional untouchability'.

CD: A Second Wave

On Gandhi's return, Congress acknowledged a spontaneous resumption of CD. Business withdrew support but terrorism spread across eastern India and, with the Depression at its deepest, rural unrest increased. This time the government responded immediately. Police arrested 120,000 people with most of the movement's leaders; Nehru was sentenced to two years. The ordinances of the new viceroy, Lord Willingdon, (1931–36) broke CD by early 1932. The shared religious outlook of Irwin and Gandhi was a thing of the past. Willingdon found him 'the most Machiavellian bargaining little humbug I have ever come across'.[32]

In June 1934 the ban on Congress was lifted and the debate began as to what lessons had been learned. CD had not had the breadth of appeal of Non-Cooperation. The big difference was the absence, the NWFP apart, of the Muslim population, some of whose spokesmen were now turning in an inward direction.

Bombay, Gujarat, Midnapur district in Bengal, and the Andhra area were most responsive, Madras and Punjab least. In the latter the government had remitted 24 per cent of the land revenue in 1931. Labour, exhausted by the great strikes of 1928 and discouraged by Congress business supporters, was not prominent. The presence of women both in demonstrations and in the prison population was notable.[33] For all, the shared hardships of the struggle and of prison had radicalized thousands.

Critically important were the upper peasants, the very class which Montagu-Chelmsford had begun to enfranchise to offset the hostility of the urban lawyers, teachers and merchants. The catastrophic fall in grain prices had stopped the flow of money back into the villages and had broken established links between local elites and the cultivators. Whether they turned for protection to Congress, or whether Congress or rival congressmen in search of constituencies turned to them, has been a matter of debate. Yet the sense that after 1919 the government was stepping back from the political arena was palpable.

The Poona Pact had aimed to heal divisions, but among the Bengali *bhadralok* politicians there was fury which expressed itself against the Muslims. In the wider national interest, the CWC had ignored their interests which were now championed in Congress by Bose. Gandhi expected them to give up 30 and Hindu Punjabis 8 of their precious seats to Untouchables.

4. The Depression: Indian Business Turns to Congress

The 1920s was a disappointing decade. The report in 1918 of the Indian Industrial Commission raised hopes with plans which by international standards were uniquely ambitious. They soon petered out. Montagu-Chelmsford assigned industry to the provinces so that a national strategy with appropriate administrative structures never developed. Public investment fell heavily. The great railway and irrigation projects were a thing of the past; except for the Lloyd Barrage in Sindh in the 1930s, by which time government investment was a quarter of what it had been even in the 1920s.

The war and international instability made Britain's financial interests a priority for London. The trend towards financial rather than industrial dominance had been evident before the war. In 1910, of the total foreign investment of £430 million in India, £158 million was in government securities, £194 million in railways with their 5 per cent guarantee, £11 million in mining and only £15 million in manufacturing and in the service sectors, especially, insurance and banking. The Fiscal Convention had assigned great powers to India, but the 1927 Currency Act partly negated them by ensuring that financial control stayed in London. With the rupee fixed at 1/6d, India, alone of the countries of the world, went to a ratio higher – 12.5 per cent – than before the war. When sterling went off gold in September 1931, Hoare, fearing an Indian debt default for which London would be responsible, blocked a plan to devalue the rupee by Sir George Schuster, the finance member. Overruled, Schuster protested at the deflationary effects of the existing ratio at a time of 'unprecedented agrarian depression…the most signal proof of India's subservience'.[34] The high exchange rate facilitated the transfer of the Home Charges but, by discouraging import substitution and making exports difficult, led to a balance of payments crisis which was averted by a massive outflow of gold, equivalent to a third of merchandise exports. With the approach of another constitutional change, monetary affairs were again taken out of the Indian political arena when a Reserve Bank was set up in 1934.

The Depression hit India hard; the fall in wholesale prices between 1929 and 1933 was greater than in any of the industrialized countries. India's share of world trade fell from 3.2 per cent in 1928 to 2.6 per cent in 1932. The second wave of the Depression between 1937 and 1939 was also unusually severe; wholesale prices in 1938 stood at 67.6 compared with 100 for 1922.

Agriculture had held up well until 1926, but in late 1930 wheat prices fell heavily with those of rice following the next year. Overall, prices fell by half between 1928 and 1933. Most exports were agricultural, those of jute fell by a third in value in the 1930s. With little coming in to money-lenders and traders, money stopped flowing back to the cultivators. Some legislation to prevent eviction for non-payment of rent was a faint response to the magnitude of the crisis, as was the 1934 Encumbered Estates Act in the UP where agrarian unrest was especially serious.

The Depression advanced trends in business already evident in the 1920s when output was worth half of what it had been before the war. British firms, which were export-oriented, experienced stagnant trade and falling profits.[35] By contrast Indian business was advancing in the 1930s, though cotton textiles, 30 per cent of manufacturing output, were hurt by the Depression and Japanese competition. In 1933 a third of Bombay's mills were idle, which gave rise to a deal with Lancashire, the Lees-Mody Pact. Indian business was quite divided; its organization, the Federation of Indian Chambers of Commerce and Industry (FICCI), was only formed in 1929. Ahmadabad, which, unlike Bombay, feared Lancashire more than Japan, reacted angrily to the pact. This did not stop the Left from denouncing Lees-Mody as a fascist compact, nor prevent the Soviet view that it was an understanding with the 'more reactionary part of the Indian bourgeoisie in the interests of British capitalism'.[36] The evidence scarcely supports the Marxist analysis that there were two elements in Indian business: the manufacturing sector, which was anti-imperialist, and a *compradore* or commercial sector linked to British interests.

The Depression accelerated another trend seen after the war whereby some businessmen lacking any point of pressure on the government began to turn to Congress. The deflationary currency ratio was a grievance and the outflow of gold, which seemed to come from enforced sales of personal savings in the villages, was offensive to national pride. There was strong dissatisfaction with the implications for India of the imperial preference established in 1932 at the Ottawa Imperial Economic Conference. Nor did Lees-Mody yield any appreciable gains. The government appeared indifferent to Indian business interests. Governor Norman of the Bank of England had told Schuster: 'Do nothing: stand fast.'[37] Willingdon's 1933 economic conference proved feebly cautious. Schuster's successor, Sir James Grigg, believed in an even tighter deflationary policy, and in 1936 ousted the more liberally minded governor of the 'independent' Reserve Bank. As Misra and Omissi have argued, the relationship at this period of government with business, British and Indian, was neither collaborative nor coercive.[38] It was neutral and focused on London's need for financial stability. But from 1936–37 the balance of trade moved in favour of India. The economic fundamentals of the imperial relationship were changing.

5. Socialism's Limited Success

In the inter-war years, socialism, as in other countries, seemed to promise more than it could deliver. Its basic idea of equality, though not alien to India, confronted a hierarchical society, where even in the 1940s there were still 10 classes on the railways. Similarly, the concept of class was for most less familiar than *jati* and the traditional forms of association. Dr Ambedkar did not lead his 60 millions of the most deprived Indians into the high-caste led Marxist parties, believing that property was not at the root of the main forms of domination: 'Why do millionaires in India' he asked, 'obey penniless *Sadhus* and *Fakirs?*[39] However, an industrial proletariat several million strong was forming on the railways and in the textile industry, but it was geographically scattered and divided.

The Communist Party of India (CPI) was founded at Tashkent in 1920 by M. N. Roy from émigré Khilafat protesters – evidence that secular and religious ideology were not incompatible. Organization in the country was difficult. The charismatic Roy was not a team player, and he spent most of the inter-war years either outside India or in prison. In 1924–25 to avoid the police he set up with the help of the famous poet, Kazi Nazrul Islam, the Bengal Peasants and Workers Party to work as a front organization inside Congress. The CPI, however, was crippled by the twists and turns of Comintern orders from Moscow. In 1928 it had to follow the ultra-left line, which prohibited cooperation with Congress or the All-India Trade Union Congress. When the Popular Front policy was adopted in 1935, the CPI was ordered back to Congress until the 1941 order to support the 'people's war'. The next year it was legalized and opposed the Quit India Movement (see Chapter 6).

Of other groups which combined Marxism and nationalism the best known was the Hindustan Socialist Republican Army. Its leader, Bhagat Singh, 'for a time' as a police report put it, 'bid fair to oust Mr Gandhi as the foremost political figure of the day'.[40] Irwin survived an attack on his train, but after Bhagat Singh threw a bomb into the CLA he was caught and executed in 1931.

Government repression was severe, especially if there was a trade union connection. The great industrial strikes of the late twenties, though fragmented and poorly organized, went on for a long time. In 1929 the government passed a Trade Disputes Act, to prohibit political strikes, and a Public Safety Act, under which dozens of trade union leaders were arrested. Roy was tried in the 1924 Cawnpore Conspiracy Case and in the bigger Meerut Conspiracy Case in 1929. In 1927 the government had been disturbed by the visit to Bombay of the Communist MP for Battersea North, S. Saklatvala, a member of the Tata business family. The writings of the British communist R. Palme Dutt were another concern; the number of students had increased by a third in a stagnant economy since Montagu-Chelmsford had put education under provincial control.

The carrot as well as the stick was used. To engage constructively with workers there was the Trade Union Act (1920) and legislation for Workers' Compensation (1923), Maternity Benefits (1929), and Payment of Wages (1933).

In Congress the socialists had a rival for political legitimacy. In the year the CPI was founded, Congress was setting up a national organization. Such was the appeal of its nationalist message that soon there were 300,000 members in the UP alone, more than the entire Bolshevik Party in its early years or the Chinese Communist Party at the time of the Northern Expedition.[41] In terms of support in the 1920s, no other colonial liberation struggle in Asia or Africa was remotely comparable to Congress.

In 1934 a Congress Socialist Party was formed. Though Nehru and Bose were not in the group they were looked to as supportive leaders. Nehru for all his mercurial radicalism did not forget that Congress was less a party than an arena where the claims of different groups were brokered. This put a check on his radicalism in practice. As the industrialist Birla explained, he 'seems to be a typical English democrat...out for giving expression to his ideology, but he realizes that action is impossible and does not press for it'.[42] He had a similar view of the Bengal Tiger: 'Mr Bose can be relied upon to help Tata Iron and Steel Works whenever necessary... His main object in labour matters is no doubt service to labour but not necessarily inimical to the capitalist.'[43]

Congress was committed to its 1931 Karachi Declaration on fundamental rights which business feared could lead to damaging outcomes under Nehru's influence. This and the burst of trade union militancy in 1935 were the background to the 1936 Bombay Manifesto, produced by 21 businessmen as a call for a propertied front to check subversive Leftism which would undermine 'the common purpose of all patriotic Indians, namely self-government for India'.[44] This implicit offer of money in return for assurances strengthened the Congress turn to constitutionalism before the 1937 elections.

Gandhi warned 'that it is most dangerous to make political use of labour until labourers understand the political condition of the country and are prepared to work for the common good'.[45] He had a vision of a world without exploitation, but it was attainable not through revolution but by patient harmony. Congress was a nationalist movement against colonial rule which class conflict would only prolong. Not all revolutionaries made the distinction. Those who seized the Chittagong armoury in 1931 declared: 'Gandhi's Raj has come!' In this sense Lenin may have been right in 1920 when he considered Gandhi to be objectively revolutionary, and Roy wrong when he persuaded Lenin to doubt 'whether an anti-imperialist movement inspired by reactionary social ideas and burdened with obscurantist religious beliefs, could be politically revolutionary'.[46]

6. Federation and the States

At the first RTC though the absent Congress was committed to the unitary constitution of the Nehru Report, the federal idea seemed for a time to have a future. The strongest support came from Conservative politicians who wanted federation to replace dominion status as the focus of debate, and consoled themselves that a large princely element would act as a brake on nationalist activity. For the Liberals, Reading concurred. Even Benn, the secretary of state (1929–31), thought it 'worth exploring, for there is a very large body of thinkers in India and England who in their secret hearts feel that "responsible" government based on parliamentary democracy is not a suitable system for India'.[47] Among Muslims, Jinnah wanted the federation 'to be a real one', though Fazli Husain's view that provincial autonomy and the new Muslim provinces must come before any discussion about a responsible centre prevailed.[48] However, it was the princes who took up the idea, aware that it gave them a veto on the form of the future central government.

The princes had been dismayed by the Indian States (Butler) Committee which reported in March 1929. It rejected their *legal* definition of paramountcy, and upheld the view expressed by Reading in a letter to the Nizam in 1926: 'The right of the British Government to intervene in the internal affairs of Indian States is another instance of the consequences necessarily involved in the supremacy of the British Crown.'[49]

In fact, the Nehru Report was much more threatening in its assumption that the states would pass under a future Indian Commonwealth. In some states democratic politics were stirring; in 1930 a States' Peoples Conference was meeting in Bangalore. Nothing could be expected from the nationalist Congress. Jawaharlal's socialist hopes for planned economic transformation inspired by the Soviet Union, had no place for a patchwork of traditional and personal governments. Although Gandhi's father had been a minister in a princely state, he was profoundly unsympathetic: 'I should resist the tyranny of Indian princes just as much as that of the English.'[50] He gave much prominence to tales of extravagance: not Baroda's universal primary education before the First World War, rather Kapurtala as a patron of Paris jewellers.

At first, there was cautious enthusiasm. Hyderabad was prepared to enter a federation on an equal footing with the provinces of British India. Mysore, too, was ready to come in. 'I am not sure...' wrote Irwin, 'that they may not have some ideas in their minds of using federation to get rid of the exercise of paramountcy.'[51] Yet for most states, the lack of constitutional development implied that entry into a federation with British India would be a distant prospect. Paragraph 58 of the Butler Report meant that there was no pressure on the states to reform their government. It stated that their relations were with the Crown conducted through the viceroy and that they could not be transferred to a responsible government of India against their wishes.

The princes were deeply divided, except in their growing desire to assert their sovereignty against paramountcy. Bikaner, representing the middling states, suggested that entry into a federation should be mediated through the Chamber of Princes, something to which the large and proud southern states would not agree. The scores of small states realised that in such an event they would disappear into larger units. More appealing to most, though not to the large and influential states, was Patiala's proposal for a *confederation* of states, which would then deal collectively with a British Indian federation. Since most states were predominantly Hindu, Muslims were expressing concern at an outcome that would greatly strengthen the Hindu element in a central government. Growing differences seemed to make federation an even more distant prospect.

Just when federation seemed to be fading as an idea, it had become a political necessity in London. In October 1931, shortly before the second RTC, the National Government was formed whose mainly Conservative supporters would only permit changes to the centre which had a strong princely element. In 1933, the year of the third RTC at which only states' ministers attended, a white paper was published declaring that in the coming Government of India Act each ruler would be asked to sign an instrument of accession declaring which elements of sovereignty could be transferred to a federal centre. It had been decided at the end of the second RTC that the federation would only come into being if agreed on by the states with over half the states' total population, provided that these included not less than half of the states individually represented in the Upper Chamber. The states would have 104 out of 260 seats in the Upper Chamber and 125 out of 375 in the Lower Chamber.

The causes of the demise of princely India have been sought in the closing days of British India, but the work of Professors Moore and Manor more plausibly redirects us to earlier times.[52] The federal proposal has raised subsequent debate about whether, had an agreement been reached, the partition of India could have been avoided. The idea of federation was probably a chimera; the decision to abandon Curzon's interventionism for a policy of non-interference in 1909 had left the states in a time-warp.

7. The Government of India Act, 1935

Churchill's opposition helped to slow down the passage through Parliament of the Government of India Bill, a 'monstrous monument of shame built by the pygmies' which with its 473 clauses and 16 schedules blocked out most other business and delayed a general election.[53] He represented the unpopularity of the National Government's policy in the constituencies and the fury of Lancashire MPs who had learnt that London would lose all say over tariffs. In 1933, Churchill almost defeated the government.

However, in 1935 Parliament passed the Government of India Act with a majority of 264; 122 MPs, of whom 84 were Conservatives, voted against the bill despite Sir Samuel Hoare's claim that it would enable India to 'take her place among the fully self-governing members of the British Commonwealth of Nations'.[54] Burma was excluded; it was henceforth to be a separate entity. The franchise was extended to about 35 million voters. Lord Lothian's Franchise Committee had considered and rejected universal suffrage, recently adopted in Ceylon. Registration criteria differed in the provinces, but the overall aim was a male-female ratio of 5:1. The Communal Award and Poona Pact percentages were kept unchanged.[55]

The British plan was to grant provincial autonomy to its friends and collaborators and to keep control of the centre where dyarchy, abolished in the provinces, reappeared. Here, defence and external affairs were kept in the viceroy's hands; monetary matters had been moved to a semi-independent Reserve Bank the previous year. Section 102 of the Act, however, gave the viceroy powers to direct the federal legislature to make laws in an emergency. The establishment of provincial self-government was almost complete, though Section 93 similarly allowed the governors to take over the administration of a province in an emergency. Dominion status was not mentioned. The plan for the centre was federation, but only after provincial autonomy had been established. The federation could only proceed after the states had agreed to enter it. They would negotiate their entry individually, while the provinces of British India would enter automatically. During the Round Table Conferences, the question of residuary powers became a bugbear. The Muslims and the Punjab government wanted them to lie with the provinces, whereas others wanted a stronger centre. There were attempts to fudge this unresolved issue by chopping up legislative powers at different levels, whilst leaving the governor-general with the discretion to assign powers in particular cases to different levels.

8. The 1937 Election

Congress was in disarray after the suppression of CD and the arrest of its leaders. The Communal Award had sown dissension in its ranks, temporarily resolved by neither accepting nor opposing it. Congress had earlier rejected the 1933 white paper on which the Government of India Act was to be based, and called for a constituent assembly where the future constitution could be decided by Indians in India. Nevertheless, the 1935 Act was to come into force on 1 April 1937 and before that elections were to be held. In response to this challenge, three trends emerged.

First, Gandhi left national politics for 'constructive work', touring the country engaged in *harijan* uplift and the promotion of *khaddar* and spinning. This was interrupted by one of India's most destructive earthquakes when

6,000 square miles of Bihar were utterly devastated. The relief organization of the Congress leader, Prasad, won national renown.

Second, mass agitation still had its supporters. Civil Disobedience had trained and politicized thousands of men and women in the towns and had damaged the legitimacy of the Raj. From the right of Congress, Vallabhbhai Patel thought that one more surge might carry the day. On the left, the socialist element, formalized in 1934 by the creation of the Congress Socialist Party (CSP) had no interest in constitutional politics.

Third, the voice of the *swarajist* wing was being heard in this vacuum. Birla, who was to contribute Rs 500,000 to the electoral fund, and other industrialists wanted Congress to represent their interests to government. After the third RTC, the government had reverted to a Simon Commission approach of working out a constitution in London. Yet, as Rajagopalachari pointed out, as well as the need to contest the federal proposals, there were possibilities in the Act. This could be seen in the localities where Congress was making steady advances in board elections and in the CLA election where in 1943 it won 44 of the 88 elected seats.

Internal reasons to participate became even more persuasive. Without focused national leadership, local Congress committees were going their own way. To curb the flourishing factionalism, the Congress's constitution of 1934 gave greater powers to the CWC which at Lucknow in 1936 authorized its parliamentary wing, the Swaraj Party, to prepare for the elections. Campaigning would draw Congress together as well as strengthen central control. Gandhi's recognition of the need to restore central authority can be seen in his support for Nehru's presidency in 1936. Though not a member of the CSP, Nehru was its champion and would, it was hoped, curb its excesses. Nehru, who had emerged as a national figure and a charismatic speaker, travelled 50,000 miles during the election campaign. Local notables flocked to join Congress. Ordinary membership rose from 640,000 in 1936 to over three million a year later. With fragmented rival parties, in many areas the choice had become simplified: Congress or the Raj.

By March 1937 the results were in.[56] Thirty-five million people or 13.3 per cent of the population were entitled to vote (instead of the 2.75 per cent that had been enfranchised since 1919), and 54.5 per cent of the electorate did so, though in the NWFP the turn-out was 73 per cent. Congress had majorities in five, later eight, of the eleven provinces, winning outright in Madras, Bihar, UP, CP and Orissa and securing dominant positions in Assam, Bombay and the NWFP. The scale of the triumph can be seen in the provincial assemblies where Congress won 711 of the 808 general seats. Most significantly, those upper peasants, who were enfranchised with the expectation that they would hold off the nationalists, had done the opposite and voted Congress.

The Depression had broken old links in the countryside. In Bihar and UP Kisan Sabhas, with links to the CSP, campaigned against the landlords. It seems that in Madras, upper peasants, losing the services and the deference of the very poor, looked for support from Congress rather than the government whose officials generally kept out of the elections. A rural magnate was reported as saying in 1936: 'The British are finished; government is not something you can give away.'[57] Having invited Congress to play the constitutional game, the government had lost and could never again plan the future without Congress participation. Equally, the scale of the victory drew Congress decisively into constitutional politics which for all but seven years, it had boycotted in the inter-war period.

However, Congress's showing in Muslim seats was meagre; of 489, it achieved only 26 victories of which 19 were in the NWFP. But the Muslim League had no reason to rejoice. There were minor successes in UP and Bombay but overall it received less than five per cent of Muslim votes. It finished with no seats in Bihar or Orissa, nor in the strongly Muslim states of Sindh and the NWFP and won only 23 per cent of Muslim seats overall. As for the two great Muslim-majority states, the League had one seat in the Punjab and – a solitary success – formed a coalition with the KPP in Bengal.

The League's massive electoral failure is often seen as a turning-point in Jinnah's career; as it was for his health, for 1937 saw the onset of the lung disease which was to kill him in 1948. Montagu-Chelmsford had marked a shift away from the elite politics of the centre at which he excelled. After he had been shouted down by Gandhi's supporters at the 1920 Nagpur Congress, he had left Congress, and in the early 1930s was living in London. On his return he revived the League and joined with Congress in the CLA to vote against the Ottawa Trade Agreement in 1935 and well as the budgets of 1935 and 1936. For the 1937 election the League offered a manifesto which championed Urdu, avoided any threats to private property, and remembered the Lucknow Pact which recalled both separate electorates and national unity.

The success of the League depended upon persuading the Muslim-majority provinces that they needed a single voice at the centre. Provincial politics suited Fazli Husain, and after his death in 1936, Sikander Hayat Khan. Reliant on a cross-communal appeal, their Unionist Party dominated the Punjab, and viewed proposed developments of a federal centre with suspicion. The politics of Bengal were fractured and complicated, but a basic difficulty was that whereas the League was dominated by landed gentry, Fazlul Haq's KPP promised the abolition of *zemindari* without compensation. Jinnah therefore depended for support on the minority provinces, for which the reserved seats were essential – though Jinnah himself seems to have believed that a safer long-term solution would come from offering joint electorates in return for a new arrangement at the centre. Reserved seats also removed the necessity of electoral organization, as he found at his cost. Jinnah could not afford to be too explicit about his tactics as he tried to convince Muslims in both majority and minority provinces, and Congress, and the British government that, despite the election results, he, through the League, was the sole spokesman for Indian Muslims.

9. Congress Raj, 1937–39

In retrospect, the Congress victory at the polls has been seen as a fatal blow to the Raj. Yet, at the time many congressmen were by no means committed to the constitutional path and it took several months to form ministries. Nehru had only entered the elections on the understanding that the object was not to take office but to undermine the constitution from within. But there was pressure from below on the leadership, and from the example of non-Congress governments being formed. Gandhi, after reassurance regarding the governors' restraint in the use of emergency powers, supported acceptance of ministerial office provided the mentality 'remains the same as in 1920.'[58] In the end, it was a way of re-asserting control by the CWC, directed by the triumvirate of Patel, Prasad and Abdul Kalam Azad, who did not take office themselves.

The viceroy, Lord Linlithgow (1936–43), has been accused of 'having found an obstacle for every solution', which only prodding from London would overcome.[59] Yet, from his perspective there was no reason to hasten the formation of these ministries. The object of the 1935 Act had been to hold off Congress with a federal centre where it would never have a majority over the minorities and the princes. Congress, of course, opposed the federation and demanded a constituent assembly. It was on this federal centre that the viceroy now fell back. Everything turned on the princes who were supposed to negotiate their instruments of accession by 1938. However, Congress's democratizing campaigns in the states throughout that year had alarmed them; and communal conflict seemed to be spreading from British India into some states, notably Hyderabad. Gandhi's *satyagraha* in Rajkot, where his father had been *diwan*, was unsuccessful, but some large states like Mysore felt threatened by these movements. In the end, Congress reversed gear, fearing that the agitation was outside the control of the CWC and could assist the Bose faction. The frightened princes did not respond to Linlithgow's offer of fiscal concessions and in September 1939 federal negotiations were suspended for the war. They knew that foot-dragging would always receive Conservative party support; the 1935 Act was better suited to the contemporary political needs of Britain than to those of India.

The formation of the Congress provincial governments has been widely identified as the point where relations with the Muslim League took an irremediably divisive turn. In much of India, Congress was now seen as the government and its organizations began replacing state institutions. 'Bande Mataram', a hymn from *Anandamath*, Bankim's novel with anti-Muslim overtones, was declared a national anthem in 1937. Notwithstanding this, Congress, in order to strengthen its claim to be a secular organization representing the nation, ran a mass contact campaign to recruit Muslim members, which the League countered with its two-*anna* membership drive. Allegations that a pre-election agreement on coalition in the UP was broken have been shown to refer to local informal understandings. Nevertheless, the UP Tenancy Act, introduced by the Congress government, was damaging to the *taluqdars*, most of whom were Muslim. This state was crucially important for the future Pakistan movement. Here, among the Muslim elite there was a sense that their standing had been irretrievably damaged by the Congress victory. In Bengal, where Congress was the largest party, a coalition with the KPP was prevented by the CWC. Jinnah, no doubt, felt bitter after his earlier cooperative approach in the CLA. The Congress doctrine stating that its governments were responsible to the electorate through the CWC seemed to rule out cooperation on principle.

Chapter 6

THE IMPACT OF WAR, 1939–1945

1. Direct Rule

When Britain declared war on Germany, India as a dependency was automatically at war too. Linlithgow has been blamed for needlessly antagonizing Congress by declaring war without consultation. Probably, the provocation was intended. In April 1939, with London's approval, another section had been added to the 1935 Government of India Act which facilitated the replacement of provincial governments by direct rule in a wartime emergency. In August Linlithgow had ignored Congress's protests at the precautionary despatch of Indian troops to Egypt, Aden and Singapore. Later in the summer of 1940 a Revolutionary Movement Ordinance was prepared which clearly had Congress in mind:

> India can now best fulfil her destiny and take her due place among the nations of the world only after the total extinction of the political party which at this vital juncture has seen fit to betray them.[1]

In deference to US opinion, 'total extinction' was excised from what was now termed the Emergency Powers Ordinance. It would be two years before Congress provided the opportunity for the use of these powers.

For Linlithgow direct rule in wartime would be more efficient than the compromises and adjustments involved in a deal with Congress and its fractious provincial governments. He was able to find Liberal and Muslim support; all but three of his Council were Indian, but not party men. As Philips has argued, 'the test of his every action was the survival of Britain and the empire'.[2]

In fact, Gandhi and especially Nehru, who had been involved in anti-fascist international politics, were not immediately antagonized by the declaration of war. However, they demanded an announcement about war aims and their relevance to India's self-governing future. It was Linlithgow's bland response which led to the CWC order to all Congress governments to resign – which they did, some reluctantly, by November – and its call for immediate independence and the summoning of a constituent assembly.

Gandhi was the initiator, though Nehru admitted that for some time he had wanted Congress to leave office because power had brought corruption and division into the fold. It had not been easy for these governments to meet expectations. The Niemeyer Award of 1936 had given 50 per cent of income tax to the provinces, but 45 per cent of income came from land revenue which could not be increased in the continuing Depression. The Congress policy of prohibition cut out an important additional source of income, in Bombay, 26 per cent of the total. The resignation of the ministries would allow the CWC to reassert control and prepare for the possibility of renewed Civil Disobedience. At the national level there was a similar tightening of CWC control when, in 1939, Gandhi forced Bose to resign from the presidency to which he had been re-elected. Bose did not share a belief in non-violence, seeing the war as an opportunity to overthrow British rule. He responded by trying to draw left and anti-imperialist elements into a Forward Bloc, but Gandhi ensured he was excluded from office for three years.

2. The Lahore Resolution

Muslims in the minority provinces, excluded in the triumphalist rush for jobs and favours responded to Jinnah's call to mark the Congress decision to resign in 1939 as a 'Deliverance Day' – as did Dr Ambedkar. Muslim support now appeared as a fallback position for a viceroy confronted by Congress electoral victory and unhelpful princes. The Muslim League with Linlithgow's encouragement began to fill the political vacuum. In October 1939, he assured Muslims that 'full weight would be given to their views and interests'. Jinnah had given him 'valuable help against Congress claims and [he] was duly grateful'.[3] It was important for world opinion that the government should have relations with Indian politicians, and the viceroy asked Jinnah for a statement of the League's 'constructive policy'.

Jinnah made agreements with the Punjab Unionists and the KPP in Bengal, which were only weakly to his advantage, because he needed some leverage. Though League membership was rising – to 2 million by 1944 – he could only claim to speak for all Muslims if he could meet the different requirements of both the majority and minority provinces. The former were relatively satisfied with the status quo of British rule at the centre. The minority provinces needed a spokesman to secure protection at the centre. Yet as Jinnah knew, separate electorates were now a poor safeguard. Even in the unlikely event of Muslims voting together, they would still be in a minority.

Jinnah's Lahore Resolution of March 1940 solved the problem. He presented Muslims not as a minority amounting to a quarter of the population, but as a nation to be treated equally. The Resolution also announced a solution to the federal problem. It proposed two federations of Muslim-majority states, one in the north-west, the other in the north-east. Existing provincial borders would be respected implying that the consequent non-Muslim minorities would be a safeguard for Muslims left in Hindu-majority states. These two federal groupings would be sovereign but there would be arrangements to cover matters in common with the other groups.

Though neither 'Pakistan' nor 'partition' were mentioned, there is a standard view, expressed by Wolpert, Anita Inder Singh and many others that this was the moment when Jinnah declared his intention and Pakistan was born. Ayesha Jalal has pointed out that there was no reference to a centre, that the proposal was highly generalized and not cast in religious form; 'this is a question of minorities and it is a political issue'.[4] His reference to protection for minorities in 'constitutions' rather than treaties suggests that Jinnah was not thinking of full separation – at least in the short run. He had earlier told his followers to prepare for another 25 years of British rule.

Designed to draw necessary support from the majority provinces, the Resolution may have been in Jinnah's mind a bargaining position for some sort of constitutional guarantees at a federal centre. What it meant, and would mean, to his followers was another matter. Muslim politics was about to be driven by popular enthusiasm rather than elite calculation. Soon, 'Pakistan' *was* mentioned, and a flag and an anthem were invented; within three years the League was in government in Bengal, Assam, Sindh and the NWFP.

Did Linlithgow exacerbate the communal division by beginning to treat Jinnah as the sole spokesman for Indian Muslims? With the invasion of Britain apparently imminent, and under pressure from Labour ministers in the coalition government, the viceroy issued his August 1940 statement to try to enlist support for the war:

> It goes without saying that they [the British Government] could not contemplate transfer of their present responsibilities for the peace and welfare of India to any system of government whose authority is directly denied by large and powerful elements in India's national life… But… they will most readily assent to the setting up after the conclusion of the war with the least possible delay of a body representative of the principal elements in India's national life in order to devise the framework of the new constitution…[5]

Churchill's redrafting had weakened it and offered hopes to Pakistan's supporters. In protest, Gandhi began a personal *satyagraha* in which 22,000 who followed his example were convicted.

3. The Cripps Mission: 22 March–12 April 1942

The Mission was the outcome of a critical moment in the war. Churchill was in Washington when on 2 January 1942 he received a telegram from Sapru and other Liberals for 'some bold stroke far-sighted statesmanship called for without delay in India, at this hour of growing danger to her safety, to enlist her wholehearted active co-operation intensifying war effort'. The Japanese attack on Pearl Harbor had brought America into the war three weeks earlier, and it was a matter of vital concern for Churchill to secure President Roosevelt's support for Britain's war effort. Leo Amery (Secretary of State, 1940–45) told Linlithgow that Winston, after being so negative when anything constructive was proposed had 'seen the red light (especially the American red light) overnight'.[6] The military reverses of early 1942 had made Churchill's own position insecure. Nominating his Labour colleague in the War Cabinet, Sir Stafford Cripps, to take a generous offer to India, Attlee declared 'There is a precedent for such action. Lord Durham saved Canada to the British Empire. We need a man to do in India what Durham did in Canada.' An insider view was that 'if he brought this Indian settlement off, Cripps would certainly replace Winston'.[7]

An unreceptive Linlithgow told Amery that this was no time to deal with the CWC which 'with the possible exception of Nehru...[is] a collection of declining valetudinarians who have no grip on the country but, who, politically are purely parasitic on Gandhi the spell-binder'. Britain should stand firm and take no chances. Singapore fell on 15 February and Rangoon on 8 March; on 9 April US forces in Bataan surrendered. The Japanese had occupied the Andaman Islands on 23 January and in early April were mounting air raids on Indian ports in the Bay of Bengal. Since India and Burma 'are in the Empire because they are conquered countries', the viceroy wrote, their sympathies were more likely to lie with Britain's enemies. Attlee found this statement 'astonishing'. 'If it were true it would form the greatest possible condemnation of our rule in India and would amply justify the action of every extremist in India.'[8]

Cripps met Nehru and the Congress president Abul Kalam Azad and offered immediate entry to the Viceroy's Executive Council; and, at the end of the war, dominion status with the right to secede from the Commonwealth. He also offered a constituent assembly elected from the provincial legislatures, with individual provinces given the right not to join, and with the states empowered to appoint representatives. Cripps and Attlee expected the long-term part of the offer to be the main inducement. Congress, however, was interested in immediate gains. The negotiation turned principally on two aspects of entry to the viceroy's council. Would this mean the formation of a Congress cabinet or just, as Churchill intended, more Indian members? Would the new Indian defence member, insisted upon by Congress, have an effective or peripheral voice in the control of the armed forces?

It has been claimed that Churchill intended the Cripps Mission to fail, a view expressed by nationalists and US observers at the time.[9] His opportunity to ensure this arose with a wrangle over the responsibilities of the defence member. A formula was found by Colonel Louis Johnson, President Roosevelt's representative, who had been drawn into the negotiations. Discovering this going on behind his back, Linlithgow appealed to London where the prime minister killed the initiative. H. V. Hodson, the reforms commissioner of the Indian government, blamed the War Cabinet for cutting the viceroy out of the negotiations and Cripps for beginning his negotiations with his maximum position and exceeding his brief by suggesting that the revised Executive Council would act like a cabinet. That brief had been drafted hastily. Amery explained how busy Churchill was with the Far Eastern Crisis and 'he has grudged the time and labour he has given to trying to do what he has never done before, master even the elements of the Indian problem'.[10]

Though the British side has been blamed for the breakdown, Peter Clarke's examination of times and dates shows that Congress had already rejected the mission.[11] Rajagopalachari and Azad were in favour as, initially, was Nehru. Even the ultra-nationalist Savarkar told the government that the Mahasabha, which supported the war, would be openly enthusiastic if the 'vivisection' clause was dropped and independence granted now. Nevertheless, the other leaders were suspicious of the usual small print in British promises. Independence was there but not named; the states' powers seemed to perpetuate princely autocracy; the right of provinces not to join sanctioned a Pakistan – though the offer was framed to divide majority from minority provinces. Amery acknowledged in a letter to the viceroy that 'the nest contains the Pakistan cuckoo's egg. But they [Congress] have got to face the fact that it is for them to find a compromise which will induce the Moslems to drop Pakistan.'[12] Cripps blamed Gandhi for the breakdown. Although he took no part in the negotiations his disapproval was well-known. He hated the idea of a divided India and of a divided Congress. His rejection of a 'post-dated cheque on a failing bank' reflected the general level of distrust.[13] The distrust was shared by Amery and his Conservative colleagues: 'most of us feel like someone who has proposed to a particularly unprepossessing damsel for family or financial reasons and finds himself lucky enough to be rejected'.[14]

The Cripps Mission reflected the need to appease Labour in the coalition government and to satisfy the Americans that something was being offered. Churchill told Cripps that 'the effect throughout Britain and in the United States has been wholly beneficial'. Although even he realized that 'in India we shall be bound by the Americans…to all the promises we have given'.[15] There could be no going back on the *de facto* offer of independence. However, like the idea of Pakistan, the terms and the timing were open to negotiation.

4. Quit India

The Cripps Mission had failed and the question of Pakistan hung unresolved. Gandhi was pondering what initiative could retain unity and meet the pressing expectations of the movement. Senior civilians were calling on the government to deflate Gandhi by ignoring him. Meanwhile plans were being laid for drastic measures against Congress if Civil Disobedience were resumed.

The news from the war-fronts was turning the slow erosion of British prestige into an avalanche of disaffection. The governor of Bombay reported that the reverses in North Africa were widely known and that panic could be expected if the German army reached the Nile valley. Japanese warships in the Bay of Bengal raised fears of invasion. Large numbers fled to India from Ceylon. Thousands left Madras when the government moved to Ootacamund in the hills. The lack of any British response to air raids panicked two-thirds of the port city of Vizagapatnam to flee inland. By the autumn the largest migration in history had occurred as 600,000 fled from Burma, 80,000 dying en route. The stories which they brought of the military and moral collapse of the eastern empire were reinforced by the trainloads of wounded soldiers passing to hideously inadequate hospitals in northern and eastern India, and by the withdrawal into Bengal and Bihar of thousands of Chinese and American troops. News of the fate of business communities in Malaya and Burma was turning Indian business against the government. As the Japanese army approached the eastern border, the Bengal government ordered the destruction of country boats on which local society and economy depended. 'Should the Japanese attempt to enter Calcutta', the inspector-general of police reported 'they would be received with garlands by the civilian population.' Nehru explained to the CWC that 'it is Gandhiji's feeling that Japan and Germany will win. This feeling unconsciously governs his decision.'[16]

Gandhi's encouragement pushed Congress to its Quit India Resolution of 8 August 1942: it called for an immediate end to British rule for the 'sake of India and for the success of the cause of the United Nations'. Some colleagues were less confident of the force of *ahimsa* in the face of Japanese aggression.

Yet Gandhi, 'the undisputed leader of a movement over which he had little command' with his 'do or die' speech caught the revolutionary mood in much of the country.[17]

In Bihar, the eastern UP, parts of Bengal and Bombay urban rioting broke out and within a fortnight the disorders had spread to the countryside and represented, in Linlithgow's words, 'by far the most serious rebellion since that of 1857'.[18] Anti-rent/revenue movements were not prominent. Repression may have pre-empted them; or the upper peasants, finding some up-turn in the rural economy, may have been integrated into Congress's national campaign. Huge crowds attacked communications and government buildings. Three hundred railway stations, 200 police stations and 1,000 post offices were destroyed. Local leadership and Kisan Sabhas seem to have directed a more or less spontaneous rebellion, though the government talked of a Japanese 'fifth column'.

Muslims mostly failed to respond, the League deploring the 'open rebellion' with the aim of 'Congress Hindu domination in India'.[19] The Punjab premier, Sikander Hayat Khan, complained of a betrayal of Indian soldiers. The response of industrial workers was muted especially where the CPI was strong, which Gandhi may have counted on. In January 1942 it had fallen into Moscow's pro-war anti-fascist line.

At this crisis of the war the government was in no mood for half measures. The leaders were arrested on 9 August, soon followed into prison by 100,000 more in a 'campaign' which required 57 battalions of troops. Whipping was extensively used on demonstrators, the RAF machine-gunned saboteurs. Two thousand five hundred people were shot dead and 66,000 detained. The UP governor admitted 'on occasions [to] methods which I cannot condone and which...nobody could defend'. By the end of August the resistance had been broken. Linlithgow expressed relief that the rebellion came when it did.[20] He feared that the autumn would bring worse news from the Caucasus and North Africa and that his Liberal councillors would wilt under intimidation.

In the short run the repression allowed the government to concentrate on the war. Quit India cooled some Labour party warmth for Congress and also strengthened what Amery called Churchill's 'Hitler-like attitude to India'. The prime minister, who declared Indians 'the beastliest people in the world after the Germans' was, Amery thought 'really not quite normal on the subject of India'.[21] In retrospect, Congress unity may have been maintained by three years in prison. It avoided the difficult response that would have been forced by the arrival in 1944 of the Indian National Army (INA) on the eastern border. Prison gave new credentials to congressmen, some of whom had been tarnished by office. The Left generally emerged deeply divided, and the field was free for the Muslim League. Though Linlithgow talked of another 30 years of the Raj, the incoming viceroy, Wavell (1943–47), knew that even if the army obeyed orders, there could never be such repression again in peacetime.

5. The Price of Victory

After the Depression years, the army, in the words of the Auchinleck Committee of 1938, was 'unfit to take the field against land or air forces equipped with up-to-date weapons'.[22] The Chatfield Committee of 1939–40 decided that it should become an imperial army again and Britain agreed through the 1939 Defence Expenditure Agreement to meet the cost of operations outside India. Numbers built up from 205,000 in 1939 to 2,250,000 in 1945 with deployments to Egypt, Sudan, Kenya, Somaliland, Aden, Palestine, Abyssinia, Iraq, Iran and to the east for the reconquest of the French and Dutch colonies. Twenty-four thousand were killed and 64,000 wounded. India's importance as a regional base can be judged by the 27 divisions and 156 RAF squadrons present there at the end of the war. Since London was now paying for the Indian army abroad, a huge sterling debt built up, reaching £1,343 million, or 20 per cent of the UK GDP, by the end of the war. The old assumption that the Indian taxpayer paid for Britain's eastern foreign policy had been turned on its head.

The economic consequences were much greater than those of the First World War and they came faster with huge price increases in the first two years. During the course of the war the money supply quintupled.

Index of relative price movements: 1939 = 100

	Rice	Wheat	Kerosene	Cotton manufactures
Dec. 1941	172	212	140	196
Dec. 1943	951	330	175	501

Source: B. R. Tomlinson, *The Political Economy of the Raj* (London: Macmillan, 1979), 94.

For the government the age of laissez-faire, diminishing since the Depression, was over. Big government had arrived with the need to control prices and secure war supplies. By 1943 India was producing more goods for the war than Australia, New Zealand and South Africa combined, worth £286.5 million by 1945.

Famine

Out of the chaos of rebellion and the scorched-earth tactics in the face of the Japanese advance there had appeared in the summer of 1942 the Bengal famine, in Wavell's words, 'one of the greatest disasters that has befallen any people under British rule and damage to our reputation here both among Indians and foreigners in India is incalculable'.[23] The loss of Burma had deprived India of 15 per cent of its rice, and a cyclone in November killed 30,000 and devastated crops in the Ganges delta. The government was claiming a real shortage, but as an explanation 'it was a search in a dark room for a black cat which wasn't there'.[24] Amartya Sen reckoned that earlier official estimates that there was just enough food to meet requirements were probably correct. To compound the other problems and the ineffective Muslim League coalition government in Bengal, the war was bringing inflation to the state. The massive influx of British and American troops, the tasks of clearing jungle and building air-strips brought higher wages for some and lifted food prices for all. A brief rise in food prices – in Calcutta by 100 per cent from March to May 1943 – was lethal for many labourers in this agrarian economy which had suffered grievously in the Depression. Three and a half million died and untold numbers had their health broken. The scale of the disaster required action from Delhi and London. Yet Linlithgow was slow to act and the new viceroy, Wavell, told Churchill that 'after a year's experience in my present office I feel that the vital problems of India are being treated by His Majesty's Government with neglect, even sometimes with hostility and contempt'.[25] If resentment at the Quit India rebellion made politicians forget Bengal and focus exclusively on the war effort, they were forced to change their minds by late 1943. The civilian economy behind the eastern battlefront was facing collapse. Troop morale, both British and Indian, was being affected by the terrible distress. To sustain India as the British base for operations from Africa to the Pacific, belated and limited action was at last undertaken.

The Indian National Army (INA)

The reliability of the army as a base for British rule was also challenged by the creation of the INA. Its small beginnings in December 1941 in Kedah, Malaya were transformed by 20,000 of the 60,000 Indian troops captured by the Japanese and by the charismatic leadership of Subhas Chandra Bose. Having escaped to Italy and Berlin from the supervision of the Calcutta police, he travelled in 1943 from Europe to Japanese-occupied South-east Asia by submarine. He essayed some combination of socialism and fascism, but his principal conviction was that Britain's danger was India's opportunity. He improved relations with the Japanese, mobilized local business support and reorganized the INA. He stressed the unity of Hindus and Muslims and raised a women's regiment named after a hero of 1857, the Rani of Jhansi.

To the cry of *Chalo Delhi* (On to Delhi), the INA joined the great Japanese offensive of spring 1944.

The advance was stopped in fierce fighting near the border at Kohima and Imphal, and the Indian and British forces began a long and devastating counter-attack. Out of defeat a retrained Indian army had arisen led by nationally minded young officers. Now, as Christopher Bayly and Tim Harper have written, Indian troops 'were used to stiffen the morale of the British in particular circumstances, reversing a generations-old practice of the Indian army at war. Here, on India's jungle-clad eastern frontier as much as in Whitehall or the Congress Working Committee, the Raj really came to an end.'[26]

Chapter 7

INDEPENDENCE, 1945–1947

1. The 1945–46 Election

Shortly after his appointment in June 1943, Wavell surprised and angered Churchill by pressing for a fresh political initiative. After the suppression of the Quit India rebellion and the sense that the war was on the turn, the prime minister was content to let things be. At the Mansion House in November 1942 he had declared that 'I have not become the King's First Minister in order to preside over the liquidation of the British Empire.'[1] Only with the end of the war in sight in September 1944 was Wavell allowed to arrange talks between Gandhi and Jinnah, which proved inconclusive. On 25 May 1945 the coalition government was dissolved. Churchill, now leading a caretaker government, probably wished to keep India out of the forthcoming election campaign, and so permitted the viceroy to repeat the short-term part of the Cripps Offer. Wavell's approach had always been: Indianization first, argue about the constitution later.

Twenty-two political leaders were invited to a conference at Simla from 25 June to 14 July 1945 to consider the representation of the main parties on the Executive Council, leaving the viceroy and the commander-in-chief as the only Britons. The CWC was released from prison for the occasion, and all offered initial welcome except for the uninvited Hindu Mahasabha which objected to parity between 'Caste Hindu' and Muslim League representatives. The viceroy's proposal was 5 Caste Hindus: 5 Muslims and 2 'minor minorities'. Jinnah's claim was that the League, despite the 1937 election results, alone represented India's Muslims. Thus, he would not allow the nomination of non-League Muslims such as Azad, the Congress president, and Khizar Hayat Khan, the Punjab premier whose Unionist government had been so helpful to Britain in the war. For Congress, claiming to be a secular party representing all parts of the Indian nation, it was also a matter of principle. Again, the communal question led to the breakdown of a conference.

Jinnah may have thought there was no hurry; the Tories would not proceed without his cooperation. But on 26 July Labour took office under Attlee after a landslide victory. Cripps's response to the failure of Simla was to announce Labour's belief not in an interim, but in a final solution where minorities would not have a veto but equally would not be forced into a constitutional settlement against their will. To clarify matters in India, Wavell called elections on 21 August, a week after Japan's surrender. Forty-one million, ten per cent of the population, were eligible to vote in polls which were staggered from December 1945 to March 1946.

Congress entered the election on its Quit India Resolution, disappointed that Wavell's response to the Labour government's announcements had been a vague restatement of Cripps without mention of independence. For the League the campaign was for Pakistan, and its exclusive right to speak for India's Muslims.

The elections revealed a stark dichotomy. The Mahasabha and the communists, who had been thought strong contenders in several provinces, did badly. Congress took 91 per cent of the non-Muslim vote and 57 of the 102 seats in the Central Assembly. It won majorities in every province except Bengal, Sindh and the Punjab. Transformed since 1937, the League established itself as the Muslim party, taking 87 per cent of Muslim votes and all 30 reserved seats at the centre and 442 out of 509 Muslim seats in the provinces. But in only two out of the five 'Pakistan' provinces, Bengal and Sindh, did the League take office. It failed in the NWFP and Assam but its advance in the Punjab was especially significant. With 79 of the 175 seats, it cut heavily into Muslim support for the Unionist-Congress-Sikh coalition that was now precariously formed. The inter-communal appeal of the Unionists since 1923 had depended on the primacy of provincial politics and an economic programme for the rural voters. British policy had changed the former; the Depression and wartime shortages had undermined the latter. The elections put partition at the top of the agenda.

2. The Cabinet Mission, March–August 1946

Labour was anxious to resolve the continuing crisis and reactivate some of its old Congress links. In February 1946 Attlee announced a Cabinet mission of Lord Pethick-Lawrence (Secretary of State, 1945–April 1947), Cripps and A. V. Alexander to assist the viceroy in arranging a constituent assembly and reconstituting the Executive Council to represent the main parties. On arrival Cripps declared: 'we want to give independence to India as quickly and as smoothly as we can... What form of Government is to replace the present regime is for India to decide.' Attlee also told the Commons on 15 March that 'we cannot allow a minority to place their veto on the advance of the majority'.[2]

Wavell, conscious that the prime minister thought him not sufficiently pro-Congress, warned the delegation of 'our extremely difficult hand to play, owing to the necessity to avoid the mass movement or revolution in India which it is in the power of the Congress to start, and which we are not certain we can control'.[3] Nehru agreed that 'If the British Cabinet Mission fails to solve the pressing problems which clamour for solution, a political earthquake of devastating intensity will sweep the entire country.'[4] When the Congress leaders had been released from jail in June 1945 they had found themselves in a new world of popular politics. Life had been transformed by the wartime inflation, the new experiences and raised expectations of millions and the excitement of the first elections for nearly ten years. When the civilian Malcolm Darling travelled through rural north-west India in the winter of 1946–47, he heard from the lips of every villager he questioned the hope and the demand for freedom.[5]

After hearing the opinions of provincial politicians, the mission concluded that an independent communal Pakistan, which would require the partition of Bengal and the Punjab, was neither desirable nor economically viable. The loss of Calcutta would be a blow in the east, and the NWFP with its current three and a half *crore* rupee annual deficit in Delhi's budget would be a crippling burden in the west. It proposed instead a Union government for defence, foreign affairs and communications, with some tax-raising powers. All other powers would rest with the provinces in a triple grouping: Section A with the Hindu-majority provinces; Sections B and C with the Muslim-majority provinces of the north-west and the north-east.

This looseness of this federal vision seemed for a time to the princes' liking, though they soon realized that the limbo into which they were consigned had its dangers. The mission statement declared that 'with the attainment of independence by British India... Paramountcy can neither be retained by the British Crown nor transferred to the new government'.[6] The Sikhs and Dr Ambedkar's Scheduled Castes Federation felt ignored.

On 5 May, the mission, Wavell, the leaders of the League and of Congress, with Gandhi in the wings, moved to Simla again to thrash out the details and to agree on the formation of an interim government. It is Ayesha Jalal's contention that the proposal had brought Jinnah fairly close to what he really wanted: equal treatment at the centre, which guaranteed Muslim interests, and the possibility of the provinces seceding into independence, here permitted after ten years. But it required his most delicate diplomacy for, though the majority-province politicians might like it, the mission statement's preamble explicitly rejected Pakistan and objections were already being raised in the council of the League from Muslim-minority provinces. The League wanted provincial groupings to be compulsory. Congress envisaged the Constituent Assembly as a sovereign body which would then decide all claims. These differences of interpretation soon surfaced. But though alarmed by Nehru's references to the NWFP with its Congress government and Assam with its Hindu majority, the League accepted the proposals on 6 June – on Cripps assurance of 16 May that Britain would not transfer power before a constitution had been framed – and Congress followed on 24 June.[7]

Shortly after, in July, the Constituent Assembly election results showed ever greater polarization with Congress taking all the general seats save nine and the League all the Muslim seats save five, and the dissatisfied Sikhs taking their four. The 93 states' seats awaited an agreement over the method of election. Jinnah, still demanding parity with Congress, would not come to a Constituent Assembly and also rejected Wavell's invitation to join the council as an Interim Government on a 6:5:3 basis, complaining of 'the Caste Hindu Fascist Congress'. Nevertheless, just as it seemed as if an arrangement could be reached, Gandhi insisted on Congress's right to nominate a nationalist Muslim, as well as shocking the mission by demanding the immediate withdrawal of British troops. Jinnah had no room for manoeuvre and when the CWC deferred to Gandhi, the agreement broke down.

Jinnah now left the constitutional path he had followed for so long. The League called for Direct Action on 16 August to achieve Pakistan. Terrible rioting broke out on that day in Calcutta. On 2 September the growing instability brought Congress into an Interim Government hitherto dependent on officials. Nehru was vice-president of the council or, to Congress, prime minister. The Sikh leader Baldev Singh was defence member. All important departments were now in Congress hands and the viceroy no longer received the secret reports of Indian Political Intelligence, as this agency now answered to Patel. The formation of the Interim Government – a moment, as Patrick French has written, 'more significant, in many ways, than the handover of power in August 1947' – was greeted across India by the black flags of the League.[8] Next month, fearing the consequences of exclusion at a time of mounting tension in the country, Jinnah, without conceding his principles, decided to enter the government with Liaquat Ali Khan, the League's secretary, as finance member. Would Jinnah reconsider the League boycott of the Constituent Assembly, set for 9 December? A brief visit of the leaders to London did not resolve matters and so the Assembly opened without the League.

3. Rising Pressure

The commander-in-chief had warned in December 1945 that 'We must be ready to deal with a well-organized revolution next spring.'[9]

Yet despite 360,000 desertions in the course of the war, army discipline was still holding, though Auchinleck knew that of the 15,740 new Indian officers 'every Indian officer worth his salt is today a nationalist'.[10] The steel frame of the ICS was coming apart. Recruitment, stopped in 1940, had been resumed in 1946 and then stopped almost immediately. Total numbers had fallen from 1201 in 1940 to 939, of whom only 429 were British in 1945. Azad declared that the British were 'now acting as caretakers'.[11]

The formation of provincial governments in early 1946, in Yasmin Khan's words, temporarily 'drew the sting out of anti-British sentiment in India'. In July Wavell told the King that 'We are in fact conducting a retreat, and in very difficult circumstances.'[12] The country was in a highly disturbed state with nearly two million workers on strike and rail and postal strikes threatened for the summer. The League's day of Direct Action inaugurated months of communal riots. They seem to have had different immediate causes. The Calcutta killings of 16–19 August which claimed the lives of 5,000–6,000 people and made 100,000 homeless were probably committed by thugs encouraged by local politicians anxious to claim the city before any future division. The slaughter of Hindus in Noakhali and Tippera in East Bengal soon after seems to have begun as a peasant revolt against Hindu landlords. Similarly, in Bihar, where 40,000 people, mostly Muslims, may have died, agrarian tensions were diverted into communal killing. The INA now proved more dangerous in defeat. The first batch of the 600 prisoners charged with 'waging war against the King' were put on trial in the Mughal Red Fort in Delhi in November 1945. The decision and the high-profile venue were soon seen as great mistakes, and a formula had to be found to drop the trials. In the meantime, Nehru and Sapru appeared for the defence, and demonstrations of support for the INA spread through many cities, most violently in Calcutta. In February 1946 a naval mutiny broke out in Bombay in which hundreds were killed as the contagion spread into the docks. Seventy-five ships were affected involving 20,000 seamen. In eastern India there was trouble in the Indian Air force. There was also civil unrest with a huge attack on a ration centre in Allahabad in February.

In September 1946 Wavell alarmed London by sending home details of a Breakdown Plan for a phased British withdrawal if the League failed to enter the Interim Government. However, when it did join, subsequent disharmony only made more urgent the viceroy's request in October for a decision regarding 'how and when we are to leave India'.[13] After visiting Bihar, Wavell admitted: 'there is little or nothing now that I can do to influence events… Machine gunning from the air is not a weapon one would willingly use, though the Muslims point out, rather embarrassingly, that we did not hesitate to use it in 1942.'[14]

Both Congress and the government needed an agreement. The endgame of British India was apparently purely elite politics; but there was a background of fear. Gandhi believed that 'we are nearing a civil war'. Nehru declared 'India is on the edge of a volcano'.[15] He had told Cripps in December 1945: 'on both sides, whatever our personal feelings in the matter, we have become the agents of powerful forces which we may influence somewhat but cannot control'.[16] Both Patel and Jinnah played an important part in persuading the naval mutineers to surrender, and Patel defended the ICS from nationalist attack. It was not only fear of political collapse. Valuable access to rationing entitlements and licences was enabling congressmen to ignore local or party accountability. To restore disciplined control, the CWC needed to take over the centre before it disintegrated.

Attlee and Cripps seem to have regarded the viceroy's warnings as the pessimism of a tired general with limited political skills. Thus, the Labour government was showing no sense of urgency in line with its bland election manifesto commitment to 'the advancement of India to responsible self-government'.[17] Wedgwood Benn thought 'Idealists in our party care much more about the African', perhaps because they were considered more amenable or more Christian.[18] When Wavell returned to meet a cabinet committee he found that one minister did not know that Sikhs lived in the Punjab, and another was astonished to hear that there were fewer than 500 British members of the ICS. It seems that the cabinet had not absorbed the implications of the 1937 election, let alone those of 1945–46 since Attlee said the 'cabinet wanted to reach the peasant over the head of the anti-British vested interest'. Cripps was convinced that the League was in decline. The foreign secretary, Ernest Bevin, grumbled that withdrawal would be seen as 'the beginning of the liquidation of the British Empire'.[19] With post-war austerity, the British public had other things on their mind and there was no public debate about India. Until agreement could be reached, Attlee was anxious to keep Indian matters out of Parliament.

What changed everything was the realization after the failure of the Cabinet Mission of the costs of maintaining, or re-establishing, the Raj. Once, India had solved Britain's balance of payments needs. Now it added to them with a £1.3 billion sterling debt. In addition, manning the British Empire took out 18 per cent of the working population. Post-war Britain was dependent on US imports but lacked the dollars to pay for them. Referring to the USA, a Treasury report warned: 'Either they would have to lend us the money for our troops [in the Middle East and India], or we should have to move our troops out.'[20] Washington, however, did not believe in empires and so in December 1946, with Bevin complaining of a 'scuttle', the cabinet, anticipating the coming dollar crisis, decided to pull out of India and, three days later, Greece and Palestine. On 20 February 1947 Attlee declared in the House of Commons:

> The present state of uncertainty is fraught with danger and cannot be indefinitely prolonged. His Majesty's Government wish to make it clear that it is their definite intention to take the necessary steps to effect the transference of power into responsible Indian hands by a date not later than June 1948.[21]

The Cripps Offer had been abandoned: there was no mention of treaty obligations or pledges. With the Interim Government breaking down, a definite time-frame replaced the usual equivocation. The question was no longer 'when' but 'to whom'. In the absence of agreement, power would be transferred to a centre, 'existing Provincial Governments, or in such other way as may seem most reasonable and in the best interests of the Indian people'.[22]

4. Lord Mountbatten

Attlee brusquely recalled Wavell thinking him too little the politician and too friendly to the League. He had feared the effect his request for an end-date would have in the House of Commons but then found that his successor insisted on one. Mountbatten arrived in Delhi on 22 March 1947 with orders to implement the transfer of power to a unitary authority. Nehru asked him: 'have you by some miracle got plenipotentiary powers? If so, you will succeed where all others have failed.'[23] He did not have such powers in a legal sense, just the confidence of Attlee and Cripps to act alone with (secret) authority to remove obstructive civilians, and the expectation that given his position as a cousin of the King, criticism from the right would be muted. To the exhausted and demoralized British bureaucracy he brought confidence and optimism and for the first time there was a press attaché, the talented Alan Campbell-Johnson, to project these feelings to the political world.[24]

He has been criticized for his partisan relations with Congress. He regarded Gandhi as an 'old poppet' and established a friendship – his wife, too – with Nehru. By contrast, relations with Jinnah were frozen as Mountbatten's charm failed to cajole him into admitting the inconsistency of making a *communal* appeal for Pakistan yet expecting to take the Punjab and Bengal with their huge non-Muslim minorities. Muslim aides to the viceroy were few. Mountbatten's indispensable assistant was the Hindu V. P. Menon, the new reforms commissioner, who also had close links with Patel. Mountbatten had been sent to secure an agreement on the rapid and controlled transfer of power to a successor government who would be friendly to future British strategic and economic interests. 'We must at all costs' wrote Cripps 'come to an accord with Congress', which had the capacity to block this.[25] The viceroy was carrying out orders; Cripps believed he had found the agent of his own policy in Mountbatten.

The announcement of 20 February 1947 intensified political competition in the majority provinces so as to achieve control by June 1948. The lapse of the Defence of India Rules made it difficult to ban uniformed groups; the Governors Conference on 15–16 April reckoned that the 'private armies' were about half a million strong.[26] The League's National Guards, the RSS and the Sikh Akalis were all on the streets. The League's campaign of Civil Disobedience brought down the Unionist-led coalition in the Punjab on 2 March, but it was not able to form a coalition government itself. Minorities were repelled by its communalism and by the uncertainty of its object. A League negotiator admitted that at that time 'he did not know what Pakistan meant'.[27] The governor, Evan Jenkins, ruled the Punjab under Section 93 as the Sikh Akali leader, Master Tara Singh, drawn sword in hand, declared 'our motherland is calling for blood and we shall satiate the thirst of our motherland with blood…I have sounded the bugle. Finish the Muslim League.'[28] The Sikhs, for long the recipients of British patronage, lacked a credible leader, as they belatedly understood their perilous position across any likely line of partition. In that month 4,000 Muslim properties in central Amritsar were burned out and not a police shot was fired. From April there was a huge flight of capital out of the province mainly from Hindu businesses. At least 5,000 people were to be killed in the Punjab before independence. Malcolm Darling, who had spent most of his career in the Punjab, returned to Britain: 'all I could say to those who asked what would happen in India was – the pessimists say anarchy, the optimists civil war'.[29] At the same time, General Ismay, Mountbatten's chief of staff, wrote: 'the situation is everywhere electric and I get the feeling that the mine may go off at any moment'. What Jenkins was to call 'the communal war of succession' had begun.[30]

Thus, even before Mountbatten arrived, partition was likely, but the government still hoped for an undivided Punjab and Bengal. A weak and impoverished Pakistan would not answer Britain's post-withdrawal strategic hopes in the region. For similar reasons, Britain hoped to avoid the division of the army, only accepting on 28 April that it was inevitable.[31] However, the CWC had accepted Patel's motion to divide the Punjab on 8 March, and recognized a similar fate for Bengal. In mid-April Mountbatten prepared Plan Balkan to transfer power to provinces which could chose India, Pakistan or independence. There has been a debate about Nehru's 'bombshell', his explosive reaction of 10 May when he – not Jinnah – was shown the proposals at Simla. Did it reflect his coming to terms with some sort of partition?[32] He certainly baulked at the fragmentation of the country, as would the other Congress leaders. They would not accept provincial choice – let alone choice for the princes – *before* a Constituent Assembly. Mountbatten beat a hasty retreat.

V. P. Menon then came up with a proposal to transfer power to two dominions. 'Dominion Status', he explained, 'would enable the Congress to have at one and the same time a strong central Government, able to withstand the centrifugal tendencies all too apparent at the moment, and to frame a truly democratic constitution unhampered by any communal considerations.' Fear of these tendencies overcame Congress reservations about dominion status. Nehru later admitted 'that we were tired men and we were getting on in years... The plan for partition offered a way out and we took it.'[33]

For the leaders it was the way to a rapid British exit with the assurance of some international diplomatic and military continuity. Just as the divisions of Indian society had prolonged British rule, now partition was the only solution which allowed a rapid British exit. Patel later claimed, as some suspected, that there had been a deal to shepherd in the states in return for acceptance of partition and cooperation over a rapid transfer of power. A visit to London and the agreement of both Congress and the League to join the Commonwealth – 'British' was later dropped – ensured that there would be no Conservative opposition.

Partition was announced on 3 June 1947. The government, observing the failure of parties to agree on a constitution, called for a 'new and separate Constituent Assembly consisting of the representatives of those areas which decide not to participate in the existing Constituent Assembly'.[34] The legislative assemblies of Bengal and Punjab would meet in two parts, representing the Muslim-majority districts and the rest and vote on partition – a simple majority in either part would be sufficient. A referendum in the Sylhet district of Assam would follow if Bengal voted for partition. To work out the details, a boundary commission was to be set up after consultation.

That day the leaders formally agreed; Jinnah would only nod his head. In the evening they broadcast to the country, and at a press conference on the 4 June Mountbatten announced a date for partition and British withdrawal: 15 August. Later that day, he met Gandhi and secured his acquiescence. The Government of India Act had taken six years before it was passed in 1935. Now, after less than six weeks, the India Independence Act proclaimed on 18 July that 'two independent Dominions shall be set up in India, to be known respectively as India and Pakistan'. The following day a train left Delhi for Karachi to establish the capital of what was to be the world's fifth biggest country.

By mid-July, Baluchistan and the NWFP had opted for the new Constituent Assembly; in the latter, 9.5 per cent of the population voted, 50.99 per cent for Pakistan. The Hindu-majority half of the Bengal Legislative Assembly voted for partition, the Muslim-majority part voted against it. There was now no time for referendums in Bengal or the Punjab; just a vote in Sylhet where 239,619 went for East Pakistan and 184,041 for Assam. Power was to be transferred to states that did not yet know their own boundaries.

The chaos of partition has been partly blamed on the short deadline of 15 August. But once again there was a partial identity of goals. Mountbatten feared that the Interim Government would break up leaving the country in chaos. Both Jinnah and Congress were under pressure to move quickly to contain fissiparous forces. The Punjab was not far from civil war. Pakhtunistan was again the cry in NWFP; local feelings in Sindh and Baluchistan were a challenge to League discipline. In Bengal, Sarat Bose (Subhas Chandra Bose's brother), and Suhrawardy were floating the idea of an independent Bengal, soon to be disowned by Congress. For the latter the Interim Government was a warning of how dysfunctional a shared centre could be. Liaquat's budget with its taxes on the rich could lead to a resurgence of the Left outside the control of the CWC. Then, too, there were the princes whose future was unresolved. If the date had been delayed, thought Rajagopalachari, 'there would have been no power to transfer'.[35]

The partial identity of interest that had brought the British government and Congress together, and kept the League apart, was expressed in the Independence Day ceremonies. On 14 August in the Pakistan capital, but still Hindu-majority city of Karachi, they were muted. 'The crowds acted as if they knew that policemen with Sten guns were on the roof of the Assembly building...' The next day, in Delhi, while Lahore and Amritsar were burning, the agony of partition was momentarily forgotten by the vast and ecstatic crowds. The BBC made positive coverage a major priority.[36]

5. The Boundary Commission

The Indian and Pakistani judges who made up the two groups for Bengal and the Punjab could not agree. So, the president, a London barrister, Sir Cyril Radcliffe, using maps and six-year-old census data in his New Delhi office, made the Awards himself in less than six weeks.

> Unbiased at least he was when he arrived on his mission
>
> ...
>
> The viceroy thinks, as you will see from his letter,
> That the less you are seen in his company the better,
> So we've arranged to provide you with other accommodation.
>
> ...
>
> The weather was frightfully hot,
> And a bout of dysentery kept him constantly on the trot,
> But in seven weeks it was done, the frontiers decided,

A continent for better or worse divided.
The next day he sailed for England, where he could quickly forget
The case, as a good lawyer must, Return he would not,
Afraid, as he told his Club, that he might get shot.[37]

Subsequently some British officials have given credence to the charge that the viceroy was not as neutral as he claimed. Nehru was allowed to hear and protest against the award of the non-Muslim Chittagong Hill Tracts to Pakistan on 12 August. Some have claimed that last-minute changes, possibly at Mountbatten's request, were made to the Punjab border where Ferozepore and Gurdaspur went to India. Radcliffe was entitled to consider 'other factors' than demography, for example these districts' relationship to the pattern of irrigation canals. But there was suspicion that Indian access to the as yet unresolved Kashmir was a consideration, as may have been a big army supply base in Gurdaspur; though it is also likely that strategic protection for the Sikh holy city of Amritsar was important.

When Radcliffe took the job a longer time-frame was in prospect and he was not required to decide before independence. In fact, the Punjab Award was ready by 9 August but Mountbatten decided that both Awards should be published two days after independence. He thus evaded a promise to Jinnah that Sikh leaders whom police believed had planned a rising would be arrested on the publication of the Awards. British troops were confined to barracks and had orders only to protect European lives. By then the responsibility lay with the Indian and Pakistani governments. But these states, just coming into being, had no presence along the 3,800 miles of new border.

Despite all warnings, the Punjab Boundary Force of 25,000 was quite inadequate to contain the explosion of anger and despair in the twelve districts of the Punjab to which it was assigned for just 32 days. One in three Punjabi males of enlistable age was, or had been, in the army, and weapons were ubiquitous. The organized character of much of the killing by roving bands has been little investigated, though questions have been raised about the role of the Sikh princely states of Patiala, Faridkot and Nabha.[38]

The populations were thoroughly mixed. Only 57.1 per cent of the Punjab was Muslim while the Hindus comprised 27.8 per cent of the population with the six million Sikhs (13.2 per cent) scattered over the large province. In the east, the Radcliffe Award left 29 per cent of West Bengal as Muslim and 29.1 per cent of East Bengal as Hindu. Partition brought the greatest migration in human history with 5.5 million Hindus and Sikhs moving east and nearly 6 million Muslims going in the other direction. The figures for Bengal are unknown and, because migration into India continued for the next two generations, difficult to estimate. At least 100,000 women were abducted.

Death was numberless. Mountbatten admitted to 200,000; other British officials put it past seven figures. In the rich and tragic literature of partition, Saadat Hasan Manto's satirical story of the transfer of lunatics, *Toba Tek Singh*, is especially poignant. Some have considered that Mountbatten's later claims for his handling of the partition belong to the same genre.[39]

6. The Integration of the States

The Instruments of Accession that Mountbatten pressed on the princes almost all led to India. On the unresolved question of the states, another partial identity of interest was forming: for Britain, haste to prevent breakdown and embarrassing requests for Commonwealth membership; for Congress, compensation for the territorial loss from partition through the British delivery of the states.

Attlee's statement of 20 February 1947, which announced the end of paramountcy, alarmed the princes. They had been consistently encouraged to trust in British support by Conservative politicians, now out of office, and by numerous opt-out constitutional arrangements. They remembered King George V in 1921 assuring them of 'My determination ever to maintain unimpaired the privileges, rights and dignities of the Princes of India. The Princes may rest assured that this pledge remains inviolate and inviolable.'[40] Cripps had specifically assured them in 1942 that with the independence of British India only their economic agreements – worth in total about £2.5 million – would have to be negotiated. He had written that Britain would not 'in any circumstances transfer paramountcy to an Indian government'.[41] Cripps envisaged that Britain could maintain the treaties through, if necessary, naval power from Ceylon or RAF air bases in friendly states. As late as April 1947 there was brief consideration in London to support an independent Travancore because of a local agreement to supply a fissionable mineral, thorium, to Britain. Amery had thought in August 1944, that British firms squeezed in an independent India might usefully relocate to states. All this, in spite of Wavell's blunt request in April 1944 to face facts: early self-government for British India was not likely to be compatible with promises to the 582 states. A year later Pethick-Lawrence pointed out that though Britain had a moral obligation, 'there is no Court in which the states can implead the sanctity of the engagements contracted with them by the Crown'.[42]

Preoccupied with other matters, Mountbatten may have thought his royal lineage, charm, and friendship with a number of the rulers would expedite business when he could find the time. Plan Balkan had seemed to offer the possibility of independence or independent grouping of states. Nehru's fierce response had led to the 3 June Plan with a strong centre and, by implication, a threatening future. Talk of possible Commonwealth membership for states was abruptly dropped. But Mountbatten probably assumed he could, if necessary, sort out remaining problems as governor-general of both states immediately after independence. This was stymied by Jinnah's announcement on 2 July that he would be Pakistan's governor-general.

The negotiations were very much a Congress affair. Mountbatten was assisted by V. P. Menon, who from 1 July was also secretary of the States Department under Vallabhbhai Patel. Nehru and Patel authorized the viceroy to assure the princes that they would no longer be required to submit to a Constituent Assembly. If they would sign Instruments of Accession before the 15 August, their sovereignty would only be diminished in three areas – defence, foreign affairs and communications – which being already out of their hands seemed to imply a transfer of paramountcy. Patel's condition was that Mountbatten brought in a 'full basket of accessions'.[43] Lord Listowel (Secretary of State, April–August 1947) told the House of Lords that the government would 'not use the slightest pressure to influence their momentous and voluntary decision'.[44] At a meeting on 25 July Mountbatten charmed and cajoled the princes, reminding them of the chequered history of his own ancestral state in the Holy Roman Empire. Privately, the talk was blunter. The *diwan* of Indore said he 'now knew what Dolfuss felt like when he was sent for to see Hitler'.[45]

By 15 August, 550 states, over 90 per cent, had joined the Indian Union. The only states of importance not in the full basket were Junagadh, Hyderabad and Kashmir. Indian 'police actions' subsequently brought in the first two; contested Kashmir, with its large Muslim majority, remains a deadly legacy of British India. Though most states were strongly Hindu, the choice of accession lay with the ruler and some might conceivably have gone for Pakistan. Jinnah's silence on the matter until the closing stages seems to reflect his belief that the Raj would last longer. Mountbatten knew that Congress was bent on a strong centre and that for them the half a million square miles and 85 million people – 24 per cent of the population of undivided India – provided a moral and physical compensation for the loss of Pakistan.

7. Independence[46]

Was it a voluntary demission or had the British been driven out? The constitutional transition in August 1947 allows competing explanations for the end of the Raj. The Whig Interpretation, from the Liberal Imperialist tradition, represents this broadly as the outcome of a progression towards self-rule from Ripon through Morley-Minto, Montagu-Chelmsford and the 1935 Act – despite evidence that constitutional changes were intended as strategies of control and not stages toward self-government. In 1947 Nye Bevan invoked this tradition when he told the cabinet: 'withdrawal from India need not appear to be forced upon us by our weakness nor to be the first stage in the dissolution of the Empire. On the contrary, this action must be shown to be the logical conclusion, which we welcomed, of a policy favoured by successive Governments for many years.'[47]

Nationalist historians have also provided continuous narratives, notably in R. C. Majumdar's *Advanced History of India* (1946). This older approach tells how Congress arose, grew to speak for the nation, accepted the constitutional challenge and swept the electoral board in 1937. After that, the British had nowhere to turn. By contrast, Sumit Sarkar and the Subaltern historians have minimized the constitutional game, which Congress only played for seven of the inter-war years. Their focus is on local resistance to colonial rule and the ever-widening public domain created by civil society. The wars and the Depression had intensified an underlying agrarian crisis since the 1880s. Once the upper peasants moved to Congress in the late 1930s, the days of British rule were numbered. By 1947 it had ceased to exist in wide areas of the country.[48]

Gandhi bridged these two nationalist worlds. He has been accused of missing opportunities by turning down Reading's offer in 1921, insisting on the resignation of the ministries in 1939, and rejecting Cripps and the Cabinet Mission. On the other hand, he understood the dangers of disunity to social harmony, political stability and to vested interests. But he was unable to prevent, and perhaps unwittingly promoted, the turn of nationalism into divisive communal paths. His challenge to the legitimacy of British rule had been relentless, but at the very end he left the Delhi decision makers to live among the strife-torn villagers of Noakhali.

Attempts to identify a critical moment on the path to freedom often assume that the initiative lay with the British. It has been suggested that the will to dominion was broken on the battlefields of the Somme and Paschendaele – as shown by the recognition of the Irish Free State.[49] Yet the loss of Ireland may, like the earlier loss of the American colonies, have strengthened the resolve to hold what was still held. A collapse of imperial confidence is not obvious in the Tory governments that dominated the inter-war period; and the brief Labour governments seemed to be more in the tradition of Liberal Imperialists than genuine anti-imperialists. In 1942 when Attlee invoked Lord Durham he was recalling a statesman who prevented the loss of Canada to the empire.

R. J. Moore has shown in his *Crisis of Indian Unity* (1974) how in the inter-war years Britain tried to hang on by one means or another. B. R. Tomlinson, too, explained that as the Raj ran out of collaborators, its approach shifted more to constitutional manipulation to find friends or balance unfriendly groups.

Meanwhile, British rule retreated to the centre, then to the controlling agencies at the centre. But the scale of the Congress victory in 1937 left the British with severely limited options. By that time the military and economic advantages of the Raj had diminished. The pull of old British firms was so weak that the transfer of power negotiations ignored them. Cripps thought they had had a good innings. In the late 1930s India had been the first colonial country where multi-nationals – ICI, Dunlop, Metal Box – set up manufacturing facilities; they could look after themselves. Real British interests had long passed from economic to financial. At the turn of the century Keynes had sarcastically noted that in the whole Indian establishment the highest-paid person below the viceroy was the government stockbroker. Between the wars, Britain had manipulated the exchange rate to gain what had earlier come from the balance of trade, but this advantage had been negated in turn by the wartime sterling debt. As Tomlinson has argued, 'The British were pushed out of India as much by the logic of their own interests as by the opposition of their nationalist opponents.'[50]

Of all the turning-points, the most plausible is the Cripps Offer. King George VI was astonished when Churchill told him over lunch in July 1942 that all parties 'were quite prepared to give up India to the Indians after the war'.[51] It followed from the promise to Nehru in 1939 at Filkins, Cripps' country house, of a constituent assembly with the return of peace. However, when Labour came to power the Quit India Rebellion had cooled their enthusiasm. Attlee now wondered how representative Congress was. Amery thought his attitude 'really hardly differs from that taken by Winston 10 years ago, namely that we cannot hand India over to Indian capitalists and exploiters'.[52] Some ministers were tougher in their determination to stay for the time being; Bevin, backed by Morrison and Shinwell, contemplated raising 'Black-and-Tan' volunteers from demobilized servicemen to support British rule. The hostile reaction to Wavell's demand for a leaving date made the viceroy think they 'were in reality imperialists and dislike any idea of leaving India'.[53]

Independence meant different things to different groups. In the late 1930s as the Pakistan demand was forming, the Self-Respect Movement and Dr Ambedkar's Untouchables were both advancing separatist claims. This reinforced British beliefs about the divided character of Indian society and shaped their understanding of promises of self-rule. The divisions seemed to guarantee distant time frames and leave open the possibility of Britain remaining as some sort of high-level arbiter. The 20 February announcement may have been unique in its no-strings character, but the cabinet had already discussed ways of tying India into a defence agreement. They had instructed Mountbatten to seek a treaty with India, which was superseded by membership of the Commonwealth, then thought of primarily in military terms.[54] There was also talk of Britain's retaining the Andaman and Nicobar Islands.

John Gallagher with his stress on the continuity of British imperialism revealed the ambiguities of the British understanding of Indian independence. The Second World War, he argued, did not bring about the end of empire. Amery, for example, thought that for Burma and other smaller countries, the future would be 'one not of Atlantic charter liberty but of increasing imperialism... I am all for encouraging the sentiment of self-government now and letting them feel their feet and the façade of independent status'.[55] The Attlee government, no less imperialistic than its Churchillian predecessor, hoped that with withdrawal there could be a switch to informal empire, to a 'new technique' to maintain imperial interests in the east. Though temporarily embarrassed, Britain was still potentially powerful; as late as 1950 production was 50 per cent higher than in Germany and two and a half times that of France. 'Quitting India has to be seen in the light of the simultaneous decision to push British penetration deeper into tropical Africa and the Middle East.'[56] However, partition and the division of the Indian army were misfortunes which threatened to crack the 'keystone of the arch of our Commonwealth defence'.[57]

In the end, the collapse came suddenly. Victory in the war and the huge build-up of forces in the subcontinent in 1945 had fed illusions that promises of self-rule were somehow compatible with future control of India's external relations. Then it became clear that Wavell's assessment of an imminent breakdown of government was not alarmist and was also held by the Congress leaders. The financial crisis in London and knowledge of America's lack of sympathy for empire made rapid withdrawal necessary, but left open the possibility for a secondary role on the world stage. The onset of the Cold War led to a partial American re-think about Britain's overseas utility. Attlee had already foreseen that 'it may be we shall have to consider the British Isles as an easterly extension of a strategic [arc] the centre of which is the American continent rather than as a Power looking eastwards through the Mediterranean to India and the East'.[58] The 'special relationship' with the USA would allow Britain to punch above its weight in the world as the revenues and *sepoys* of India had once done.

8. Partition: Two Nations?

The 'two-nation' theory of Muslims and Hindus in India has a long history, forcefully expressed when Congress was forming in the 1880s by Syed Ahmed Khan, and as the basis of the League's position in the next century. Though responding to the forms of British rule, the claim was based on pre-British realities: the Muslim conquests; conversions; and eighteenth-century revivalism. It assumed a unity apparently at odds with the fractured complexity of the Indian Muslim population and with evidence of much social integration and syncretic practices which some have thought so characteristic of the country. Aziz Ahmad began a modern debate between separatists and integrationists represented by Imtiaz Ahmad. It is also a reminder of nostalgia for the departed glories of Muslim rule and the connections with the currents of belief in the wider Islamic world.[59] For its proponents what mattered was belief in Muslim unity. Partition was then a natural and desired outcome once it was clear that the foreign rulers were leaving.

This unity was often assumed in the formation of British policy, which permitted separate electorates in local government after 1882, mandated them nationally in 1909 and, despite misgivings, extended them in 1919 and 1935. This, and the other ways in which British rule shaped and exploited identities, have formed the basis of allegations of 'divide and rule' and in the last phase, 'divide and quit'.[60] Partition thus followed from the way Britain governed India; from the British dependence on Muslim political support during the war and even from an alleged desire to leave a South Asia weakened by internal antagonisms. Against this, it might be said that 'divide and rule' was just that and not a preparation for withdrawal. Although at the very end partition was necessary for a rapid British exit, British politicians considered their strategic interests required a united India.

Farzana Shaikh has pointed out that the earlier Whig representation of interests had suited Muslim notables.[61] However, following trends in Britain after the First World War, the representation of people replaced that of interests. At this point, Muslims became vulnerable, the more so since separate electorates removed the pressure to organize political parties. Numbers began to matter and in an age of provincial politics Muslims were permanent minorities almost everywhere. In addition, the encroaching assumptions of liberal democracy were at odds with Muslim political values, where the basic building bloc was the community not the individual. It may be then that some fundamental assumptions came to the surface: the importance of the *ummah*, the worldwide community of believers; the superiority of the Muslim way of life; and the belief that Muslim populations should live under Muslim governments.

There is a view expressed by Stanley Wolpert and others that the connection between nation and state was relatively unproblematic.[62] Here, Jinnah was repelled by Gandhi's turn to mass politics at Nagpur in 1920 and the inevitable use of Hindu religious language, of promises of *Ram Rajya*. These fears came to fruition in the 'Congress Raj' of 1937–39. They drove Jinnah to the 1940 Lahore Resolution of Muslim nationhood and, though Pakistan was not mentioned by name, to the implication that Muslims must have their own state. He had to use language guardedly because of the difficulty of reconciling Muslim-majority and Muslim-minority provincial interests, because of the uncertain time-frame of British rule and, above all, because of the electorate weakness of the League. But despite the suddenness of British withdrawal, the goal of Pakistan was achieved, though not in the form ideally desired.

Ayesha Jalal's revisionist attack has denied the necessary or intended connection between nation and state. In her account, Jinnah wanted a constitutional settlement at the centre which, regardless of numbers, would recognize and guarantee Muslim interests. In this he spoke for the 35 million Muslims in the minority provinces, but not for Bengal or the Punjab. Until the last moment Unionists and the KPP were suspicious of politics at the centre and relatively satisfied with their provincial world. The contradictions between these supporters forced on Jinnah ambiguous language, as did his apparently secular beliefs and the communalist nature of the Pakistan claim. The latter would leave the minority provinces stranded in India and force the partition of Bengal and Punjab, both of which were economically vital to a Pakistan. When, in April 1942, Rajagopalachari suggested, to his colleagues' horror, that Congress should respond positively to the Pakistan demand and that plebiscites might be held in Muslim-majority *districts*, he drew from Jinnah the riposte that he was only 'offering a shadow and a husk-a maimed, mutilated and moth-eaten Pakistan'.[63]

Thus, Jalal argues, Jinnah's Pakistan was a bargaining counter for a federal state with self-governing provinces and guarantees at the centre. Referring to the Lahore Resolution in his presidential address in 1943 at Delhi, Jinnah declared: 'They [cries of 'Hindus'] started damning the resolution on the grounds that it was Pakistan... You know perfectly well that Pakistan is really a word which is really foisted upon us and fathered on us by some sections of the Hindu press and also by the British press.'[64] All this accounts for his otherwise strange rejection of the Cripps Offer, which seemed to allow a communal Pakistan, implying a partitioned Bengal and Punjab, and his acceptance of the Cabinet Mission Plan with its federal unpartitioned provinces – significantly with opposition from some League colleagues. In June 1947 he actually proposed that both Constituent Assemblies meet in Delhi. Early in 1946 Nehru, noticing that Pakistani sentiment was strongest in Muslim-minority provinces, told Cripps: 'It seems clear that Jinnah is not after Pakistan but something entirely different.'[65]

If Pakistan was Jinnah's bargaining counter, why did he not lower his bid at the very end? Miscalculation has been suggested as a possible explanation. British encouragement during the war and in the Cripps Offer may have left him unprepared for the sudden decision to withdraw in 1946–47. He seems also to have overestimated British promises to the princes and realized too late that there would not be a post-independence patchwork of states, some of which would be friendly to Pakistan or to a decentralized subcontinent.

He may also have underestimated the pressures that were driving Congress towards acceptance of partition, even if some expected it to be short lived. Birla had backed the idea since 1942 and Hindu business realized that a strong centre was necessary for their 1944 Bombay Plan for industrial reconstruction.[66] At the centre, experience of the Interim Government, with Liaquat Ali Khan's 'anti-business' budget, convinced Congress that cooperation with the League was impossible. Nehru's appointment of a Congress Muslim, Asaf Ali, to be the first Indian ambassador to the USA scarcely breathed a spirit of compromise.

At the end of 1946 the Bengal Partition League with Mahasabha and business support was founded for a Hindu West Bengal. In Bengal it was not only the Mahasabha that wanted partition. Religious and social separation ran deep. Sarat Chandra Chatterji in his famous novel *Srikanta* (1915) refers to the schoolfellows of his eponymous hero as Bengalis and Muslims.[67] A similar outlook could be found among Muslim spokesmen, for example the *zemindar*/politician Nawab Ali Chaudhuri who declared that there was no common sentiment of nationality between Muslims and Bengalis. Many *bhadralok* with their *zemindari* connections feared a permanent majority representing poor Muslim cultivators or an independent Bengal under a radical populist government of Suhrawardy and Sarat Bose. When Fazlul Huq fell in 1943, having failed on his promise of the abolition of *zemindari* without compensation, he left a rising hostility towards Hindus among the upper peasants. An influential earlier writer, Wilfred Cantwell Smith, had related Muslim communalism to economic backwardness.[68] Partition was the only way Congress could come to power in Bengal. Gandhi's political influence was waning and the party leaders had more or less accepted the inevitability of cutting off 'the diseased limb', as Patel put it.[69]

Jinnah's lofty eminence – much more than head-and-shoulders above his colleagues – has made him a prime candidate for the Great Man Theory of history. Nehru thought him 'one of the most extraordinary men in history'.[70] Had negotiations been spun out until after his death in September 1948, would there have been a Pakistan? Evidence for his secularity or otherwise is equally ambiguous. The image of the *Quaid-e-Azam* (Great Leader) is a westernized one, with his monocle and command of English as immaculate as his Savile Row suit. But just as the Nehru jacket or Gandhi's *dhoti* broke down barriers between public space and the Indian home, so Jinnah's appearance after 1937 began to reflect national, or communal, self-assertion. Speaking Urdu more frequently, he often wore a *sherwani* coat, a *karakuli* cap and then began to abandon the UP *churidar pajama* for the baggy Punjabi *shalwar*. Though born into a Shia Khoja family, it has been claimed that he was really Sunni by the end of his life. Some biographers have explained Jinnah's movement in a communalist direction in these years as a discovery of his roots in response to the slights and set-backs of the inter-war years: conviction not tactics, in response to the threat of a Hindu *raj*.[71]

An important reason why Jinnah could not compromise in the final days was that he was riding a tiger. As his colleague Jamil ud-din Ahmed told him it was not possible to pull back 'after having sworn on the Quran to fight and die for undiluted sovereign Pakistan'. His friend, F. K. Khan Durrani, complained that 'At present one must shout with the crowd or get lynched by the crowd, and the feeling has been created that one who is not a Leaguer is worse than a kafir and should be hanged like a dog forthwith.'[72] In April 1946 the League strengthened the wording of the Pakistan Resolution from two Muslim states to a 'sovereign, independent Muslim state'.[73] When Iqbal made his famous Pakistan address in 1930, the League's quorum had to be reduced from 75 to 50. But by 1944 there were over 2 million members and the League's National Guards were reckoned at almost 100,000. According to Nehru the secret of his leadership was to 'avoid taking any positive action which might split his followers'.[74]

The debate about the mass appeal of the idea of Pakistan was usefully shaped some years ago by Professors Paul Brass and Francis Robinson.[75] Both approaches are carefully nuanced but they incline towards the opposite poles of *instrumentalism* and *primordial feeling*. Brass pointed especially to the Muslim elite of the UP whose insecurity drove them to mobilize wider Muslim support using religious appeals and a communal vision of self-rule. In doing this they 'chose "divisive rather than composite symbols" as the focus of political action'.[76] Robinson, rejecting the idea of conscious manipulation, argues that people draw on the symbols and sentiments around which their life is already structured, reinforcing them as they proclaim them. The inclination to do so was prompted by a general turn to the politics of identity. A villager who had recently learned to read told Malcolm Darling: 'I now know who I am.'[77] By the 1940s calls for Pakistan were widespread and passionate. In South India it was supported by both the Muslim poor, who had nothing to gain, and by the business classes who had much to lose. Most important was the spread of the idea into the Punjab countryside by landholders and *pirs* (local religious leaders). Resentment at Hindu moneylenders, as of Hindu *zemindars* in Bengal, the overthrow of established values and expectations from the surging inflation of the war, and the fear of the unknown from the collapsing Raj all encouraged faith in the restorative justice of a unified Islamic state and society. Was this nationalism or communalism? Writing of these times, Gyanendra Pandey has argued that 'nationalism was nothing more than communalism driven into secular channels'.[78]

CONCLUSION

The historian J. R. Seeley in his best-selling *The Expansion of England* (1883) cautioned readers against the vulgar error of assuming that India is 'in any practical sense of the word a possession of England... When we speak of India as "our magnificent dependency" or "the brightest jewel in the English diadem" we use metaphors which have come down to us from primitive ages.' He did not assume that Britain had conquered India with a purpose or a sense of mission. Nevertheless, 'there are some deeds which, though they had better been not done, cannot be undone'. Thus, there were responsibilities subject, in British eyes, to the 'condition of our Indian Empire that it should be held without any great effort'.[1] Here was one of the paradoxes of British rule: great pretensions but government on a low income that never in peacetime exceeded seven per cent of national income. The limited impact on the majority of the population may be judged from the following table:[2]

	Literacy rate	Life expectancy at birth	
		Men	Women
1901	6.2	20.1	21.8
1911	7.0	23.9	23.4
1921	8.3	20.1	20.9
1931	9.2	28.1	27.8
1941	15.1	33.1	31.1

References to what Britain *gave* India are equally unhelpful, and they reveal a gulf between a widespread British assumption that the Raj, despite serious reservations, was a good thing and a near consensus in India that it was indefensible. In the last generation the dominant theory of colonialism, associated with Frantz Fanon and Edward Said, has stressed the *totality of conquest*. India and Indians, as the 'other', have been in the hegemonic grip of Orientalist discourse. However, D. R. Nagaraj has reminded us of other models for the relationship.³ There is also the belief in a '*persistence of a "cultural soul"*', a conviction that the spiritual superiority of Asian civilization would survive the age of political domination. It is associated with the work of the art historian A. K. Coomeraswamy, but its wider appeal is evident from the Theosophical Society and the western fascination with eastern spirituality.

This points to the third model of *multiple interactions*, which has occurred cumulatively over many years between India and Britain, perhaps especially Scotland, from where so many officials and traders came. If Britain 'gave' the English language to India, a study of the reciprocal gift from Indian languages already filled a massive volume when *Hobson-Jobson* was published in 1886. When Seeley called one of his chapters 'The mutual influence of England and India' most of his readers would have assumed that the flow of influence was mainly eastward and indeed modern historians have questioned, in Peter Hennessey's words, the depth of the 'imperial imprint in the wax of collective British memory'.⁴ Yet today, with the resurgence of India and the large south Asian population in Britain, the opposite seems the case. We are now more aware of the influence of ICS ideals on social reformers such as William Beveridge, the father of the welfare state, and perhaps of similar inspiration behind the policy of multiculturism in contemporary Britain.

British rule was the principal conduit by which western influence entered the country. To give one example, print replaced palm-leaf manuscripts, making possible an egalitarian access to knowledge regardless of caste.⁵ The French Revolution, the Italian *Risorgimento* and Soviet Russia excited intellectuals whose fathers had been moved by Edmund Burke, but nationalism took its own forms, with the sense of religious community especially dominant. As three-fifths of the subcontinent were unified, the modern state arrived, with its standing army and urban-based central executive. The appearance of its features, such as the much-vaunted legal system, often differed from the reality. In the mid-nineteenth century, the civilian J. H. Nelson had noted the gulf between the legal maxims of British Indian law taken from the ancient texts and daily practice and expectation. To many, British magistrates, linguistically and culturally uncomprehending, made the courts a lottery, though not for Europeans.

Because the Raj did not end in collapse or defeat, commentators have stressed the elements of continuity across 1947. There were elements from Mughal days, the salt tax and the land revenue arrangements among them.

However, what is usually meant is continuity from the last decade of British rule. Two hundred and fifty clauses of the 1935 Act went straight into the Indian constitution in 1950. There was the strong state with its policy-making bureaucracy, the communal approach to representation and entitlement and, after the death of laissez-faire, the trend towards economic planning.[6] The Congress ministries after 1937 prefigured the machine politics of free India. Pakistan inherited the militarized bureaucracy of the twentieth-century Punjab, as well as British personnel as governors, chiefs of staff and nearly 500 army officers. Indian relations with Britain remained friendly but wary, and Commonwealth membership was one of the paths by which India and Pakistan re-entered the world stage. British investment actually rose after independence, and India remained a principal market for British industrial goods. The economic legacy, above all poverty, was more difficult to change.

Partition, despite meeting the aspirations of some, destroyed the lives and livelihoods of millions. The northern cities were filled with refugees. Resident populations as well as those driven across the face of the subcontinent and of the earth experienced exile and a sense of dislocation.

Democracy, in the form of universal suffrage, was not inherited. It was chosen for the 1950 Indian general election when Nehru took the 'biggest gamble in history'.[7] Congress and the Muslim League were not revolutionary organizations, and they facilitated the transfer of power. Nevertheless, the Freedom Movement had destroyed the legitimacy of British rule. For a fifth of humanity, whatever the inherited political, economic and psychological distortions, 14–15 August 1947 was a turning point in history. As Nehru told the Constituent Assembly on the 14 August:

> Long years ago we made a tryst with destiny, and now the time comes when we shall redeem our pledge, not wholly or in full measure, but very substantially. At the stroke of the midnight hour, when the world sleeps, India will awake to life and freedom.[8]

How does British rule compare with other modern imperialisms? D. A. Low's rating would appear to be: middling. In his summary, most benevolent was that of the USA, not in Hawaii, but in the Philippines, for which in 1916 Congress passed the Jones Act promising 'independence as soon as stable government can be established'. Less so was that of the French. Ho Chi Minh thought that 'the Gandhis and de Valeras would have long since entered heaven had they been born in one of the French colonies'. Least benevolent of all were the Dutch in the East Indies exemplified by governor-general de Jonge who declared in the early 1930s: 'We have ruled here for 300 years with whip and club and we shall be doing so in another 300 years.'[9] The broad brush-stroke cannot cover all circumstances: the potential economic and strategic value of the colony; the different times and circumstances of acquisition; the relative numbers of European officials and settlers. Comparisons with India must consider the scale of the operation, with its dependence on collaborators, and the political culture of the home country. The ending, however, was strikingly different from the French case. Horrific upheavals in north India were not paralleled by threats to British political stability. As J. G. A. Pocock has written about the earlier loss of the American colonies, there was a readiness to sacrifice colonial empire to domestic constitutional order, a 'capacity for losing an empire without caring very deeply'.[10]

Few would now dispute Seeley's claim that 'In a history of modern England it [India] deserves a prominent place in the main narrative, and not the mere digression or occasional notice which our historians commonly assign to it.'[11] Apart from the intrinsic interest of Indian history, there is India's role as the second centre of the British Empire and its increasingly evident direct and indirect influence on many aspects of British life. The complexity of this relationship has always been marked by ambiguity. The authoritarian and exploitative Raj proclaimed a basis in liberal values, enshrined in the Queen's Proclamation of 1858; hence, perhaps, the limited and selective attachment of many of its sternest Indian critics. Even in the heyday of high imperialism, western racist assumptions could produce inclusive statements. The door of the Indian Institute in Oxford bore an inscription in modern Sanskrit with the translation: 'This building, dedicated to Eastern sciences, was founded for the use of Aryas (Indians and Englishmen) by excellent and benevolent men desirous of encouraging knowledge.'[12]

APPENDIX A

	Prime Minister	Secretaries of State for India
1859–65	Lord Palmerston: Whig	Sir C. Wood
1865–66	Lord Russell: Whig-Lib.	Sir C. Wood, 1865–66
		Earl de Grey (later Ripon), 1866
1886–67	Lord Derby: Con.	Lord Cranborne (later Salisbury)
	B. Disraeli,1868: Con.	
1868–74	W. Gladstone: Lib.	Duke of Argyll
1874–80	B. Disraeli: Con.	Lord Salisbury, 1874–78
		Lord Cranbrook, 1878–80
1880–85	W. Gladstone: Lib.	Lord Hartington, 1880–82;
		Lord Kimberley, 1882–85
1885–86	Lord Salisbury: Con.	Lord Randolph Churchill
1886	W. Gladstone: Lib.	Lord Kimberley
1886–92	Lord Salisbury: Con.	Viscount Cross
1892–94	W. Gladstone: Lib.	Lord Kimberley
1894–95	Lord Rosebery: Lib.	Sir H. Fowler
1895–1902	Lord Salisbury: Con.	Lord G. Hamilton
1902–1905	A. J. Balfour: Con.	Lord G. Hamilton, 1902–1903;
		W. St. John Brodrick, 1903–1905
1905–1908	Sir H. Campbell-Bannerman: Lib.	J. Morley
1908–15	H. H. Asquith: Lib.	J. Morley, 1908–10, 1911;

(Continued)

	Prime Minister	Secretaries of State for India
		Lord Crewe, 1911–15
1915–16	H. H. Asquith: Coalit.	A. Chamberlain
1916–22	D. Lloyd George: Coalit.	A.Chamberlain,1916–17;
		E. Montagu, 1917–22
1922–24	A. Bonar Law, 1922–23: Con.	Viscount Peel
	S. Baldwin, 1923–24: Con.	
1924	J. R. MacDonald: Lab.	Lord Olivier
1924–29	S. Baldwin: Con.	Lord Birkenhead, 1924–28;
		Viscount Peel, 1928–29
1929–31	J. R. MacDonald: Lab.	W. Wedgwood Benn
1931–35	J. R. MacDonald: National	Sir S. Hoare
1935–37	S. Baldwin: National	Marquess of Zetland
1937–40	N. Chamberlain: National	Marquess of Zetland
1940–45	W. S. Churchill: National	L. S. Amery
1945	W. S. Churchill: Caretaker	L. S. Amery
1945–50	C. R. Attlee: Lab.	Lord Pethick-Lawrence, 1945–April 1947;
		Lord Listowel, April–August 1947

Viceroys

1856–62	Lord Canning (viceroy from 1858)
1862–63	Lord Elgin
1863–69	Lord Lawrence
1869–72	Lord Mayo
1872–76	Lord Northbrook
1876–80	Lord Lytton
1880–84	Lord Ripon
1884–88	Lord Dufferin
1888–94	Lord Lansdowne
1894–99	Lord Elgin
1899–1905	Lord Curzon
1905–10	Lord Minto
1910–16	Lord Hardinge
1916–21	Lord Chelmsford
1921–26	Lord Reading
1926–31	Lord Irwin (later Halifax)
1931–36	Lord Willingdon
1936–43	Lord Linlithgow
1943–February 1947	Lord Wavell
February–August 1947	Lord Mountbatten

APPENDIX B

The population of India, excluding Burma, from Kingsley Davis, *The Population of India and Pakistan* (Princeton: Princeton University Press, 1951) 27.

Census	Population in 1,000s	Estimated population in 1,000s
1871	203,415	255,166
1881	250,160	257,380
1891	279,593	282,134
1901	283,870	285,288
1911	303,041	302,985
1921	305,730	305,679
1931	338,171	338,171
1941	388,998	388,998

CHRONOLOGY

1858	Government of India Act
1859–61	Indian Law Codes
1869	Suez Canal opened
1871	Education Resolution
1875	Alwar Despatch
1876–78	Famine in south India
1877	Empress of India
1878–80	Second Afghan War
1878	Vernacular Press Act
1879	Deccan Agriculturists' Relief Act
1879	Statutory Civil Service
1881	Rendition of Mysore
1882	Local Government Resolution
1883	Ilbert Bill
1885	Indian National Congress founded
1885	Panjdeh incident
1885	Third Burma War
1886	Kayasth Caste Conference
1886	Muslim Educational Conference
1892	Age of Consent Act
1892	Indian Councils Act
1893	Durand Line
1903–1904	Tibet invasion
1905	Partition of Bengal

1906	All-India Muslim League founded
1907	Anglo-Russian Entente
1908	Alipore Bomb Trial
1908	Allahabad Convention
1909	*Hind Swaraj* published
1909	Indian Councils Act
1911	Partition of Bengal revoked
1911	Capital moves from Calcutta to Delhi
1914	India entered First World War
1915	Defence of India Act
1915–16	Indian Home Rule Leagues
1916	Lucknow Pact
1916	Kut el-Amara surrender
1918	Montagu-Chelmsford Report
1919	Rowlatt Acts
1919	Amritsar Massacre
1919	Government of India Act
1919	Fiscal Autonomy Convention
1919	Third Afghan War/Afghan War of Independence
1919	All-India Khilafat Committee
1920	Hunter Commission
1920	Communist Party of India founded
1920	Non-Cooperation
1920	Nagpur Congress
1921	Moplah rebellion
1922	Lloyd George's 'steel frame' speech
1923	Swaraj Party formed
1923	Bengal Pact
1924	Cawnpore Conspiracy Case
1925	RSS founded
1925	Self-Respect Movement founded
1927	Simon Commission
1927	Currency Act
1929	Indian States (Butler) Committee

1929	Meerut Conspiracy Case
1929	Lord Irwin's Declaration
1930	First Round Table Conference
1930	Civil Disobedience
1931	Karachi Declaration on Fundamental Rights
1931	Statute of Westminster
1931	Chittagong Armoury Raid
1931	Delhi Pact
1931	Second Round Table Conference
1931	Communal Award
1932	Poona Pact
1932	Civil Disobedience: second phase
1933	Third Round Table Conference
1933	Lees-Mody Pact
1933	White paper on constitutional future
1934	Congress Socialist Party formed
1934	Reserve Bank of India
1935	Ottawa Trade Agreement
1935	Government of India Act
1936	Bombay Manifesto
1937	General election
1939	India enters Second World War
1940	Lahore Resolution
1942	15 February: Singapore falls to Japanese
1942	March–April: Cripps Mission
1942	8 August: Quit India Resolution
1943	Subhas Chandra Bose reorganizes INA
1945	June–July: Simla Conference
1945–46	General election
1946	March–August: Cabinet Mission
1946	July: Constituent Assembly elections
1946	16 August: League called for Direct Action
1946	Congress (Sept.) and League (Oct.) joined Interim Government
1946	September: Wavell's Breakdown Plan

1947   20 February: Attlee's House of Commons declaration

1947   22 March: Mountbatten arrives in India

1947   April: Mountbatten's Plan Balkan

1947   3 June: Partition announced

1947   18 July: India Independence Act

1947   14–15 August: Pakistan and Indian independence

NOTES

Introduction

1 Appendix B.

2 C. H. Philips (ed.), *The Correspondence of Lord William Cavendish Bentinck, Governor-General of India, 1828–1835*, 2 vols (Oxford: Oxford University Press, 1977), vol. 1, 310–11; vol. 2, 806.

3 Ibid., II: 806.

4 P. J .Marshall, *Problems of Empire: British India 1757–1813* (London: George Allen and Unwin, 1968), 30–31.

5 Thomas Macaulay, *Minute on Education* (1835), reprinted in Philips, *Correspondence*, vol. 2, 1403ff.

6 Ibid.

7 Ibid.

8 Quoted by Eric Stokes, *The English Utilitarians and India* (Oxford: Clarendon Press, 1959), 88.

9 Christopher Herbert, *War of No Pity* (Princeton: Princeton University Press, 2008), 89, 104–5. For a selection of interpretations by contemporaries and historians, see Ainslee T. Embree, (ed.), *India in 1857* (Delhi: Chanakya Publications, 1987). See also Rosie Llewellyn-Jones, *The Great Uprising in India, 1857–8: Untold Stories Indian and British* (Woodbridge: Boydell Press, 2007) and a wide range of studies from a left perspective in P. C. Joshi (ed.), *Rebellion 1957* (New Delhi: National Book Trust, India, 2009).

10 Cubbon to Officiating Secretary, Foreign Department, 3 June 1860, Harrison Papers, fol. 28, Isle of Man Record Office.

11 Eric Stokes, *The Peasant and the Raj* (Cambridge: Cambridge University Press, 1978).

12 V. D. Savarkar, *The First Indian War of Independence, 1857* (London: n.p., 1909).

13 Karl Marx and Friedrich Engels, *The First Indian War of Independence* (Moscow: Progress Publishers, 1968), 15.

14 Queen Victoria, 'Proclamation', 1 November 1858, in C. H. Philips and B. N. Pandey (eds), *The Evolution of India and Pakistan, 1858–1947: Select Documents* (London: Oxford University Press, 1962), 10–11.

15 G. O. Trevelyan, *The Competition Wallah* (London; reprinted from Macmillan's Magazine, 1864), 54.

16 Philips, *Correspondence*, vol. 1, 549.

1. Crown Rule to 1880

1   S. Gopal, *British Policy in India, 1858–1905* (Cambridge: Cambridge University Press, 1965), 61.

2   Ronald Robinson, 'Non-European foundations of European Imperialism: Sketch for a theory of collaboration', in Roger Owen and Bob Sutcliffe (eds), *Studies in the Theory of Imperialism* (London: Longman 1972) 117–41. See also D. Omissi and A.-M. Misra, 'Co-option and Coercion in India, 1857–1947', *Contemporary Review* 6.3 (1992): 536–52.

3   David Gilmour, *The Ruling Caste* (London: John Murray, 2005).

4   Quoted in Maria Misra, *Vishnu's Crowded Temple* (London: Allen Lane, 2007), 75.

5   Philips and Pandey, *Evolution of India and Pakistan*, 10–11.

6   J. M. Compton, 'Open Competition and the Indian Civil Service,1854–1876', *English Historical Review* 83.328 (1968): 265–84.

7   Trevelyan, *Competion Wallah* (London; reprinted from Macmillan's Magazine, 1864), letter 1.

8   Compton, 'Open Competition and the Indian Civil Service'.

9   Ibid.

10 Anil Seal, *The Emergence of Indian Nationalism* (London: Cambridge University Press, 1971), 134.

11 George Pottinger, *Mayo: Disraeli's Viceroy* (Wilton: Russell, 1990), 192.

12 Seal, *Emergence*, 138–9.

13 Sumit Sarkar, *Modern India, 1885–1947* (Basingstoke: Macmillan, 1989) 44ff. Ranajit Guha (ed.), *Subaltern Studies: Writings on South Asian History and Society* (Delhi and Oxford: Oxford University Press, 1982–99).

14 Sir George Chesney, *Indian Polity* (London: Longmans, Green & Co., 1894), 268–70.

15 W. W. Hunter, *A Life of the Earl of Mayo*, vol. 1 (London: Smith Elder, 1875), 187.

16 Niall Ferguson, *Empire* (London, Allen Lane, 2003) 174.

17 J. S. Gewal, *The Sikhs of the Punjab* (Cambridge: Cambridge University Press, 1990), 28ff.

18 C. U. Aitchison, *Lord Lawrence* (Oxford: Clarendon Press, 1892), 153.

19 Judith Brown, *Modern India* (Delhi: Oxford University Press, 1985), 137.

20 C. A. Bayly, *Indian Society and the Making of the British Empire* (Cambridge: Cambridge University Press, 1988), 198–9.

21 Peter Hardy, *The Muslims of British India* (Cambridge: Cambridge University Press, 1972), 93; Seal, *Emergence of Indian Nationalism*, 305.

22 Francis Robinson, *Separatism among Indian Muslims: The Politics of the UP Muslims, 1860–1923* (Cambridge: Cambridge University Press, 1974), 89.

23 Hardy, *Muslims of British India*, 98.

24 Robinson, *Separatism among Indian Muslims*, 346.

25 Hardy, *Muslims of British India*, 72.

26 Aitchison, *Lawrence*, 135.

27 C. U. Aitchison, *A Collection of Treaties, Engagements and Sunnuds, Relating to India and Neighbouring Countries Compiled by C. U. Aitchison, Under-secretary to the Government of India in the Foreign Department* (Calcutta: G. A. Savielle and P. M. Cranenburgh, Bengal Print Co., 1862–65).

28 Philips and Pandey, *Evolution of India and Pakistan*, 10–11.
29 Wood to Lawrence, 18 July 1864, Wood Papers, British Library.
30 Correspondence Regarding the Comparative Merits of British and Native Administration in India, 1867, H 44, Political and Secret Department Library, IOR [India Office Records], British Library.
31 I. F. S. Copland, 'The Baroda Crisis of 1873–77: A Study in Government Rivalry', *Modern Asian Studies* 2.2 (1968): 97–123.
32 Secret Despatch, 9 September 1875, no. 24, with enclosures, IOR, British Library.
33 Salisbury to Disraeli, 10 January 1976, Hughenden Papers.
34 Lytton to Disraeli, 30 April 1976, Hughenden Papers.
35 Gopal, *British Policy*, 114.
36 David Cannadine, *Ornamentalism* (London: Allen Lane, 2001); Salisbury to Lytton, 7 July 1876, Salisbury Papers microfilm, British Library.
37 Note by Lytton, 17 May 1876, Lytton Papers, British Library; see also, D 61,4 April 1873, Secret and Political Memoranda, IOR, British Library.
38 Salisbury to Lytton, 2 November 1876, Salisbury Papers microfilm, British Library.
39 C. L. Tupper, *Our Indian Protectorate* (London: Longmans, 1893), 61.
40 Lady Betty Balfour, *The History of Lord Lytton's Indian Administration, 1876–80* (London: Longmans, 1899), 2.
41 Seal, *Emergence of Indian Nationalism*, 132.
42 Lytton to Sir H. Norman, 5 December 1876, with Lytton to Carnarvon, 29 November 1876, Carnarvon Papers, National Archives.
43 Balfour, *History*, 29.
44 Ira Klein, 'Who Made the Second Afghan War?' *Journal of Asian History* 8 (1974): 97–121.
45 Ibid.
46 R. Bosworth Smith, Life of Lord Lawrence, vol. 2 (London: Smith Elder, 1883), 649.
47 Balfour, *History*, 381.
48 Klein, 'Who Made the Second Afghan War?'
49 Balfour, *History*, 359.
50 Ibid., 413, 430.
51 G. E. Buckle, *Life of Benjamin Disraeli*, vol. 4 (London: John Murray, 1910–20), 485–6. John Lowe Duthie, 'Lord Lytton and the Second Afghan War: A Psychohistorical Study', *Victorian Studies* 27.4 (1984): 461–73.
52 They were levied as follows, with agricultural incomes exempt: income tax – 1860–65; licence tax on professions and trades – 1867; certificate tax – 1868; licence tax – 1869–73; income tax – 1886. B. R. Tomlinson, *The Economy of India, 1860–1970* (Cambridge: Cambridge University Press, 1993), 152. Unless otherwise stated, economic figures are drawn from this source.
53 Peter Robb, *A History of India* (Basingstoke: Palgrave Macmillan, 2002), 162.
54

Value of foreign trade in *lakhs* (100,000) of rupees (annual average)

	Imports	Exports
1849–50 – 1853–54	15.85	20.02
1859–60 – 1863–64	41.06	43.17

(*Continued*)

	Imports	Exports
1869–70 – 1873–74	41.30	57.87
1879–80 –1883–84	61.81	80.41
1889–90 –1893–94	88.70	108.67
1899–1900 –1903–1904	110.69	136.59
1904–1905	143.92	174.14

Exchange rate	
1870	Rs 1 = £0-2s-0d
1885	Rs 1 = £0-1s-7d
1892	Rs 1 = £0-1s-3d

Source: *Imperial Gazeteer* (Calcutta, 1907), vol. 3, 268.

	Population (millions)	Urban population (%)
1871	249.44	8.7
1881	254.51	9.3
1891	276.69	9.4
1901	280.87	10.0
1911	298.20	9.4
1921	299.63	10.2

See also Appendix B.

55 B. M. Bhatia, *Famines in India* (New Delhi: Asia Publishing House, 1963), 45.
56 CAB 41/8/1, 8th, Royal Archives at Windsor Castle, 1837–1901, microfilm, IOR, British Library.
57 David Arnold, 'Cholera and Colonialism in British India', *Past and Present* 113 (1986): 118–51.
58 Balfour, *History*, 193.

2. Liberal Imperialism, 1880–1899

1 David C. Potter, *India's Political Administrators, 1919–1983* (Oxford: Clarendon Press, 1986), 122–3.
2 Philips and Pandey, *Evolution of India and Pakistan*, 59.
3 R. J. Moore, *Liberalism and Indian Politics, 1872–1922* (London: Edward Arnold, 1966), 25.
4 Ibid., 30.
5 Ibid., 48.
6 Nicholas Tarling (ed.), *Cambridge History of South East Asia*, vol. 2 (Cambridge: Cambridge University Press, 1992), 40.
7 Moore, *Liberalism and Indian Politics*, 47.

8 Ibid.

9 Ibid., 49.

10 *Oxford Dictionary of National Biography*, 'Gallagher, John Andrew (1919–1980)' and, following, as part of the same entry, Ronald Robinson, (1920–1999). See also, R. Robinson and J. A. Gallagher, 'The Imperialism of Free Trade', reprinted in John Gallagher, *The Decline, Revival and Fall of the British Empire* (Cambridge: Cambridge University Press, 1982), 1–18.

11 Mayo thought of him as a 'collaborator' and 'one of the ablest and wisest men in India.' For Lytton he was the 'one native whom I believe to be positively dangerous... [he]has successfully studied English society, English institutions, and English character with the deliberate purpose of playing us off against ourselves.' Mayo to the Duke of Argyll, 2 March 1969, Mayo Papers, Cambridge University Library; Lytton to Lord Ripon, 8 June 1880, Lytton Papers, British Library.

12 House of Commons, *East India (Native States under the Administrative Control of Political Agents: Return for Five Years, 1898–1902* (London: HMSO, 1906) extracted from page 3.

13 John Westlake, 'The Native States of India', *Law Quarterly Review* 26 (1910): 312–19.

14 C. L. Tupper (comp.), *Indian Political Practice* (Calcutta: Office of Superintendant of Government Printing, India,1895–1901), vol. 2, para. 260; and vol. 3, para. 475.

15 *Indian Law Reports*, I.A.XXIV (1897), 137; *International Law Reports* (1912), Pro. Div. 92; *Gazette of India*, no. 1700E, 21 August 1891.

16 See note before the preface to the second edition.

17 Salisbury to Lytton, 13 July 1876, Lytton Papers, British Library; Cannadine, *Ornamentalism*, 21.

18 Tupper, *Indian Political Practice*, vol. 1, para. 129 – see also, Tupper, *Our Indian Protectorate*, 356; Sir Charles Dilke, *Greater Britain* (London: Macmillan, 1872), 552.

19 Mss Eur F92/3, Lee-Warner Collection, British Library; below, Mss Eur 38/3/70, Bowring Albums, British Library.

20 *Mysore Census*, vol. 1 (1891), 238–9.

21 Holeya tanaka ota
   Doreya tanaka doru (Kannada)

22 Moore, *Liberalism and Indian Politics*, 37.

23 Anthony Denholm, *Lord Ripon, 1827–1909* (Cambridge: Cambridge University Press, 1982), introduction (no pagination); Philips and Pandey, *Evolution of India and Pakistan*, 50.

24 Moore, *Liberalism and Indian Politics*, 33.

25 Lucien Wolf, *Life of the First Marquess of Ripon*, vol. 2 (London: John Murray, 1921), 98.

26 Seal, *Emergence of Indian Nationalism*, 156.

27 Preface to Gallagher, *Decline, Revival and Fall*, xii.

28 Wolf, *Life of the First Marquess of Ripon*, vol. 2, 119.

29 Moore, *Liberalism and Indian Politics*, 38.

30 Edwin Hirschmann, *White Mutiny* (New Delhi: Heritage Publishers, 1980), 12. The Indigo Commission Report (1861) had revealed coercive management of plantation labour. In 1871–72 when the Criminal Procedure Code was being re-written, Fitzjames Stephen had warned the Legislative Council that the existing system 'extends practical immunity to English wrongdoers'.

31 C. E. Buckland, *Bengal under the Lieutenant-Governors*, vol. 2 (Calcutta: S. K. Lahiri and Co., 1902), 781.

32 Hirschmann, *White Mutiny*, 179.

33 Sumanta Bannerjee, *The Parlour and the Streets: Elite and Popular Culture in Nineteenth-Century Calcutta* (Calcutta: Modern Book Agency, 1998), 177; Hirschmann, *White Mutiny*, 181–2.

34 Philips and Pandey, *Evolution of India and Pakistan*, 57.

35 Bipin Chandra Pal, *Memories of My Life and Times* (Calcutta: Modern Book Agency, 1932), 411.

36 H. J. S. Cotton, *New India* (London: K.Paul, 1904), 42.

37 *Oxford Dictionary of National Biography*, 'Dutt, Romesh Chunder [Rameshchandra Datta] (1848–1909)'.

38 Cotton, *New India*, 55.

39 William Dalrymple, *The White Mughals* (London: Harper Collins, 2002).

40 Philips, *Correspondence*, vol. 2, 978.

41 Seid-Gholam-Hossein Khan, *Seir Mutaqherin*, vol. 3 (Calcutta,1789; reprinted Lahore: Sheikh Mubarak Ali, 1975), 161–2.

42 Kenneth Ballhatchet, *Race, Sex and Class under the Raj* (London: Weidenfeld and Nicolson, 1980).

43 Tupper, *Indian Political Practice*, vol. 1, para. 79.

44 Wolf, *Life of the First Marquess of Ripon*, vol. 2, 101.

45 J. M. Compton, 'British Government and Society in the Presidency of Bengal, c. 1858–1880', DPhil dissertation, University of Oxford (1968), ch. 2.

46 Eric Stokes's review of Ballhatchet, *Race, Sex and Class* in *London Review of Books* 2.7 (1980); Cotton, *New India*, 47.

47 Lord Northbrook to Queen Victoria, 11 August 1873, Northbrook Papers, British Library.

48 Sir Edward Cook, *The Life of Florence Nightingale*, vol. 2 (London, 1913), 343.

49 John R. McLane, *Indian Nationalism and the Early Congress* (Princeton: Princeton University Press, 1977), 93.

50 Jawaharlal Nehru, *An Autobiography* (London: Bodley Head, 1949), 27.

51 McLane, *Indian Nationalism*, 107, 72.

52 Hardy, *Muslims of British India*, 129. To protect his position, the Syed was prepared to cooperate with Hindu landowners in the United Indian Patriotic Association.

53 McLane, *Indian Nationalism*, 162.

54 D. Omissi, *The Sepoy and the Raj, 1860–1940* (Basingstoke: Macmillan, in association with King's College London, 1994), 10.

55 S. R. Mehrotra, 'The Early Indian National Congress, 1885–1918', in B. R. Nanda, *Essays in Modern Indian History* (Delhi: Oxford University Press,1980), 42–64 (52).

56 J. P. Misra, 'Lord Lansdowne and the Indian National Congress', *Indo-British Review* 1.3 (January to March 1969): 22–39.

57 Gordon Johnson, *Provincial Politics and Indian Nationalism: Bombay and the Indian National Congress* (Cambridge: Cambridge University Press, 1973), 19; Philips and Pandey, *Evolution of India and Pakistan*, 69, 131–2.

58 McLane, *Indian Nationalism*, 157.

59 Mehrotra, 'Early Indian National Congress', 61.

60 Though M. M. Bhownagree was elected a Tory.

61 Valentine Chirol, *Indian Unrest* (London: Macmillan, 1910), xiii; quoted in McLane, *Indian Nationalism*, 157.

62 Johnson, *Provincial Politics*, 193.

63 John Gallagher, Gordon Johnson and Anil Seal (eds), *Locality, Province and Nation: Essays on Indian Politics, 1870–1947* (Cambridge: Cambridge University Press, 1973), 6n.

64 C. A. Bayly, 'Patrons and Politics in North India', 29–68.

65 D. A. Washbrook, 'Gandhian Politics', *Modern Asian Studies* 7.1 (1973): 107–15.

66 Rajat K. Ray, 'Three Interpretations', in Nanda, *Essays in Modern Indian History*, 1–39.

67 Tapan Raychaudhuri, 'India, 1858 to the 1930s', in Robin W. Winks (ed.), *The Oxford History of the British Empire*, vol. 5 (Oxford: Oxford University Press, 1999); see also, Tapan Raychaudhuri, 'Indian Nationalism as Animal Politics', *Historical Journal* 22.3 (1979): 747–63.

68 Strachey, *India* (London, 1888) 5, 8.

69 Dilke, *Greater Britain*, 559–60.

70 Quoted from the *Bengalee* in McLane, *Indian Nationalism*, 159.

71 Quoted in Bipan Chandra, *Modern India* (New Delhi: National Council of Educational Research and Training, 1981), 195.

72 Brown, *Modern India*, 116. R. C. Dutt in his *Economic History of British India* (London, 1902) complained that 'The poverty of the Indian population at the present day is unparalleled in any civilised country' (vi).

73 Discussed in Eric Stokes, 'The First Century of British Colonial Rule in India', *Past and Present* 1.58 (February 1973): 136–60.

74 R. K. Ray, 'Political Change in British India', *Indian Economic and Social History Review* 14.4 (1977): 493–577.

75 Karl Marx and Frederick Engels, *Selected Correspondence* (Moscow: Progress Publishers, 1965), 337.

76 Bipan Chandra, *Nationalism and Colonialism in Modern India* (New Delhi: Orient Longman, 1979), 23.

77 For the beginnings of a modern debate about the Indian economy under British rule see Morris D. Morris et al., *Indian Economy in the Nineteenth Century: A Symposium* (Delhi: Indian Economic and Social History Association, 1969); see, also, the introduction to Tomlinson, *Economy of Modern India*.

78 S. Bhattacharyya, *Financial Foundations of the British Raj* (Simla, 1971), 'Statistical Appendix', 308, 319.

79 Bipan Chandra, *The Rise and Growth of Economic Nationalism in India* (New Delhi: People's Publishing House, 1966), 282.

80 K. N. Chaudhuri, 'India's Internal Economy in the Nineteenth Century: An Historical Survey', *Modern Asian Studies* 2.1 (1968): 31–50.

81 Sarkar, *Modern India*, 55.

82 Kenneth W. Jones, *Socio-Religious Reform Movements in British India* (Cambridge: Cambridge University Press, 1989), 45.

83 Christophe Jaffrelot, *The Hindu Nationalist Movement in India* (New York: Columbia University Press, 1996), ch. 1.

84 Stanley Wolpert, *Tilak and Gokhale* (Berkeley: University of California Press, 1977), 81.

85 Ibid., 101.

86 McLane, *Indian Nationalism*, 339.

3. The Consequences of Lord Curzon: India or the Empire, 1899–1916

1 David Dilks, *Curzon in India*, vol. 1 (London: Rupert Hart-Davis, 1969), 248.

2 David Gilmour, *Curzon* (London: John Murray, 1994), 221.

3 Kenneth Rose, *Superior Person* (London: Weidenfeld and Nicolson, 1969), 190.

4 Moore, *Liberalism and Indian Politics*, 76; Rose, *Superior Person*, 327.

5 Dilks, *Curzon in India*, vol. 2, 129.

6 Sarkar, *Modern India*, 104.

7 House of Commons, *East India (Famine): Report of the Indian Famine Commission, 1901* (London: HMSO, 1901), 10.

8 Sarkar, *Modern India*, 105: Brown, *Modern India*, 120.

9 Derek Waller, *The Pundits* (Lexington: University Press of Kentucky, 1990), 192.

10 P. L. Mehra, 'The Younghusband Expedition: an Interpretation', *Journal of Indian History* 33.98, part 2 (1955): 201–28; *Journal of Indian History* 39.115, part 1 (1961): 137–62.

11 Glen Wilkinson, '"There Is No More Stirring Story": The Press Depiction and Images of War during the Tibet Expedition, 1903–04', *War and Society* 9.2 (1991): 1–16.

12 See Peter Fleming, *Bayonets to Lhasa* (Oxford: Rupert Hart-Davis, 1985); Patrick French, *Younghusband* (London: Harper Collins, 1995); S. G. Mishra, 'The Younghusband Expedition and the Maharaja Sham Sher', *The Quarterly Review of Historical Studies* 15.1 (1975–6): 44–60.

13 W. S. J. F. Brodick, Earl of Midleton, *Records and Reactions, 1856–1939* (London: John Murray, 1939) 200–201.

14 Kenneth Young, *Arthur James Balfour* (London: G. Bell, 1963), 237.

15 McLane, *Indian Nationalism*, 134, 92.

16 Gilmour, *Curzon*, 273.

17 John R. McLane, 'The Decision to Partition Bengal in 1905', *Indian Economic and Social History Review* 2.3 (1964): 221–37; Sarkar, *Modern India*, 107.

18 Sarkar, *Modern India*, 107.

19 Bankimchandra Chatterji, *Anandamath, or the Sacred Brotherhood*, trans. Julius J. Lipner (Oxford: Oxford University Press, 2005), 84.

20 Nirad C. Chaudhuri, *Autobiography of an Unknown Indian* (London: Macmillan, 1951), 222.

21 Ibid.

22 Bengal was reckoned to be a little worse than these figures for the All-India Price Index:

1890–94	1904	1906	1908
100	106	129	143

23 A. P. Kannangara, 'Indian Millowners and Indian Nationalism before 1914', *Past and Present* 40 (July 1968): 147–64.

24 Sumit Sarkar, *The Swadeshi Movement in Bengal, 1903–08* (New Delhi: People's Publishing House, 1973), 65.

25 Sarkar, *Modern India*, 135.

26 Sarkar, *Swadeshi Movement*, 347; Sarkar, *Modern India*, 135ff.

27 P. Pattabhi Sitaramayya, *The History of the Indian National Congress, 1885–1935* (Madras: Working Committee of the Congress, 1935), 89.

28 Wolpert, *Tilak and Gokhale*, 238.

29 Johnson, *Provincial Politics and Indian Nationalism*, 175.

30 Morley to Minto, 23 November 1906, Morley Papers, British Library.

31 Moore, *Liberalism and Indian Politics*, 92.

32 Hardy, *Muslims of British India*, 167.

33 S. R. Ashton, *British Policy towards the Indian States, 1905–1939* (London: Curzon Press, 1982), 40.

34 S. A. Wolpert, *Morley and India, 1906–10* (Berkeley: University of California Press, 1967); Stephen E. Koss, *John Morley at the India Office, 1905–1910* (New Haven and London: Yale University Press, 1969).

35 17 December 1908, House of Lords, *Parliamentary Debates*, 4th series, vol. 198 (1908), col. 1985.

36 Philips and Pandey, *Evolution of India and Pakistan*, 191.

37 Robinson, *Separatism among Indian Muslims*, 149; M. N. Das, *India under Morley and Minto* (London: Allen and Unwin, 1964), 151.

38 Reforms Despatch, 10 October 1908, in Das, *India under Morley and Minto*, appendix 1.

39 Hardy, *Muslims of British India*, 163.

40 Das, *India under Morley and Minto*, passim; S. R. Wasti, *Lord Minto and the Indian Nationalist Movement, 1905–1910* (Oxford: Clarendon Press, 1964) passim; Robinson, *Separatism among Indian Muslims*, 168.

41 Amalesh Tripathi, *The Extremist Challenge* (Bombay: Orient Longmans, 1967) 142; Rajat K. Ray, *Social Conflict and Political Unrest in Bengal, 1875–1927* (Delhi: Oxford University Press,1984) 174ff.; Peter Heehs, *The Bomb in Bengal* (Delhi: Oxford University Press, 1993); Hiren Chakrabarti, *Political Protest in Bengal* (Calcutta: Papyrus, 1992); Sarkar, *Swadeshi Movement*, 469; Indulal Yajnik, *Shyamaji Krishnavarma* (Bombay: Lakshmi Publications, 1950) 134.

42 Sarkar, *Swadeshi Movement*, 87.

43 Tripathi, *Extremist Challenge*, 61.

44 Ibid.

45 The novel was published in 1916 and is translated in the Penguin Classics series. Satyajit Ray directed a film of the same name in 1985.

46 Wasti, *Lord Minto and the Indian Nationalist Movement* (Oxford: Clarendon Press, 1964), 90.

47 Yajnik, *Shyamaji Krishnavarma*, 135.

48 Ibid., 122.

49 Morley to Minto, 19 September 1907; see also Morley to Minto, 22 November 1907, Morley Papers, British Library.

50 Morley to Minto, 23 Apr 1908, Morley Papers, British Library.

51 J. H. Broomfield, 'The Vote and the Transfer of Power: a study of the Bengal General Election,1912–13', *Journal of Asian Studies* 21.2 (1962): 163–81; Ray, *Social Conflict*, 202ff. The *bhadralok* politicians were no more successful with the Legislative Council of a re-united Bengal. Broomfield has seen this as a great opportunity for the Moderates to secure progressive participation in government. He blames their failure to replace the incumbents who had not boycotted the first elections on the inability of the Indian Association to get organized and speak the language of grass roots politics. Ray stresses the power of newly organized British business and the way the government's electoral categories were only responsive to parochial and communal sentiment.

52 As recommended by the 1909 Decentralization Commission.

53 For the details, R. J. Moore, *Crisis of Indian Unity* (London: Clarendon Press, 1974), 19–20.

54 Alan H. Adamson, 'The Impact of Indentured Immigration on the Political Economy of British Guiana', in Kay Saunders (ed.), *Indentured Labour in the British Empire, 1834–1920* (London: Croom Helm, 1984), 42–3.

55 Hugh Tinker, 'Into Servitude: Indian Labour in the Sugar Industry, 1833–1970', in Shula Marks and Peter Richardson (eds), *International Labour Migration: Historical Perspectives* (Hounslow: Maurice Temple Smith for the Institute of Commonwealth Studies, 1984), 81.

56 W. K. Hancock, *Survey of British Commonwealth Affairs*, vol. 1 (London: Oxford University Press, 1937), 183.

57 Quoted by Judith M. Brown, *Gandhi: Prisoner of Hope* (New Haven and London: Yale University Press, 1989), 56.

58 M. K. Gandhi, *Hind Swaraj and other Writings*, ed. Anthony Parel (Cambridge: Cambridge University Press, 1997), xiii, xv, 73–4.

59 Ibid. 39, xxxix.

60 Ibid., 66.

61 Wolpert, *Morley and India*, 250.

62 Morley to Minto, 12 November 1908, Morley Papers, British Library; Brown, *Gandhi: Prisoner of Hope*, 74.

63 Disraeli, *Speech…at the Crystal Palace, June 24, 1872* (Wiesbaden: Franz Steiner Verlag GmbH, 1968).

64 Sir Richard Temple, *India in 1880* (London: John Murray, 1881), 496–7.

65 Gopal, *British Policy*, 120–21.

66 Martin Gilbert, *Servant of India* (London: Longmans, 1966), 154.

67 S. D. Waley, *Edwin Montagu* (London and Bombay: Asia Publishing House, 1964), 301.

68 Walter Lawrence, *The India We Served* (London: Cassell, 1928), 42–3.

69 Thomas Metcalf, *Imperial Vision* (London: Faber, 1989), 226.

70 Partha Mitter, *Much Maligned Monsters* (Oxford: Clarendon Press, 1977), 270.

71 Morley to Minto, 6 July 1906, Morley Papers, British Library.

72 Ibid.

73 Rudyard Kipling, 'Pagett, M. P.', in *Rudyard Kipling's Verse: Definitive Edition* (London: Hodder and Stoughton, 1940), 26–7.

74 Morley to Minto, 8 October 1907, Morley Papers, British Library.

75 Morley to Minto, 11 July 1907, Morley Papers, British Library.

76 Morley to Minto, 22 November 1907, Morley Papers, British Library.

77 Heehs, *Bomb in Bengal*, 23.

78 John Beames, *Memoirs of a Bengal Civilian* (London: Chatto and Windus, 1961), 156.

79 Francis G. Hutchins, *Illusion of Permanence* (Princeton: Princeton University Press, 1967), 158.

80 Kipling's letter as frontispiece to Lawrence, *The India We Served*.

81 Paul Smith, *Lord Salisbury on Politics* (Cambridge: Cambridge University Press, 1972), 376.

82 Kipling, 'Recessional', in *Rudyard Kipling's Verse*, 328–9.

4. The First World War, 1914–1922

1 Britain's contribution was 6.2 million men, Canada's 600,000, Australia's 450,000 and New Zealand's 221,000.

2 As numbers picked up in the late nineteenth century, the Indian government had taken an active interest, appointing Thomas Cook as sole agent for the transport of

pilgrims and then tried to regulate their health through a Native Passenger Shipping Act. F. E. Peters, *The Hajj* (Princeton: Princeton University Press, 1994). Because of the resonance of the word 'mutiny', the army preferred 'riot' or 'emeute'.

3 Nicholas Tarling, '"The merest pustule": The Singapore Mutiny of 1915', *The Journal of the Malaysian Branch of the Royal Asiatic Society* 55.2 (1982): 26–59.

4 B. R. Tomlinson, 'India and the British Empire, 1889–1935', *Indian Economic and Social History Review* 13.3 (1975): 339–80.

5 Kingsley Davis, *The Population of India and Pakistan* (Princeton: Princeton University Press, 1951), appendix B.

6 Nehru, *Autobiography*, 36; Rajat K. Ray, 'Political Change in British India', *The Economic and Social History Review* 14.4 (1977): 493–517.

7 *India's Contribution to the Great War* (Calcutta, 1923), 67, 234.

8 S. R. Mehrotra, *India and the Commonwealth, 1885–1929* (London: George Allen and Unwin, 1965), 113.

9 Rumbold, *Watershed in India*, 91.

10 Lord Hardinge, despatch, 25 August 1911, in Philips and Pandey, *Evolution of India and Pakistan*, 90–91.

11 Moore, *Crisis of Indian Unity*, 113.

12 D. A. Low (ed.), *Soundings in Modern South Asian History* (London: Weidenfeld and Nicholson, 1968), 5.

13 By the secretary of state, a civilian (Lord Meston), Sinha and the Maharaja of Bikaner.

14 Mehrotra, *India and the Commonwealth*, 79.

15 Philips and Pandey, *Evolution of India and Pakistan*, 264.

16 A. Zimmern, *The Third British Empire* (London: Humphreys Milford, 1926).

17 Mehrotra, *India and the Commonwealth*, 110.

18 Ibid.

19 Sugata Bose and Ayesha Jalal, *Modern South Asia: History, Culture, Political Economy*, 2nd ed. (New Delhi: Oxford University Press, 2004), 110.

20 R. Kumar (ed.), *Essays on Gandhian Politics* (Oxford: Oxford University Press, 1971), 60.

21 Ibid., 3.

22 Tim Coates, *The Amritsar Massacre* (abridged) (London: Stationery Office, 2000), 57, 75–6.

23 Quoted by Tomlinson in 'India and the British Empire, 1889–1935'.

24 *Parliamentary Debates*, House of Commons, 5th series, vol. 157 (1922) cols 1513, 1517.

25 Keith Jeffrey, 'An English Barrack in the Oriental Seas', *Modern Asian Studies* 15.3 (1981): 369–86.

26 Rumbold, *Watershed in India*, 115.

27 Alfred Milner quoted by J. A. Gallagher, 'Nationalisms and the Crisis of Empire,1919–21', *Modern Asian Studies* 15.3 (1981): 355–68.

28 Quoted by Jeffrey in 'An English Barrack'.

29 Clive Dewey, 'The End of the Imperialism of Free Trade', in Clive Dewey and A. G. Hopkins (eds), *The Imperial Impact: Studies in the Economic History of Africa and India* (London: Athlone Press, 1978), 35–67.

30 Gopal Krishna, 'The Khilafat Movement in India: the First Phase', *Journal of the Royal Asiatic Society* 1–2 (1968): 37–53.

31 Mehrotra, *India and the Commonwealth*, 193n.

32 Sarkar, *Modern India*, 197; Partha Chatterjee, 'Gandhi and the Critique of Civil Society', in Ranajit Guha (ed.), *Subaltern Studies III* (Delhi: Oxford University Press, 1984): 153–95 (53).

33 Gandhi, *Hind Swaraj*, 73; Brown, *Gandhi: Prisoner of Hope*, 124.

34 Sumit Sarkar, 'The Conditions and Nature of Subaltern Militancy: Bengal from Swadeshi to Non-Co-operation, c.1905–1922', in *Subaltern Studies III*, 271–320 (289).

35 Gail Minault, 'Urdu Political Poetry during the Khilafat Movement', *Modern Asian Studies* 8.4 (1974): 459–71.

36 Martin Gilbert, *The World in Torment: Winston S.Churchill, 1916–22* (London: Minerva, 1990), 405, 408.

37 Stanley Wolpert, *A New History of India*, 7th ed. (New York and Oxford: Oxford University Press, 2004), 287, 304; Mehrotra, *India and the Commonwealth*, 115.

38 Gallagher, 'Nationalisms and the Crisis of Empire'.

39 D. N. Dhangare, 'Conflict, Religion and Politics', *Past and Present* 74 (1977): 112–41; L. Hardgrave, 'The Mappilla Rebellion, 1922', *Modern Asian Studies* 11.1 (1977): 59–99.

40 Bernard Lewis, *The Emergence of Modern Turkey* (Oxford: Oxford University Press, 1961), 263.

41 Moore, *Crisis of Indian Unity*, 14.

42 Gopal Krishna, 'The Development of the Indian National Congress as a Mass Organization, 1918–23', *Journal of Asian Studies* 25.3 (1966): 413–30. Though the delegates were still predominantly lawyers and professionals, the social range was widening. The Muslim percentage rose to 10.9 in 1921 but fell back the next year to 3.6. Furthermore, women increased their percentage from a negligible base to 3.1 in 1923.

43 Ibid.

44 P. C. Bamford, *Histories of the Non-Co-operation and Khilafat Movements* (Delhi: Government of India Press, 1925; reprinted Delhi: Deep Publications, 1974), 49, 59.

45 Rumbold, *Watershed in India*, 317.

46 Gopal Krishna, 'The Khilafat Movement in India: The First Phase', *Journal of the Royal Asiatic Society* 100 (1968): 37–53.

47 His ban on machinery was not total. He thought Mr Singer invented his sewing machine out of love for his wife. It saved her work and did not involve the exploitation of others. Partha Chatterjee, *Nationalist Thought and the Colonial World* (London: Zed Books, for the United Nations University, 1986), ch. 4.

48 R. K. Ray, review of *Jawaharlal Nehru*, vol. 1 by S. Gopal, *Indian Economic and Social History Review* 14.2 (1977): 273–82.

49 Ramachandra Guha, *An Anthropologist among the Marxists and other Essays* (New Delhi: Permanent Black, 2001), 92.

5. Dyarchy and Depression, 1922–1939

1 John Gallagher, 'Congress in Decline: Bengal 1930 to 1939', in Gallagher, Johnson and Seal (eds), *Locality, Province and Nation: Essays on Indian Politics, 1870–1947* (Cambridge: Cambridge University Press, 1973), 6n.

2 Mrs Besant's Theosophical Society was headquartered in Madras city and had 132 of its 200 branches in the province. She controlled newspapers and could influence educational charities. Also, Christopher Baker, 'Non-Cooperation in South India', in C. J. Baker and D. A. Washbrook (eds), *South India*, (Delhi: Macmillan, 1975).

3 Quoted in Sarkar, *Modern India*, 159.

4 Gopal, *Indian Economic and Social History Review* 14.3 (1977): 406ff.

5 D. A. Washbrook, *The Emergence of Provincial Politics: The Madras Presidency, 1870–1920* (Cambridge: Cambridge University Press, 1976), 296.

6 Eugene Irshchick, *Politics and Social Conflict in South India* (Berkeley and Los Angeles: University of California Press, 1969); Robert L. Hardgrave, *The Dravidian Movement* (Bombay: Popular Prakashan, 1965).

7 Mushirul Hasan, 'Communalism in the Provinces: A case study of Bengal and the Punjab, 1922–26', *Economic and Political Weekly* 15.33 (1980): 1395–1406; David Page, *Prelude to Partition* (Delhi: Oxford University Press, 1982).

8 Hardy, *Muslims of British India*, 204.

9 Hasan, 'Communalism in the Provinces'.

10 Ayesha Jalal, *The Sole Spokesman* (Cambridge: Cambridge University Press, 1985), 12n.

11 Erik Barnouw and S.Krishnaswamy (eds), *Indian Film* (New York: Oxford University Press, 1980); P. Shah, *The Indian Film* (Bombay: Motion Picture Society of India, 1950);William Mazzarella, 'Making Sense of the Cinema in Late Colonial India', in Ravinder Kumar and William Mazzarella (eds), *Censorship in South Asia* (Bloomington: Indiana University Press, 2009); David Page and William Crawley, *Satellites over South Asia* (New Delhi: Sage Publications, 2001); Lakshmi Subramanian, 'The Reinvention of a Tradition: Nationalism, Carnatic Music and the Madras Music Academy, 1900–1947', *Indian Economic and Social History Review* 36.2 (1999): 131–63; Mihir Bose, *A History of Indian Cricket* (London: Deutsch, 1990); Ramachandra Guha, *A Corner of a Foreign Field* (London: Picador, 2002).

12 Deepak Kumar, 'Racial Discrimination and Science in Nineteenth Century India', *Indian Economic and Social History Review* 19.1 (1982): 63–82.

13 Earl of Birkenhead, *Halifax* (London: Hamish Hamilton, 1965), 222.

14 Philips and Pandey, *Evolution of India and Pakistan*, 286–7.

15 J. A. Gallagher and Anil Seal, 'Britain and India between the Wars', *Modern Asian Studies* 15.3 (1981): 387–414.

16 Martin Gilbert, *Prophet of Truth: Winston S. Churchill, 1922–39* (London: Minerva, 1990), 353, 370.

17 Nehru, *Autobiography*, 195.

18 Sitaramayya, *History of the National Congress*, 605.

19 Sharif al-Mujahid, 'Jinnah and the Congress Party', in D. A. Low (ed.), *Congress and the Raj: Facets of the Indian Struggle, 1917–47* (London: Heinemann Educational, 1977).

20 Page, *Prelude to Partition*, 205.

21 Judith M. Brown, *Gandhi and Civil Disobedience* (Cambridge: Cambridge University Press, 1977), 109.

22 Mushirul Hasan, '"Congress Muslims" and Indian Nationalism: Dilemma and Decline, 1928–43', *South Asia* 8, 1–2 (1985): 102–20. See also Mukulika Bannerjee, *The Pathan Unarmed* (Oxford: James Curry, 2000) ch. 2.

23 S. Gopal, *The Viceroyalty of Lord Irwin, 1926–31* (Oxford: Clarendon Press, 1957), 61.

24 Gilbert, *Prophet of Truth*, 390.

25 Brown, *Gandhi and Civil Disobedience*, 246.

26 Ravinder Kumar, 'The Poona Pact', *South Asia* 7.2 (1984): 87–101.

27 B. R. Tomlinson, *The Indian National Congress and the Raj, 1929–42* (London: Macmillan, 1976), 17.

28 Guha, *Anthropologist among the Marxists*, 98.

29　Christophe Jaffrelot, *Dr Ambedkar and Untouchability* (London: C. Hurst, 1980), 67

30　Ibid., 62.

31　Of 17 candidates in the 1937 elections, 11 succeeded in reserved seats and three in general constituencies.

32　Brown, *Gandhi and Civil Disobedience*, 279.

33　The poet Sarojini Naidu was active in Congress campaigns for women's suffrage and social uplift.

34　Dieter Rothermund, *India in the Great Depression, 1929–1939*(New Delhi: Manohar Publications, 1997), 44.

35　Of the 50 largest firms, 39 were still British.

36　Partha Sarati Gupta, *Imperialism and the British Labour Movement, 1914–1964* (London: Macmillan, 1975), 224.

37　Rothermund, *India in the Great Depression*, 105.

38　Misra and Ommissi, 'Cooption and Coercion'.

39　Jaffrelot, *Dr Ambedkar and Untouchability*, 77.

40　Sarkar, *Modern India*, 269.

41　Raychaudhuri, 'Indian Nationalism and Animal Politics'.

42　Misra, *Vishnu's Crowded Temple*, 198.

43　Rajnarain Chandavarkar, *Imperial Power and Popular Politics* (Cambridge: Camrbridge University Press, 1998), 302.

44　Claude Markovits, *Indian Business and Nationalist Politics, 1931–1939* (Cambridge: Cambridge University Press, 1985): 110.

45　Ibid., 267.

46　Sarkar, *Modern India*, 287; M. N. Roy, *Memoirs* (Bombay: Allied Publishers, 1964), 499–500.

47　Moore, *Crisis of Indian Unity*, 150.

48　Jalal, *Sole Spokesman*, 11.

49　Ashton, *British Policy towards the Indian States*, 112.

50　Gandhi, *Hind Swaraj*, 77.

51　Ashton, *British Policy towards the Indian States*, 137.

52　R. J. Moore, 'The Making of India's Paper Federation,1927–35', in C. H. Philips and Mary Doreen Wainwright (eds), *The Partition of India: Politics and Perspectives,1935–47* (London: Allen and Unwin, 1970); James Manor, 'Gandhian Politics and the Challenge to Princely Authority in Mysore, 1936–47', in Low, *Congress and the Raj*.

53　Philips and Wainwright, *Partition of India*, 595.

54　R. J. Moore, *Crisis of Indian Unity*, 298.

55　Untouchables received 7 seats out of 156 in the Council of State, 19 out of 250 in the CLA and 151 of the 1,585 in the provincial assemblies.

56　There were many independents, some of whom changed allegiances, so precise figures are not secure.

57　Low, *Congress and the Raj*, 480.

58　Chatterjee, *Nationalist Thought*, 111.

59　Philips and Wainwright, *Partition of India*, 17.

6. The Impact of War, 1939–1945

1　Quoted in Misra, *Vishnu's Crowded Temple*, 209. See, also, R. J. Moore, *Escape from Empire* (Oxford: Clarendon Press, 1983), ch. 1.

2 Philips and Wainwright, *Partition of India*, 17.

3 Jalal, *Sole Spokesman*, 48–9.

4 Wolpert, *New History of India*, 287, also, Anita Inder Singh, *The Origins of the Partition of India, 1936–47* (Oxford: Oxford University Press, 1987); Jalal, *Sole Spokesman*, 55–61.

5 Philips and Pandey, *Evolution of India and Pakistan*, 371.

6 Nicholas Mansergh (ed.), *The Transfer of Power, 1942–7*, vol. 1 (London: HMSO, 1970), 295.

7 Quoted in Eric Stokes, 'Cripps in India', *Historical Journal* 14.2 (1971): 427–34; Clarke, *Cripps Version*, 289.

8 *Transfer of Power*, vol. 1, 60, 49, 111.

9 R. J. Moore, 'The Mystery of the Cripps Mission', *Journal of Commonwealth and Political Studies* 11.3 (1973): 195–213; see also R. J. Moore, *Churchill, Cripps and India, 1939–45* (Oxford: Clarendon Press, 1979).

10 H. V. Hodson, *The Great Divide* (London: Hutchinson, 1969), 103–4 and ch. 9; Stokes, 'Cripps in India'.

11 Clarke, *Cripps Version*, ch. 4.

12 *Transfer of Power*, vol. 1, 396.

13 Stokes, 'Cripps in India'; there are a number of slightly different versions attributed to Gandhi.

14 John Barnes and David Nicholson (eds), *The Empire at Bay: The Leo Amery Diaries, 1929–1945* (London: Hutchinson, 1988), 794.

15 *Transfer of Power*, vol. 1, 739; R. A. Butler, *The Art of the Possible: The Memoirs of Lord Butler* (London: Hamilton, 1971), 112.

16 Christopher Bayly and Tim Harper, *Forgotten Armies: The Fall of British Asia, 1941–45* (London: Allen Lane, 2004), 167; Sarkar, *Modern India*, 390.

17 *Transfer of Power*, vol. 2, 621; Gyanendra Pandey (ed.), *The Indian Nation in 1942* (Calcutta: Centre for Studies in Social Sciences, 1988), 5.

18 *Transfer of Power*, vol. 2, 853.

19 Ibid., 771.

20 Ibid., vol. 6, 1019; vol. 2, 739.

21 Wavell, *Journal*, 89; Barnes and Nicholson, *Empire at Bay*, 750, 842.

22 Gallagher and Seal, 'India between the Wars'.

23 Wavell to the secretary of state and to the prime minister, telegram, 9 February 1944, Wavell, *Journal*, 54.

24 Amartya Sen, *Poverty and Famines* (Oxford: Clarendon Press, 1981), 80.

	Wage Index	Foodgrains Index
1939–40	100	100
1941–42	115	160
1942–43	125	385

Source: Sen, *Poverty and Famines*, 64.

Sen's judgement of food availability has been challenged by Madhusree Mukerji, *Churchill's Secret War* (New York: Basic Books, 2010).

25 Wavell to the prime minister, 24 October 1944, Wavell, *Journal*, 94.

26 Bayly and Harper, *Forgotten Armies*, 381.

7. Independence, 1945–1947

1 Martin Gilbert, *Road to Victory: Winston Churchill, 1941–1945* (London: Minerva, 1986), 254.
2 Clarke, *Cripps Version*, 406; Philips and Pandey, *Evolution of India and Pakistan*, 378.
3 Wavell, *Journal*, 232.
4 *Transfer of Power*, vol. 6, 1117.
5 Malcolm Darling, *At Freedom's Door* (London: Oxford University Press, 1949), passim.
6 Philips and Pandey, *Evolution of India and Pakistan*, 381.
7 See review of Moore, *Escape from Empire* by Anita Inder Singh, *Journal of Commonwealth and Comparative Politics* 22.1 (1984): 102–3.
8 Patrick French, *Liberty or Death* (London: HarperCollins, 1997), ch. 16.
9 *Transfer of Power*, vol. 6, 581.
10 Nicholas Owen, 'More than a Transfer of Power: Independence Day Ceremonies in India, 15 August, 1947', *Contemporary Record* 6.3 (1992): 415–51.
11 *Transfer of Power*, vol. 6, 581; Owen, 'More than a Transfer of Power'.
12 Yasmin Khan, *The Great Partition* (New Delhi: Penguin/Viking, 2007), 46; Wavell, *Journal*, 494.
13 *Transfer of Power*, vol. 8, 840.
14 Wavell, *Journal*, 374.
15 E. W. R. Lumby, *The Transfer of Power in India, 1945–7* (London: Allen and Unwin, 1954), 118; *Transfer of Power*, vol. 6, 1117.
16 Nicholas Owen, 'Responsibility without Power: The Attlee Government and the End of British Rule in India', in Nick Tiratsoo (ed.), *The Attlee Years* (London: Pinter, 1991), 167–89.
17 Owen, 'Responsibility without Power'.
18 Gallagher, *Decline, Revival and Fall*, 144.
19 Owen, 'Responsibility without Power'.
20 Wm Roger Louis and Ronald Robinson, 'The Imperialism of Decolonization', *Journal of Imperial and Commonwealth History* 22 (1994): 462–511.
21 Philips and Pandey, *Evolution of India and Pakistan*, 392–3.
22 Ibid.
23 Wavell, *Journal*, xii.
24 R. J. Moore, 'The Mountbatten Viceroyalty: A Review Article', *Journal of Commonwealth and Political Studies* 22.2 (1984): 204–15; Alan Campbell-Johnson, *Mission with Mountbatten* (London: Hamish Hamilton, 1985).
25 Clarke, *Cripps Version*, 451.
26 Lionel Carter (ed.), *Mountbatten's Report on the Last Viceroyalty* (New Delhi: Manohar, 2003), 97.
27 Jalal, *Sole Spokesman*, 238.
28 Moore, *Escape from Empire*, 328.
29 Darling, *At Freedom's Door*, 302.
30 *Transfer of Power*, vol. 12, 512.
31 *Transfer of Power*, vol. 10, 419.
32 Moore, *Escape from Empire*, 270–73; Hugh Tinker, 'Incident at Simla, May 1947. A Moment of Truth?', *Journal of Commonwealth and Comparative Politics* 4.4 (1970): 349–58.

33 Quoted by Asim Roy, 'The High Politics of India's Partition', in Mushirul Hasan (ed.), *India's Partition* (New Delhi: Oxford University Press, 2009), 102–32.

34 Philips and Pandey, *Evolution of India and Pakistan*, 397–411.

35 Campbell-Johnson, *Mission with Mountbatten*, 298.

36 Owen, 'More than a Transfer of Power'.

37 W. H. Auden, 'Partition' (1966), in *Collected Poems*, ed. E. Mendelson (London: Faber, 2007), 803–4; Neil Duxbury, 'Lord Radcliffe Out of Time', *Cambridge Law Journal* 69.1 (2010): 41–71; Lucy P. Chester, *Borders and Conflict in South Asia* (Manchester: Manchester University Press, 2009); Hugh Tinker, 'Pressure, Persuasion, Decision: Factors in the Partition of the Punjab,15 August, 1947', *Journal of Asian Studies* 36.4 (1977), 695–704.

38 Robin Jeffrey, 'The Punjab Boundary Force and the Problem of Order, August, 1947', *Modern Asian Studies* 8 (1974): 491–520; Paul Brass, 'The Partition of India and Retributive Genocide in the Punjab, 1946–7', *Journal of Genocide Research* 5.1 (2003), 71–101.

39 Toba Tek Singh is translated in Hasan (ed.), *India's Partition*; Joya Chatterjee, 'The Making of a Borderline: The Radcliffe Awards for Bengal', in Ian Talbot and Gurharpal Singh (eds), *Region and Partition* (Oxford: Oxford University Press, 1999), 168–202.

40 *Transfer of Power*, vol. 6, 101.

41 Ibid., vol. 4, 901.

42 Ibid., vol. 6, 1140.

43 H. V. Hodson, *The Great Divide* (Karachi: Oxford University Press, 1985), 368.

44 Ian Copland, 'The Princely States, The Muslim League and the Partition of India in 1947', *International History Review* 13.1 (1991): 38–69.

45 Nicholas Mosley, *The Last Days of the British Raj* (London, Weidenfeld and Nicolson, 1961),174; Ian Copland, 'Lord Mountbatten and the Integration of the Indian States: A Reappraisal', *Journal of Imperial and Commonwealth History* 21.2 (1993): 385–408.

46 H. V. Brasted and Carl Bridge, 'The Transfer of Power in South Asia: An Historiographical Review', *South Asia* 17.1 (1994): 93–114.

47 Nicholas Owen, 'More than a Transfer'.

48 Sarkar, *Modern India*, ch. 7.

49 Rumbold, *Watershed in India*, 1.

50 B. R. Tomlinson, 'India and the British Empire 1935–1947', *Indian Economic and Social History Review* 13.3 (1976): 331–49.

51 John W. Wheeler-Bennett, *King George VI* (London: Macmillan, 1958), 703.

52 John Barnes and David Nicholson (eds), *The Empire at Bay. The Leo Amery Diaries, vol. 2, 1929–1943* (London: Hutchinson, 1988), 1035.

53 Wavell, *Journal*, 399.

54 Anita Inder Singh, 'Imperial Defence and the Transfer of Power in South Asia, 1946–7', *International History Review* 4.4 (1982): 568–88.

55 Barnes and Nicholson, *Empire at Bay*, 876.

56 Gallagher, *Decline Revival and Fall*, 144.

57 Ibid., 145.

58 Wm Roger Louis and Ronald Robinson, 'The Imperialism of Decolonization', *Journal of Imperial and Commonwealth History* 22.3 (1994): 463–511.

59 Aziz Ahmad, *Studies in Islamic Culture in the Indian Environment* (Oxford: Clarendon Press, 1964); Imtiaz Ahmad (ed.), *Caste and Social Stratification among Muslims in India* (Delhi: Manohar, 1978).

60 B. N. Pandey, *The Break-up of British India* (London: Macmillan, 1969); Moon, *Divide and Quit* (London, Chatto and Windus, 1962); Anita Inder Singh, *Origins of the Partition of India* (DPhil thesis, University of Oxford, 1981). All these stress the importance of British encouragement of the Muslim League during the war.

61 Farzana Shaikh, *Continuity and Consensus in Islam: Muslim Representation in Colonial India, 1860–1947* (Cambridge: Cambridge University Press, 1989).

62 Stanley Wolpert, *Jinnah of Pakistan* (New York: Oxford University Press, 1984).

63 Jalal, *Sole Spokesman*, 121.

64 Roy, 'The High Politics of India's Partition'.

65 *Transfer of Power*, vol. 6, 855–6.

66 Claude Markovits, 'Businessmen and the Partition of India', in Mushirul Hasan (ed.) *Inventing Boundaries* (New Delhi and Oxford: Oxford University Press, 2000).

67 But translated as Hindu and Mussalman in the Penguin India translation (New Delhi: Penguin, 1993) , 4.

68 Joya Chatterji, *Bengal Divided* (Cambridge: Cambridge University Press, 1994); William Cantwell Smith, *Modern Islam in India: A Social Analysis* (London: Gollancz, 1946).

69 Roy, 'The High Politics of India's Partition'.

70 Jalal, *Sole Spokesman*, 250.

71 Akbar S. Ahmad, *Jinnah, Pakistan and Islamic Identity* (London: Routledge, 1997); Wolpert *Jinnah*, passim.

72 Quoted by Nicholas Owen in 'War and Britain's Political Crisis in India', in Brian Brivate and Harriet Jones (eds), *What Difference did the War Make?* (Leicester: Leicester University Press, 1993).

73 Farzana Shaikh, 'The Making of Pakistan', *Modern Asian Studies* 2.3 (1986).

74 Jalal, *Sole Spokesman*, 250; see also Yasmin Khan, *Great Partition*, 53.

75 Paul R Brass. 'Elite Groups, Symbol Manipulation and Ethnic Identification among the Muslims of South Asia', and Francis Robinson, 'Islam and Muslim Separatism', in David Taylor and Malcolm Yapp (eds), *Identity in South Asia* (London: Curzon Press, 1979), 35–77, 78–112.

76 Ibid., 79.

77 Darling, *At Freedom's Door*, 349.

78 Gyanendra Pandey, *Constructions*, 235.

Conclusion

1 Sir J. R. Seeley, *The Expansion of England*, 3rd ed. (London: Macmillan, 1900), 212, 224, 263.

2 Tomlinson, *Economy of India*, 4. Over the same period, the figures for Britons went from under 50 to over 60. In the USA. white Americans had a similar expectancy, with black Americans' expectancy rising from just over 30 to just over 50.

3 D. R. Nagaraj, 'Introduction', in Ashis Nandy (ed.), *Exiled at Home* (Delhi: Oxford University Press, 1998), 1–21.

4 Henry Yule and A. C. Burnell, *Hobson-Jobson: A Glossary of Colloquial Anglo-Indian Words and Phrases* (London: John Murray, 1886); Seeley, *Expansion of England*, course II, lecture 5; Peter Hennessey, *Having it so Good* (London: Penguin, 2007), 274.

5 A. K. Ramanujan, 'Is there an Indian Way of Thinking', in Vinay Dharwadker (ed.), *The Collected Essays of A. K. Ramanujan* (New Delhi and Oxford: Oxford University Press, 1999), 34–51.

6 David Washbrook, 'The Rhetoric of Democracy and Development in Late Colonial India', in Sugata Bose and Ayesha Jalal (eds), *Nationalism, Democracy and Development* (Delhi, 1997), 36–49.

7 Ramachandra Guha, *India after Gandhi* (London: Macmillan, 2007),127ff.; see also Sunil Khilnani, *The Idea of India* (London: Hamish Hamilton, 1997), passim.

8 Sarvepalli Gopal (ed.), *Jawaharlal Nehru: An Anthology* (Delhi: Oxford University Press, 1980), 76–7.

9 D. A. Low, 'Introduction', in *Britain and Indian Nationalism: The Imprint of Ambiguity, 1919–42* (Cambridge: Cambridge University Press, 1997).

10 Richard Bourke, 'Pocock and the Presuppositions of the New British History', *Historical Journal* 53.3 (2010): 747–70.

11 Seeley, *Expansion of England*, 215.

12 Thomas R. Trautmann, *Aryans and British India* (Berkeley and London: University of California Press, 1997), 5.

GLOSSARY

Ahimsa	non-violence
Anjuman	association
Babu	term of respect attached to a personal name in Bengal: pejorative designation for a Westernized *bhadralok*
Bhadralok	'cultured people'; mostly higher-caste Bengali Hindus who in the nineteenth century developed a rich hybrid culture from their engagement with the West
Chattri	umbrella-shaped pavilion or turret
Crore	10,000,000
Dharma	religious and moral obligation in Hinduism
Diwan	prime minister
Dhoti	single piece of cloth worn as male dress
Durbar	holding a court
Fatwa	authoritative opinion in Islamic law
Hajj	the Muslim pilgrimage
Harijan	'people of God': Gandhi's name for the Untouchable castes
Hartal	closure of shops and offices as a form of passive resistance
Jati	family group: sub-caste

Jihad	striving for perfection; holy war
Jirga	decision-making council
Khalifa	successor to the Prophet Muhammad, title of Ottoman Sultan
Kisan	cultivator
Lakh	100,000
Mahatma	great soul, as Gandhi was known
Mofussil	provinces, as opposed to presidency cities
Quaid-e-Azam	great leader, as Jinnah was known
Raj/rajya	rule
Ram Rajya	rule of Lord Ram: peace and truth
Sabha	association, assembly
Samiti	association
Sanad	document conveying rights, titles
Satyagraha	holding on to truth
Sepoy	Indian soldier
Swadeshi	of one's own country
Swaraj/swarajya	self-rule
Taluqdar	land-tax collector with proprietorship in the land, especially in the UP
Ulema	Muslim law doctors
Ummah	the world-wide community of Muslim believers
Varna	four-caste division of Hindu society

FURTHER READING

The endnotes refer to specialized topics, and to the documentary collections by Philips and Wainwright and *The Transfer of Power* series, to which might be added the Indian equivalent of the latter, *Towards Freedom*, 1938–46 published by the ICHR. Below is a brief list of more general books which in turn offer guidance for further enquiry.

General

Sunil Khilnani, *The Idea of India* (London: Farrar, Straus and Giroux, 2003); Sumit Sarkar, *Modern India, 1885–1947* (Basingstoke: Macmillan, 1989).

There are a number of surveys of longer periods of Indian history that have chapters on the period of Crown rule: Judith M. Brown, *Modern India: The Origins of an Asian Democracy* (Oxford: Oxford University Press, 1985); and Maria Misra, *Vishnu's Crowded Temple: India since the Great Rebellion* (London: Allen Lane, 2007), which has much material not found in the other surveys.

The following are more condensed: Sugata Bose and Ayesha Jalal (eds), *Modern South Asia: History, Culture, Political Economy* (London: Routledge, 2011); Herman Kulke and Dietmar Rothermund, *A History of India* (London: Routledge, 2010); Claude Markovits (ed.), *A History of Modern India, 1480–1950* (trans. from French, London: Anthem Press, 2002); Barbara D. Metcalf and Thomas R. Metcalf, *A Concise History of Modern India* (Cambridge: Cambridge University Press, 2002); Peter Robb, *A History of India* (Basingstoke: Palgrave Macmillan, 2002); Stanley Wolpert, *A New History of India* (New York and Oxford: Oxford University Press, 2004).

Politics

Anil Seal, *The Emergence of Modern Nationalism: Competition and Collaboration in the Later Nineteenth Century* (Cambridge: Cambridge University Press, 1968); Sarvepalli Gopal, *British Policy in India, 1858–1905* (Cambridge: Cambridge University Press, 1965); Jim Masselos (ed.), *Indian Nationalism: A History* (New Delhi: Sterling Publishers, 2005); R. J. Moore's brief and useful *Liberalism and Indian Politics, 1872–1922* (London: Hodder & Stoughton, 1966) and his more thorough studies: *Crisis of Indian Unity, 1917–1940* (Oxford: Clarendon Press, 1974) and *Escape from Empire: Attlee Government and the Indian Problem* (Oxford: Oxford University Press, 1983).

For the Official British Presence

David Gilmour, *The Ruling Caste: Imperial Lives in the Victorian Raj* (London: Pimlico, 2005); David Cannadine, *Ornamentalism: How the British Saw Their Empire* (London: Penguin, 2001); and Kenneth Ballhatchet, *Race, Sex and Class under the Raj* (London: Littlehampton Book Services, 1980).

First World War

Sir Algernon Rumbold, *Watershed in India, 1914–22* (London: Athlone Press, 1979).

Second World War

Christopher Bayly and Tim Harper, *Forgotten Armies; The Fall of British Asia, 1941–45* (London: Allen Lane, 2004).

Biographies

David Gilmour, *Curzon* (London: Papermac, 1995).

Judith M. Brown and Anthony Parel (eds), *The Cambridge Companion to Gandhi* (Cambridge: Cambridge University Press, 2011) provides a guide to the library of works on Gandhi. His own *An Autobiography: The Story of My Experiments with Truth* was first published in 1927; see also his grandson Rajmohan Gandhi's *Gandhi: The Man, his People and the Empire* (London: Haus Publishing, 2007).

Nehru's own *An Autobiography: Jawaharlal Nehru* was first published in 1926. S. Gopal's three-volume life of Nehru was abridged into one volume (Delhi: Oxford University Press, 1989); there is also M. J. Akbar's *Nehru: The Making of India* (London: Viking, 1988) and much else.

For Subhas Chandra Bose, see Leonard Gordon, *Brothers Against the Raj: A Biography of Indian Nationalists Sarat & Subhas Chandra Bose* (New York and Oxford: Rupa & Co., 1990); and his great nephew Sugata Bose, *His Majesty's Opponent: Subhas Chandra Bose and India's Struggle against Empire* (Cambridge, MA and London: Belknap Press, 2011).

Rabindranath Tagore's own *My Reminiscences* (London: Laurier Books Ltd, 1991); Krishna Dutta and Andrew Robinson, *Rabindranath Tagore: The Myriad-Minded Man* (London: Tauris Parke Paperbacks, 1995).

Philip Ziegler, *Mountbatten* (London: Smithmark Pub, 1985).

Ayesha Jalal's revisionist study of Jinnah, *The Sole Spokesman: Jinnah, the Muslim League and the Demand for Pakistan* (Cambridge: Cambridge University Press, 1985).

The Economy

B. R. Tomlinson, *The Economy of Modern India, 1860–1970* (Cambridge: Cambridge University Press, 1993) and *The Political Economy of the Raj 1914–1947* (London: Palgrave MD, 1979); for a wider human perspective, see David Arnold, *Colonizing the Body: State Medicine and Epidemic Disease in Nineteenth-Century India* (Berkeley: University of California Press, 1993).

The States

Barbara N. Remusack, *The Indian Princes and their States* (Cambridge: Cambridge University Press, 2004).

Independence and Partition

John Gallagher, *The Decline, Rise and Fall of the British Empire* (Cambridge: Cambridge University Press, 1982); Alan Campbell-Johnson, *Mission with Mountbatten* (London: New Age International Ltd, 1985); Joya Chatterjee, *Bengal Divided: Hindu Communalism and Partition, 1932–1947* (Cambridge: Cambridge University Press, 1994); Patrick

French, **Liberty or Death: India's Journey to Independence and Division** (London: Harper Collins UK, 1997); Yasmin Khan, **The Great Partition: The Making of India and Pakistan** (New Delhi: Penguin/Viking, 2007); a number of indispensable articles are gathered in Mushirul Hasan (ed.), **India's Partition: Process, Strategy and Mobilization** (New Delhi: Oxford University Press, 2009); Francis Robinson, **Islam and Muslim History in South Asia** (Oxford: Oxford University Press, 2000).

For the Brass-Robinson debate: David Taylor and Malcolm Yapp (eds), **Political Identity in South Asia** (London: Curzon Press, 1979); Farzana Shaikh, **Continuity and Consensus in Islam: Muslim Representation in Colonial India, 1860–1947** (Cambridge: Cambridge University Press, 1989); Alex von Tunzelmann, **Indian Summer: The Secret History of the End of an Empire** (London: Picador, 2007).

A few novels, in chronological order, which give a flavour of their times: W. D. Arnold, **Oakfield; or, Fellowship in the East** (reprint; Leicester: Leicester University Press, 1973); Bankimchandra Chatterji, **Anandamath, or The Sacred Brotherhood**, trans. by Julius J. Lipner (Oxford: Oxford University Press, 2005); Rudyard Kipling, **Kim,** and his verse about ordinary British soldiers (many editions available); Rabindranath Tagore, **The Home and the World** (London: Macmillan, 1919); E. M. Forster, **A Passage to India** (many editions available); Sarat Chandra Chatterji, **Srikanta** (New Delhi, Penguin, 1993); Paul Scott, **The Raj Quartet** (London: William Heinemann, 1976); Saadat Hasan Manto, **Selected Stories** (New Delhi: Penguin, 2007).

QUESTIONS

Chapter 1

1. The 1860s and 1870s have been seen as decades of lost political opportunity. But it is unrealistic to believe that the promises of the Queen's Proclamation could have been implemented. Do you agree?
2. The Second Afghan War was an unmitigated disaster for which Lord Lytton has been unfairly blamed. He was carrying out the orders of Disraeli's government. Do you agree?
3. Crown rule provided Indians with a framework of fair and effective government from 1858 to 1914. Discuss.

Chapter 2

4. Was the Ilbert Bill controversy a turning point in the history of British India?
5. Were the manifestations of Indian nationalism before the First World War largely driven by government initiatives?
6. Was economic exploitation more important than political frustration in the emergence of a nationalist movement, 1858–1914?

Chapter 3

7. Was Lord Curzon principally responsible for the appearance of militant nationalism?
8. British rule, 1858–1914, served British interests. Discuss.
9. The Morley-Minto reforms were conservative measures looking back to the late Victorian representation of interests. They were not early preparations for Indian self-rule. Do you agree?

Chapter 4

10. 'It was only on the Somme and at Passchendaele that the [British] desire for dominion began to die.' (Sir A. Rumbold)

    'If anyone imagines that England would let India go without staking her last drop of blood, this is a sign of absolute failure to learn from the world war.' (A. Hitler in *Mein Kampf*)

    Which opinion offers a better guide to an understanding of the Montagu-Chelmsford reforms?
11. The period from the Lucknow Pact to the Khilafat Movement was the 'magic moment' of Hindu-Muslim unity. Do you agree and, if so, why didn't it last?
12. Gandhi's greatest contribution to the cause of Indian freedom was completed by the early 1920s. Discuss.

Chapter 5

13. Gandhi's leadership hindered as well as advanced the achievement of a united independent India. Discuss.
14. Divisions within the nationalist movement were a greater obstacle to Indian independence than British imperialism. Discuss.
15. Do you agree that the Great Depression was the main cause of the growth of support in the inter-war years for Indian independence?
16. The princes' failure to participate in the federal schemes of the 1930s ensured their own demise and made partition more likely. Discuss.
17. Do you agree that with the Congress triumph at the 1937 general election the days of the Raj were numbered?

Chapter 6

18. After the promises of the Cripps Mission, the Raj was effectively over. Discuss.
19. Was the Quit India Movement a success or a failure?

Chapter 7

20. Was Britain driven out of India or was it a voluntary departure?
21. 'Whatever caused the end of empire, it was not the Second World War' (John Gallagher). Why, then, did Britain withdraw from India?
22. Did Jinnah want partition?
23. Do you agree that British policies since the early twentieth century had set the scene for partition?
24. Was the haste of the 15 August deadline the principle cause of the violence of partition?

INDEX

Numbers in boldface refer to information in tables.

Lightning Source UK Ltd.
Milton Keynes UK
UKOW05f1852131013

219001UK00001B/60/P